Thrive By Design

Your Guide to Abundant Living

ANDREW LORD

Blueprint Life Academy

THRIVE BY DESIGN

CONTENTS

Dedication — x
Acknowledgements — xi
A Note From the Author — xiii
I know why you're here… — xv
How to Read This Book — xvii

1
MAXIMISED IDENTITY

| 1 | The Maximised Life | 2 |

| 2 | Let's Get One Thing Straight | 9 |

| 3 | Where Do You Belong? | 17 |

| 4 | Found | 22 |

| 5 | A Tool for the Journey | 27 |

| 6 | A Quantum Leap | 33 |

7	Your First Mission	35
8	More Adventures	43

2
MAXIMISED MINDSET

9	Welcome to the Dojo	60
10	Your Amazing Brain	63
11	Neurochemistry Insights	71
12	The Happy Mind	81
13	The Growth-Focused Mind	95
14	The Positioned Mind	113
15	The Abundant Mind	125
16	Mind Mapping	134
17	Design Thinking	140

3
MAXIMISED LIFESTYLE

18	The 6 Lifestyle Domains	148
19	The Anatomy of Strategy	150
20	Fun & Adventure	158
21	Health & Fitness	166
22	Romantic Connection	177
23	Family Life	189
24	House & Garden	199
25	Work, Business & Finances	204
26	Mastering Your Calendar	216
27	Habits & Systems	223

MAXIMISED IMPACT

28	Don't Settle	232
29	Brokenness before Breakthrough	235
30	The Wilderness	242
31	Bigger Than You	245
32	Stepping Up	249
33	Impact is a Process	255
34	You Will Face Resistance [But You've Got This!]	265
35	Who Are You Going to Serve?	275
36	Impact Through Education	279
37	No Wrong Place	287

Resources   291
Notes   293

Copyright © 2023 by Andrew Lord | Blueprint Life Academy

All rights reserved. No part of this book may be reproduced in any manner whatsoever without written permission except in the case of brief quotations embodied in critical articles and reviews.

Cover image: Eberhard Grossgasteiger

First Printing, 2022

For my mum and dad, who first sowed the seed that I have something of value to offer...

I am forever grateful.

ACKNOWLEDGEMENTS

I always think that I can do big things on my own.

I am always wrong.

This book, like any creative project, didn't just happen because I decided it would. It was the result of hours of input, from clients, from friends, from podcast interviews, and from people who I haven't met in person but who boldly pursued their own creative endeavours and have brought into the world an inspiring piece of art. Their Work. To all these people I am incredibly grateful.

In the process of bringing this book to life, there were some contributions that are worthy of special mention.

Sofia, this book would not exist without you. This is not my story, it is ours. I'm so grateful to be sharing it with you. Thank you for your unfailing love.

To Bella-Rose, Emmalia, Liliana, Christall-Star, and Rohan, you continually inspire me to live bigger and love better. You are more precious to me than life itself. I know that the penning of these pages has meant less time together, but I hope as you grow older you realise, that this book was not just for my clients, it is for you too. You have all taught me so much in your own unique ways. You have shaped who I am and this book is an extension of that learning. I hope that in the years to come this book brings you wisdom and encouragement as you each go out and live your own lives to the full.

I have shared my journey with countless amazing people. I marvel at how blessed I am to have so many beautiful people in my corner. Friends. Family. It is impossible to mention you all by name, but as you read this, I hope you realise, "hey, he's talking about me now!" and that warm glow of connection fills you from the inside out.

To Roy, Lloyd, Sarah, Terry, and Ross, who contributed to the Lifestyle Design chapters. Thank you for sharing your stories.

To John Coomer and Kylie Zeal for your candid feedback through the editing process. All your critiques and encouragements are much appreciated.

To the 'Brains Trust' – Mark, Peter & Trish, Joanne, Claire, Janne & Geoff, Jason, Suzie, Katwin, Mick & Ange, John & Adelle, Nick, Anne, and Tom – you are an incredible group of people. Each of you have, in your own way, helped me to refine this book – not just with your feedback, but also your kind words of encouragement. You have kept me on track. Thank you.

And to the Book Ambassador crew who joined in the launch so that we could reach as many people as possible. A book is only as good as the people who read it and I am proud to say that my readers are the best!

A NOTE FROM THE AUTHOR

Thank you for investing in yourself by purchasing this book. In doing so you join a growing community of life-inspired men and women who are determined to stand for more than merely 'getting by'.

I know you have a dream. I know you want to live a life worthy of the calling in your heart.

In this book, you'll hear stories from my life and friends I've connected with along the way. I share these stories to illustrate one thing – YOU can do it too!

I pray that within these pages you find not only inspiration, but motivation and methods that you can use to turn energy into action. All great stories begin with a dream – but without action, that's all they will be.

Your life was meant for more than that.

To get full access to downloadable resources and support documents described in this book, go to: www.thrivebydesignbook.com/resources

I KNOW WHY YOU'RE HERE...

I know because I was once looking for the same thing. And when he found me, he told me, I wasn't really looking for him. I was looking for an answer.

It's the question that drives us... It's the question that brought you here. You know the question just as I did... The answer is out there... and it will find you, if you want it to.

TRINITY – THE MATRIX

You're here because you know something.
You've known it your whole life.
You're looking for something – but what? It's unclear. Hidden.
Let me tell you what it is.
You were born with greatness inside. You have a calling. Everything you've done, everything you are, your gifts, your talents, your hopes, your dreams, and desires are all pointing to one thing – they are pointing to YOU!
The real you. A God-breathed miracle designed with passion and purpose.
This book is about making what's real on the inside, true in your life.
This book is about fulfillment through authenticity.
This book is about you.

HOW TO READ THIS BOOK

This book has 4 parts, which I will guide you through.

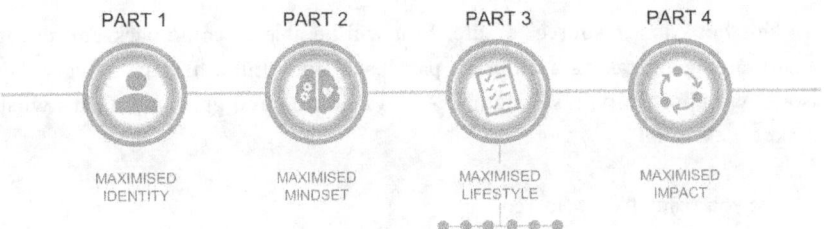

Part 1 is a personal discovery adventure. It's best if you have a pen and journal handy and are able to spend some time in uninterupted thought.

Part 2 is a training regime. You will learn AND you will do. Don't skip the practical component if you want to get the most out of this section.

In Part 3, you don't need to read every chapter. In fact, it's best if you don't. CHOOSE a path based on what matters most to you right now.

Do you remember the old 'choose your own adventure' books from when you were a kid? It's kind of like that.

Fun & Adventure | Health & Fitness | Romantic Connection

Family Life | House & Garden | Work, Business & Finance

Which one matters most to you right now?

Part 4 is a challenge to think bigger. It may not be for right now, but sooner or later you will be compelled to give back to your community. This section will show you how.

This book is a resource for life. You will be able to come back and use it again and again, taking a different path each time. Life's like that. Every day is a new opportunity. It's dynamic. Always shifting and growing. That's what makes it exciting!

Are you ready to get started?

1

MAXIMISED IDENTITY

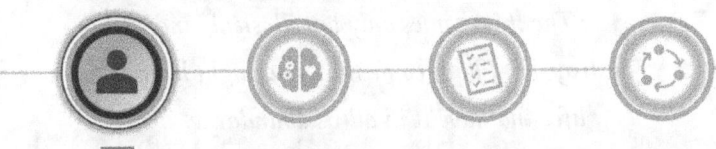

| 1 |

The Maximised Life

> *The thief comes only to kill, steal, and destroy, but I have come that you might have life, and have it in all its abundance.*
>
> **JESUS – THE BOOK OF JOHN**

What do you think of when you hear about someone living a 'Maximised Life'?

I'm guessing visions of a ruggedly good-looking solopreneur in brand-name activewear, their brow glistening with non-fragrant sweat, standing atop Mt Kilimanjaro, which they decided to climb on the weekend. They calmly take in the spectacular sunset, enjoying the endorphin rush of yet another success, before being whisked away by private helicopter to their Insta-perfect family and their high-paying corporate job, where they use divinely appointed insights to make million-dollar decisions every day. They are constantly praised, promoted, and envied by lesser mortals… like us.

Sound about right?

The booming self-help industry, of which life coaching is a part, is worth billions of dollars and there is a vested interest in maintaining such an easily marketable image of success. However, of all the clients I've worked with, people I've interviewed, and students I've taught over the past 20+ years – all of them define 'success' in a much deeper way.

Michael Crossland, a courageous cancer survivor who has shared the stage with the likes of Tony Robbins and the Dalai Lama, and has inspired millions with his story says, "Success is about how big your heart is, not how big your house is." [1]

Matt Defina, head of programs for The Man Cave[2], shared with me, "Success is having the courage to be yourself and having the tools to avoid falling into society's stereotypes."[3]

Oprah Winfrey says, "Success is synonymous with fulfillment – doing the thing that aligns with your inner voice." [4]

I have asked the "*What does success mean to you?*" question hundreds of times, and despite the infinite variety of descriptions that reflect the rich diversity of humanity, one truth consistently emerges – **success happens on the inside first**.

'The Maximised Life' is a catchy term we use in my coaching practice to describe living at your best. That's our goal. But this isn't some superficial treatment. It's not a glossy makeover. It's not just a change in schedule or even in attitude. It's much bigger than that. The Maximised Life requires you to be all in. It's a wild, white-knuckle ride filled with creative possibilities. It's fun, and frustrating, all at the same time. It's being truly alive – being human in a way that only you can.

No one can tell you how to be you – that's something you need to discover for yourself. What I *can* give you is a framework that will guide your journey of self-discovery and show you how to design your own personalised plan for whole-hearted, abundant living.

The best way to do this is from the inside out. By living an authentic life that aligns your heart, mind, faith, actions, and attitude. A life that radiates truth from the core of your being.

In this book I'm going to help you make *the big shift*. From crippling doubt and despair about your own worth. From feeling alone and misunderstood, to clarity, confidence, and a strong sense of divine purpose. A self-belief that compels you to take action!

If, when you read this, you're filled with hope, then you're in the right place. You might be sceptical. You might have doubts about yourself and the process. That's OK. Keep reading and see what unfolds. Right now, you're at the perfect place – on earth, and in history to be doing what you've been called to do. No matter what it is. Building a youth program or school to mentor young people; making a big career shift to do something you've always dreamed of; being a better mum or dad so your kids grow up filled with love and acceptance – with this book in your hands, and a willingness to persevere, you have everything you need to change your world.

Let me tell you what's coming up:

In Part 1: **Maximised Identity**, we will be diving deep into the core of your being to discover gems of truth. You'll learn secrets about yourself that, one moment, have you shaking your head with wonder and disbelief, the next minute, have you nodding yes! – because you've never heard something so right!

I will show you how to safely preserve these truths, lest they evaporate in the choking heat of self-doubt or get lost in the unforgiving labyrinth of self-sabotage. You will return to these truths often, draw from their wisdom, and get closer to understanding the Call – your personal mission.

In Part 2: **Maximised Mindset** we begin your training. Resilience, happiness, hope, creativity, perception, courage, and more.

Mastering mindset requires unlearning the old and laying down new programming ready for the challenges that lie ahead. I'll be sharing stories from my own journey and from others to help you better understand important transitions we all must undergo on our path to a maximised sense of self.

In Part 3: **Maximised Lifestyle** we make it real. The invisible becomes visible. Ethereal, conceptual ideas become goals, strategy, and action. Hope and dreams take form. You will choose your path and visit one of the six different worlds – the 'lifestyle domains' where you will meet various different mentors to help you on your way.

And finally, in Part 4: **Maximised Impact**, the ripples continue outward. The gifts you uncover are not for you alone. They are for you to share with others. That's why you found them. We're going to look at what it takes to lead well, and create a positive culture in your family, school, or organisation. I'm going to show you how you can scale your positive impact by educating and empowering others.

Please understand, the Maximised Life is NOT about having it all together. It's not about being born rich or gifted or having all the right words at the right times. It's not about attaining to a level of perfection where everything suddenly gets easy. No, the Maximised Life is marked by challenge, setbacks, and struggle. These are the necessary human experiences that enable us to expand and grow and they set the stage for breakthrough, triumph, and celebration!

Alex Kendrick, writer and director of the film Facing the Giants, said: *"If we could write the script for our own lives, it would probably make a really boring movie!"*[5] We'd have a job we loved. We'd never make mistakes or face struggle. We'd win the lottery – twice. Our partner would be flawlessly beautiful, and they would never disagree with our point of view. The kids would never argue. We would find exercise effortless and remarkably effective at toning our already genetically gifted physique...

Would you go and see that movie?

No! There's no arc. No messy middle. No struggle. No story.

In the first century, there was a guy called Paul. He was a spiritual teacher, prolific letter-writer, and eventually martyred for his all-in faith. He also reinforced the 'inside-out' definition of success. He points out that we've been entrusted with a secret truth from heaven and that there really is no point making value judgements about good or bad here and now because our *internal motives* are what matter most. He says, there will be a day when: *"He [God] will bring to light what is hidden in darkness and will expose the motives of men's hearts"*; and *"at that time each [person] will receive his praise from God."* [6]

Did you catch that last part?

One day, at the end of this life, you're going to be asked a simple question: "Did you do it?"

Do what?

The *thing*. You know, that thing I put inside you to do. Did you find it? Did you DO IT?

If the answer is yes, then I imagine the grandstands of heaven are going to erupt. Roars of joy and celebration will echo into eternity. I like to think there will be a highlights reel of your life playing on a big screen somewhere, and all of a sudden, you will get it. You will see the parts that were important – the actions that were motivated by love and inner-conviction and truth. Then, the King, the creator of the universe, the one who set it all up, will turn to you and say, proudly and simply – "Well done."

That will be a pretty awesome moment.

In this book I'm going to show you how to live with this kind of undefeatable hope. How to turn adversity into action, and struggle into strength. How to live YOUR Maximised Life.

IT'S AN ONGOING QUEST

A past client and fellow coach, Tom Schumann asked me while I was writing this chapter: "Do you still struggle with the things that you teach about? I mean, I have clients, and I tell them they have to overcome resistance – to feel the fear and do it anyway. And yet, I still face challenges that scare me. I know it's just fear, but I still don't want to face it! Do you get that?"

My answer was – Yes.

There are 2 states – *comfortable or growing*. Often, we're aiming for comfortable, but if you want to keep growing (essential for the Maximised Life) then you'd better get used to being uncomfortable. If you're comfortable, then you're not growing – and when things in nature stop growing, they die.

I know this book won't be for everyone.

This book IS about a better life – but if you're looking for the '10-steps to…' – wealth, fame, whatever – you're going to be disappointed. Sorry.

This is not a set of *'hacks'* to get one single result out of life or other people. It's not a quick fix. If your aim is to avoid tough situations or get comfortable, then this isn't the book for you. Probably best that you know now.

The Maximised Life is not a 'recipe' or a set of 'rules'. It follows a pattern, which I'm excited to share with you, but it's a practice, a habitus. A vibrant lifestyle you design with care, then master, not an hollow formula to follow.

People might think – hey, he's written a book about the Maximised Life, he must have his stuff sorted.

Um. No.

Like anyone, my life is a work in progress. I am continually learning, growing, and uncovering the next exciting step. I'm not sharing the principles in this book, because I've got all the answers; I'm sharing this journey with you because I've failed and fallen enough times to know that there is ALWAYS a way to get back up. There is ALWAYS hope. And I believe, there is ALWAYS, the master storyteller, behind the scenes, waiting for the perfect time to turn these big falls into something amazing.

So, if you're feeling brave… Let's go on an adventure!

| 2 |

Let's Get One Thing Straight

*Owning our worthiness is the act
of acknowledging that we are sacred.*

BRENÉ BROWN

Have you ever held a baby while it slept? Or maybe peeked your head into its room, not wanting to wake them, but you're captivated by the absolute peace and contentment of that small, beautiful creation. I always used to volunteer to 'check on the baby' when our kids were little (especially the oldest before any exhaustion had set in). My wife would find me standing at the door, mesmerised. She'd smile knowingly and we'd stand there together in silence for a little while, marvelling at what had happened to us. I could have watched her forever.

Why?

What is it about these tiny humans that is so disarming and engaging?

If we were to consider their value from a practical point of view, they would definitely come up short. They don't help out. They don't contribute financially. Their attempts at communication are confusing and sometimes downright rude! They insist on being served. They don't feed themselves. They demand you do it for them AND clean up everything at the other end too! Yeah, from a pragmatic perspective, you'd have to agree, they're pretty useless – right?

And yet, there they are – a miracle.

A yawn or gurgle is enough to make you gasp or bring a tear of joy to your eye.

What is going on here?

When I run a coaching workshop or presentation, I like to do this exercise. I first saw it done by my friend, Matt Purcell at the Royal Retreat. I hold up a fifty dollar note. Snap it up few times, smell it, hold it up to the audience and ask, "Who wants it?" All the hands in the room shoot up.

"Alright," I say, "here's the deal. If you want it, stand up." The crowd all get to their feet. Game on!

"IF, at any time, you decide you want to opt out of this game, if you decide you don't want the fifty dollars you can just sit back down, OK?" The audience nods collectively; confident and greedily eyeing their fifty-dollar prize.

"What if," I ponder, "I took this fifty dollars, dropped it on the floor and stepped on it?" For effect I drop the money and stomp on it, then pick it up, dust it off and hold it high again for all to see. "Stay standing if you still want this fifty dollars?" I ask. Nobody moves.

"OK. What if, I was very rude to this fifty dollars?" I ask, and I take the fifty dollar note off to the side of the stage and say, "Fifty dollars, you are the dumbest fifty dollars I have ever seen! You're not worth enough to be impressive like One Hundred Dollars, and you're not popular like Twenty dollars! You're just boring! Not only that you're ugly! Yellow! Poo-yellow! What sort of a banknote is poo-yellow! No one would ever want or appreciate you! Look, you've even got a little tear in the corner! Fifty dollars – you are a loser!" My face is flushed as I end my abusive rant, but I clear my throat, stand back up, straighten my jacket, and compose myself. I step back toward the middle of the stage and in a much more professional tone ask the audience; "Who still wants this fifty dollars?" There are a few giggles in the audience, but everyone remains fixed. The insults have not deterred them. They are still determined they want that fifty dollars.

Then I lean toward the participants standing in front of me as though I'm about to let them in on a secret. "Let me tell you something I don't tell many people." I look around as though someone might hear us. "When I present to groups like this, I get a little nervous. And when I get nervous, [pause] I sweat." Some people in the audience shift awkwardly with this new information. "Now, what if, I take this fifty dollars here..." I hold up the fifty dollars, "...and I rub it in my armpit." And I proceed to insert the fifty dollars under my jacket into my sweaty armpit. I reproduce the note from the recesses of my armpit, taking a theatrical sniff of the freshly unminted note, recoiling in mock disgust.

"Aww!" a few exclaim.

Some girls in the front row take their seats, discreetly covering their noses from an imaginary smell wafting their way. Most of the room, however, is still standing.

"OK, what if..." I pause. "What if I walked out of here, up the hallway, and into the men's toilet?" There are a few audible groans in the audience. One or two quietly take their seat, not wanting to be complicit in what's about to come next. I continue. "I walk into one of the stalls, and, *accidentally* drop the fifty dollars into the bowl. I don't want to get it out, because the person before me forgot to flush," [more groans] "so I flush it. Down, down, down it swirls.

Through the darkness, coming across all sorts of horrible and unspeakable things along the way. It's gone." I pause again. Silence. A few people in the audience shift uncomfortably, not sure what this means for our game and the prize they were hoping for.

"A few weeks later, it's a sunny day and I'm walking along town beach. There are a few pieces of driftwood and seaweed that have been washed up on the sand and I look up the beach and notice a crumpled yellow thing sticking out of a pile of seaweed. I walk up to the debris, bend down, and pick it up, and I notice that it has a little tear in the corner just like the fifty dollars I lost two weeks earlier. I check the serial number (which I had written down) and guess what? Yep. It's the same fifty-dollar bill. It's clean. It's dry. Apart from a small tear in the corner there is no evidence that it's ever been mistreated."

I hold up the fifty dollars note and ask quietly, "For the last time now, who still wants this fifty dollars?"

More than 90% of the audience is still standing and so I turn and ask, "Why? You know where this fifty dollars has been! You know the horrible things that have happened to it and yet you still want it – why?" Invariably someone always steps forward and states matter of factly, "But it's still fifty dollars. It's still *worth* fifty dollars."

"That's right," I agree. "No matter what has happened to it, the fifty-dollar note is still *worth* fifty dollars."

I turn to the audience and say, "You are the same. You have *value*. You have *worth* because of who you are. No matter what has happened to you. No matter your imperfections. No matter if someone has been rude to you, or called you names and told you that you're worthless. It doesn't matter if you've been mistreated, smeared, stepped on, or even rejected, forgotten, and left for dead. No matter what happened to you, you still have *intrinsic value* because you are a human being. You have been created with value – understand?"

The audience nods solemnly as they accept the weight of this truth. I pass the fifty dollars to the audience member who had spoken up and articulated this simple truth and ask the others to give them a round of applause as everyone takes their seat. In the light of this truth, no one feels like they've lost. All intuitively know that this single, simple revelation far outstrips any monetary value and they sit down satisfied.

Back in 2011, Mel Robbins gave a popular TED talk quoting the scientists who have calculated the chance of you being you, as (approximately) 1 in 400 trillion – that's a 1 out of 400,000,000,000. Dr. Ali Binazir, who works at Harvard and has degrees from Berkeley and Cambridge, was in the audience and decided he wanted to crunch the numbers for himself. His results were even more astounding. Given the number of humans on the earth at any given time, he calculated the odds of your parents meeting, and staying together long enough to have a child. He factored in the odds of your ancestors meeting, and then their ancestors, and then their ancestors, and so on… Based on Binazir's figures[1], the chance of you being born is about $1:10^{2,685,000}$

So, that's a 1 with 2,685,000 zeros after it.

How small is that you ask?

Well, let's put it this way. Binazir points out that the number of atoms in an 80kg male body is 10^{27} (that's 1 with 27 zeros after it). That's a lot of atoms. But that's nothing compared to the number of atoms that make up the earth – that's 10^{50} (that's a 1 with 50 zeros after it). Not enough? OK – the number of atoms that make up the known universe (at last count) is 10^{80} – yep, that's a 1 with 80 zeros after it. Still with me?

Now let's go back and look at the chance of you being born – you being you – that's a 1 with TWO MILLION, SIX HUNDRED AND EIGHTY-FIVE THOUSAND zeros after it!

Boom! (My head just exploded).

A miracle is defined as 'an event so unlikely that it could be considered statistically impossible'. We didn't even take into account the chances of you stumbling across this book on the day you did, at the right time in your life so that you would pick it up and start reading it! It's probably a good thing I didn't do these figures before I started to write this book! I would have seriously considered not bothering if I knew the odds of us connecting were so ridiculously small!

And yet, here you are – a miracle.

Are you getting this?

Despite all the odds, you are alive, you're here, and you're **completely unique**. Even if you don't agree with Binazir's maths, you have to acknowledge, there is no one, in all the billions of people that we share the planet with, who is quite like you. There never has been, nor there ever will be anyone with your combination of personality, skills, strengths, gifts, and experience. 'Unique' is an understatement. You are freaking amazing!

Let's talk about value.

Value = Demand/Supply   OR   V = D/S

(Don't freak out at the formula, this is a pretty basic concept)

Economics 101 – Value is given by the relationship between supply and demand.

If something is hard to get, and a lot of people want it (e.g.: diamonds or gold) then it naturally has a high value. And if something is easy to come by, and not a lot of people are asking for it, then the value is low (like dirt) – right?

We've established that you're rare. In fact, the chance of you being you, is basically zero. Virtually impossible. And yet here you are. That means even if you only make a difference to ONE person in some small way, the **value** of that is infinite. You are PRICELESS!

Brené Brown has spent more than 2 decades studying shame (which she relates directly to a sense of unworthiness) and uncovered its most powerful antidotes; empathy and vulnerability. From her research, which includes thousands of personal stories, there emerged an understanding of how the 'whole-hearted' live. In her 2010 TED talk she describes ONE distinguishing feature that sets apart these whole-hearted individuals from those who struggle constantly and live in a perpetual state of: 'Am I good enough?'. The key difference is that the first group **believe** they are worthy of love and belonging – while the other group doesn't.[2] It is that simple.

As we move through this book, we're going to be talking a lot about 'taking action' because action is what shapes reality. It's what rewires your neural pathways, reforms habits, and changes the results you've been getting from ordinary to amazing. Life changing work for sure, BUT – I don't want you to think for a second, that this 'work' is what makes you special or gives you your value. Far from it. You are amazing, special, loved, and valuable – just as you are!

Even if you choose to do none of the activities listed in this book. Even if you stop reading after this chapter. Even if you choose not to believe it is true – it still is. You are incredible. Miraculous. And of infinite worth. Don't ever forget it.

It's one of the universe's paradoxical mysteries – you have infinite potential within you; and yet, just as you are, you are enough. You are already worthy of love and belonging. You cannot add to or take away from that worthiness with your work or efforts, and yet, here I am, about to ask you to **take action** in the chapters that follow. How does that make sense?

Here it is. We don't build the Maximised Life to find or earn love and belonging; we do it to *express* love and belonging. Living fully is an act of gratitude. It is the natural response to the gift of life we've been given! As we express it, we see it made real and it can reinforce for us what we believed, but it isn't the actions that make it true. Truth is truth, whether it gets expressed or not. You have value whether you take action or not. But your actions make your inner-truth *experienceable* – and that is a whole new level of awesome!

| 3 |

Where Do You Belong?

> *It's easy to stand in the crowd.*
> *It takes courage to stand alone.*
>
> **MAHATMA GANDHI**

Have you ever felt out of place? At school? At work? Or even around the people you love?

Feeling isolated, marginalised, or misunderstood is a common human experience.Ironically, if you're feeling lonely – you're not alone.[1,2]

We all want to belong. We all want to feel that we are part of a tribe – a family. The word *'be-longing'* means to 'be' [in the state of] 'longing' [the object of one's desire]. We want to be wanted. In this chapter we're going to explore the tension of loneliness that forces us to reflect more deeply on who we are.

Given loneliness is such a universal experience, it might seem silly to define it, but just to be clear, we're not talking about social isolation, as in, having minimal contact with other people. Loneliness can happen in the middle of a crowded party. It is a subjective state that signals your personal relationships are not what they should be (or what you want them to be).[3] Struggling to find meaningful connections with those around you is like being in a stuffy room without enough oxygen. Your mood gets flat. Your energy becomes low and lethargic. I've seen people spend years in this state with stoic resolve. Ignoring the signs, hoping it will pass. Others run gasping to escape. Maybe you know what I'm talking about?

1 in 4 adults feel this way about half of the time and about half of adult Australians feel this way at least once a week.[2] Recent research from the global health company Cigna suggests some startling numbers – that 3 in 5 adult Americans (61%) report feeling lonely, with a range of linked and contributing wellbeing factors, including: higher stress, greater likelihood of illness, a negative satisfaction level with their social interactions and personal relationships.[3] Prolonged loneliness can severely impact a person's mental health leading to an increased risk of depression and suicide.[2,4]

Loneliness sucks.

But like most pain it has a positive role to play. Those acute feelings of loneliness are our *coalmine canary* warning us we need to make some changes. Rebecca Saxe, a brain researcher from MIT compares loneliness to hunger, and points out how feeling socially isolated triggers an acute desire for social engagement to restore the balance.[5] We want to be connected. We want to be understood and accepted.

I've spent most of my adult life at extreme ends of the loneliness spectrum. Either feeling like I'm on an alien planet trying to communicate with the locals and fit in. Or, in that magic zone where people seem to just 'get me' and I can enjoy the warmth of mutual connection.

It's tempting to set up camp in that comfortable place. It feels so much safer there – but I have learned that loneliness is part of the journey. It's a part of growth. Staying where you are never challenged is how you give up your authentic self.

I left for university at 18. Out of home for the first time and pumped to be off on this new adventure. I remember my mum trying not to cry as she helped me settle into my room. I felt for her a little, but I couldn't get the smile off my face. Not even for mum's sake. We both knew it was probably overdue. I think they just put up with me in the final months as a last show of parental sacrifice and a testament to the value they placed on education. I'm still not sure if those tears arose from the significance of the occasion, concern for my future, or just relief that the job was done!

My first day, I managed to catch the bus (which I'd never done in a city before), find my lecture hall, (which I'd also never done before) and actually enjoyed my first concepts of design lecture. Then came a practical session. I remember sitting next to a Korean international student, Kim. Very polite. Full of friendly intent but his English was more hand gesture than discernible words.

The task was to draw and render 4 solid figures – a prism, pyramid, sphere, and cylinder. I got busy drawing and shading. I enjoyed it. I loved art exercises like this and found it easy to get into the zone. Then I noticed out of the corner of my eye, Kim's work. His sphere appeared to literally be hovering above the page!

My mind started racing. *"Oh my God! I thought I could do this, but I can't! Did you see his sphere? It's incredible. I don't draw like that. I don't think I could ever draw like that! I don't belong here!"* I was awash with shame. Who was I to think I could compete at this level? In comparison to Kim's, my drawings were like the dirty smudges of a first grader who'd never used crayons before. I swallowed hard. I took some deep breaths. I could feel panic rising. I was hot. I wanted to run, but there was nowhere to go. Oh shit, I thought. I'm not meant to be here! I'm way out of my league and soon everyone is going to know it!

I was outwardly composed, but inside all the failures of my past were piling up like a train wreck in my mind – an irrational flood of jumbled memories: My poor entrance score for university (that somehow was still enough to get into the design course I wanted); that critical basketball game in the State Cup, when I travelled 10 hours to play and sat the whole game on the bench; that day I found out the girl I'd just asked out the week before, had left town with her family! (The word was her family's business had failed, they'd declared bankruptcy and left town, but my mates assured me disappearing was just the easiest way to avoid having to break up with me in person). An overwhelming sense of disappointment clouded around me and my throat began to tighten with tears. "What a loser!" I thought. A final declaration from inside me driving home the overwhelming sense of condemnation, not just of my efforts, but of me as a person.

Thankfully the session ended and there was no show-and-tell. I gathered up my stuff and got out of there fast. I caught the wrong bus and took an extra hour to get back to my dorm. Alone in my room I laid on my bed and wondered what just happened? Slowly but surely time and solitude slowly released the grip of anxiety. I just lay there. The storm had passed, but my mind kept scrambling. How was I going to go back? More to the point, *why* was I going to go back? Was this really me or just an elusive pipedream? Maybe I'd just conjured this idea of 'being a designer' up to somehow give myself a sense of validity? Maybe it was just naivety and arrogance that had got me this far and failure was inevitable and imminent? Was this *really* what I wanted, or was I being led astray by a nefarious trickster in my head? Perhaps there was a better path – a safer path?

But my mind drew blank. There was nothing else.

I mustered the courage to show up again the next day.

And the next. And the next…

The days became easier. I kept going.

4 years later, I graduated. 2 Distinctions, a Credit, and a Pass. A year ahead of more than half the students who sat in that room on Day 1. Some of them never finished at all.

Kim went back to Korea 6 months after starting. He was a brilliant artist but finding his way in a foreign country must have been incredibly tough. Ironically, the catalyst for my own imposter crisis, he probably felt very alone. I guess we weren't that different after all. I admire his courage just for showing up.

Have you ever felt like a misfit in your own life?

The big question is, are you willing to face it again?

The Maximised Life is not found in the comforts of home and staying ordinary. To find it, we must venture outside the boundaries of who we already are and discover who we might become. It is scary, and painful trials are inevitable. That is the path to self-discovery. For those brave enough to venture there, the Maximised Life awaits…

| 4 |

Found

Your real, new self will not come as long as you are looking for it. It will come when you are looking for Him.

C.S. LEWIS

In my early years, studying at uni, I did a lot of thinking and self-reflection about what I wanted to stand for. I had a lot of ideas – more than enough for 10 lifetimes. It hit home to me how precious life is. I wanted mine to count. Even back then, I had a sense of the 'Call' and I wanted to honour that. Honour comes from the same root word as honest and it means being respectable, worthy of trust, pure. Heart, mind, and actions aligned.

With that desire for integrity humming in the back of my mind, my second year of uni, I found myself sitting among strangers on a church pew one Easter Sunday. Having grown up in a small, tight knit community church with my family, the motions of the service were all very familiar, but I still felt like an imposter there. I didn't know any of the people and realised that this was the first time since the last holidays I'd set foot inside a church building or given

God much thought at all for that matter. In the busyness of my new life, I'd become a 'holidays-Christian'. I wasn't living aligned with my core values. In the next few weeks, I asked my friend Steve, with whom I'd had some deep talks about spiritual things before, "Hey are you going to church?". He told me he was, and so I asked if I could come along.

The next week, 9am Sunday morning, I jumped into a car with Steve and 2 pretty girls – Rachel and Kate. This was turning out better than I expected! We attended the gathering which was upbeat and engaging. There were some 'fairly enthusiastic' participants there (not like my old community church out West!) but nothing off-putting, and at the end of the service, the pastor (also called Steve) came and said 'Hi'. He told me they were having a church camp that weekend and I was welcome to join them. "Maybe" I shrugged. "Well, the offer is there", he said, and we left.

I played basketball on a Friday night and Steve had gone home for the weekend, so Kate arranged to pick me up with a friend. We drove out to a hall which seemed like it was in the middle of nowhere. It was dark but there was light and music coming from a small building. When we went inside, it wasn't what I expected! It was carpeted, the furniture was pushed to the sides and there were people in all sorts of disarray! Some were bent over laughing, some looked stoned or drunk and others were lying blissfully on the floor. Some sat in chairs with their heads bowed serenely, others were making weird cackling sounds, while a few were full-on bawling their eyes out, tears streaming down their faces!

Gulp. Not belonging just went to a whole new level!

Kate seemed undeterred and keen to get inside. She pulled on my arm, but I was frozen in the doorway. "Umm, I'm going to go for a walk" I told her. "C'mon", she pulled on my arm, tilting her head to the side and smiling at me in a disarming way. Her soft insistence was reassuring, and I trusted her, but I stood firm. "I'm OK", I said nonchalantly, "I'm just going to have a walk and stretch my legs" (I had been pretty cooped up in the car ride out). "OK", she shrugged happily and walked in, leaving me standing in the doorway.

I quickly slipped back outside and took a deep breath. Phew! That was weird.

Although it was odd, it somehow also felt very natural. People just being themselves. Unashamed. I walked out into the night, out of the dirt carpark and into an adjoining paddock. It was a cloudless night and we were a long way from the city, so the stars were bright. I walked for a while, then sat down, looking up at the stars. I felt calm, but also curious. Something in me wanted to go back.

After about 30 minutes this curiosity was starting to nag at me. I prayed a simple prayer. "God, if this is you, please show me". As soon as the words were out of my mouth, right at that moment, a shooting star appeared in the sky, but it didn't vanish quickly like a normal shooting star would, it burned slowly across the sky, staying visible for about 3 seconds before it faded and disappeared!

"Woah!" I gasped and got up quickly. I walked back across the paddock, resolved to go back inside. Maybe I'd seen a sign in the heavens, or maybe I just didn't want to get hit on the head with space junk! Either way, I walked back into the hall and saw that the room was now quieter but even more dishevelled than before.

Steve (the pastor guy) was right there. He'd just helped an elderly couple sit/fall onto the floor. Seeing me walk in, he came over to me and smiled warmly. "Can I pray for you?" he asked respectfully. "Sure" I said with a resigned, unenthusiastic shrug (what was I going to say? – "No, piss off old man, leave me alone"). I closed my eyes and Steve placed his hands on my shoulder. Right away I felt a warm, reassuring presence around me. The God-friend I'd known forever, the one I'd just been talking to outside under the stars, now reappeared and enveloped me with a new level of affection I didn't realise was possible. The caring guardian who had been watching over me all these years, was now hugging me, and the sense of acceptance was overwhelming. My legs got weak, and I wanted to sit down. Without opening my eyes, I understood. The scattered mess of people around me suddenly made sense. The compulsion to surrender weighed heavily on my body and so I sat down. Then lay down. I felt at peace. I rested and enjoyed that moment.

I shared my experience with Kate later that evening, and with my mum on the phone when I got home. I knew life had changed. I had found the path. My path. Or perhaps the path had found me?

BEFORE WE BUILD

Any building needs a solid foundation. It's the same with our lives. Have you ever thought about the word 'Foundation'? It is made up of 'found' (to be revealed, discovered, made known), and 'ation' – a suffix meaning the result of or taking 'action'. It's a *discovery* made real with *action*.

Have you been found? Are you living out that 'found-ness'?

You're about to learn some deep truths about yourself, but your story does not exist in isolation. We are all players in a much bigger story. I'd be remiss if I didn't tell you that spiritual awareness was important. More than important. Essential.

Brené Brown's research defines 'Spirituality' as: "...recognising and celebrating that we are all inextricably connected to each other by a power greater than all of us, and that our connection to that power and to one another is grounded in love and compassion. Practicing spirituality brings a sense of perspective, meaning, and purpose to our lives."[1]

My ongoing personal transformation and the work I do with all my clients (including nonbelievers) is built on the fact that pulsating deep within every person is a unique call to adventure, and that life is a process of learning and discovery orchestrated by a loving creator. Accepting this truth releases me from the fear of screwing up. I know that I'm always playing a bigger game. I know that I don't always have to understand every part of the story. I just need to play my part. And I know that every circumstance can be turned to my advantage. This makes me bullet-proof in the face of adversity. You don't need to see meteorites falling from the sky or feel the literal weight of God's love pushing you to the floor – but you *do* need an encounter with Spirit. If you're not sure how, just get alone, get quiet, and use the same words I did: "God, if this is you, please show me".

You might be surprised at what happens next...

| 5 |

A Tool for the Journey

Imagination is more important than knowledge. Knowledge is limited, but imagination can take you everywhere.

ALBERT EINSTEIN

As human beings we co-exist in two different realms at the same time.

There's the physical realm, which we can see and taste and touch. This is where we take action and observe the outcomes of those actions. Most would argue, this is 'reality' – after all, it's the domain of science, which since the enlightenment period of the 17th and 18th centuries has been the authority on what is 'truth' or not. It is a practical place governed by cause and effect. You've heard the axioms: "*What you reap you will sow.*" "*What goes up, must come down.*" It's safe and predictable. Its rules are logical and clear-cut. And we like it that way! When we look at successful people, the idea of 'hacking' or reverse-engineering their habits in the hope that we can emulate their results makes sense.

Then there is the conceptual realm. This is the realm of thought and belief. The realm of our internal dialogue, our hopes, dreams and visions of what is possible. In the conceptual realm we are not limited by physics. We can travel through time and alternate universes. We can conjure resources, become a new person, invent new products, and if it doesn't work out, reverse time and try it all over again. In the conceptual realm, days can pass in seconds, or we can ponder a single moment for weeks on end. The conceptual realm is where children play and learning happens, but it can also be a place of dangerous illusions. Self-doubt, fear, past wounds, and toxic emotions can cloud our judgement and choke out the truth of love and belonging. But we don't usually take it too seriously. After all, it's not 'real' is it...

Is it?

Many great thinkers through the ages have argued that the conceptual realm is where life is *most* real. Plato said, "Reality is created by the mind, we can change our reality by changing our mind." George Orwell emphatically declares, "Reality exist in the [collective] mind and nowhere else." Rene Descartes famously ties his ability to function in the conceptual realm to the very nature of his existence: "I think, therefore I am." Siddhartha Gautama, spiritual teacher, and founder of the Buddhist tradition acknowledges both the conceptual and the physical world when he says: "Our life is shaped by our mind; we become what we think." You can see in the Buddha's statement, an awareness of both, but primacy is placed on the inner world.

The Maximised Life begins at our core. The deepest, purest part of ourself where heaven's song still echoes in the chambers of our heart. This chapter is about unlocking the tool you need to find it.

That tool is your imagination.

IMAGINATION

When I bring this up at workshops there is **always** resistance. Maybe you groaned a little yourself when you read that last line? What is it about creativity that makes us so uncomfortable? In my time coaching people through the creative process, I've heard all of the pushbacks. Let's take a look at some...

Firstly (and maybe this is the root reason), so many people say: "I don't think I can do that. I'm just not that creative."

Most adults perpetuate the self-fulfilling prophecy that they are just 'not creative'. A study by Robert Mc Garvey shows that 84% of kindergarten children rank highly in creativity, and by second grade that percentage (of high creativity) has dropped to just 10%.[1] What happened? What drastic reshaping of the mind takes place in the years aged 5 to 7 to get this astounding change in capacity?

One obvious answer is 'they started school'. In the world's most watched TED talk, 'Do Schools Kill Creativity', education thought leader, Sir Ken Robinson shares how the human resource of creativity is being systematically squandered and diminished in schools.[2] Practices, which we rarely give a second thought, have established themselves in schools since the industrial revolution. These systems are designed to promote uniformity, conformity, and obedience. Robinson says: "Imagination is the source of every form of human achievement. And it's the one thing that I believe we are systematically jeopardising in the way we educate our children and ourselves."[2] On the bright side, if creativity can be unlearned, then it can also be relearned again too. You CAN be creative – if you allow yourself to be.

This leads us to another common objection. The *'I'm too old for this*' defence. Creativity seems a bit frivolous. A bit unscientific or childlike to say, *"let's use our imagination."* I've had workshop participants say: "I know you work with young people and get great results there, but I'm past that! I'm an adult with pressures and responsibilities! I don't have time to play games."

If you're thinking the same thing right now, then let me assure you – imagination is what ALL great success stories begin with.

It's exactly the same process that engineers use to build bridges. It's how effective corporate CEOs conceive new solutions to take their companies to the next level. It's how teachers create new learning experiences to engage students and change their lives. It's how politicians design new policies that shape the fabric of our society. Imagination is what great humans do best.

If it helps, try using the word 'Vision' instead of 'Imagination. It sounds a lot more 'adult' but it's using the same mental-muscles.

Edward de Bono says, "There is no doubt that creativity is the most important human resource of all. Without creativity, there would be no progress, and we would be forever repeating the same patterns". [3]

The third reason I get pushback on the conceptual realm as a starting point is its inherent vulnerability. When we reveal something of ourselves, we are exposing ourselves to others judgement and critique. That's scary. What if they don't like it? Our creativity is a part of who we are. It's a very short leap from "they don't like my ideas or my work" to "they don't like ME!"

When we open the hatch to dive into the deeper parts of ourselves, it is pretty scary. We don't know what we're going to find.

"What if I'm called to be a podiatrist and I hate the sight of feet!"

Or, worse still, *"What if I look inside and there's nothing much down there at all?"*

Or, the opposite, *"What if I get lost in the sea of possibilities? If the conceptual realm has unlimited possibilities, how am I supposed to handle that? How will I know which idea is right?"*

Trust me. You're going to be OK. I guarantee that when you find your core, not only will it feel as right for you as anything ever has before, but you will be stunned by the breath-taking beauty that is inside you.

The final pushback on using imagination and creative process comes from what Stephen Pressfield describes in his book, *The War of Art* as, 'Resistance'. (We will look at this phenomenon in more detail in Part 2). Pressfield describes Resistance as a natural negative force that's sole purpose is to stop the advancement of human creativity and evolution.[4] It is as real as gravity or bad weather or decay.

All creative projects come with a corresponding force of resistance. Like the shadow of a tree. When the light shines, the shadow also appears. And the bigger the aspiration, the bigger the shadow. It's human nature to resist change. We all have a natural inner inertia that wants us to stay put. Stationary is always more comfortable than moving. To move takes effort. It takes willpower. It takes faith.

With all these reasons why imagination/creativity might pose a problem for us, it's pretty natural to ask the question; is it really necessary? I mean, if we step back from the edge of this airy-fairy 'conceptual realm' and get logical again for a minute, wouldn't it make more sense to take a practical approach? Why don't we just look at success in the physical realm and start with that? Reverse engineer it. Bigger house, better job, more wealth, happy family, hotter bodies, and more intimate relationships – did I miss anything? Facebook and Instagram never lie, right? It seems that the physical world is where it's at!

Taking action IS important. It is what creates the results we're after. But if the action is hollow, if it's not motivated by love, if you're just following someone else's recipe or formula, then you are constantly going to find yourself missing the mark and feeling like a fraud. Empty. Lost. Not belonging in your own life – and that REALLY sucks. I've been there. I think you have too.

No. The only way forward is down. A creative process of tapping into your true self.

| 6 |

A Quantum Leap

The reality is, you're not really lost.
Your true self is right there, buried...
Finding yourself is actually returning to yourself.
An unlearning. An excavation.
A remembering who you were before the world got its hands on you.

EMILY MCDOWELL

Are you alone right now?

(Wait, that wasn't meant to sound creepy!)

What I mean is, as you read, do you have **time and space** to pause and ponder without interruption? Do you have a quiet space? Are you comfortable? Do you have some water, a journal, and a comfy place to sit?

If you're on a bus or train or a place crowded with other people, I would encourage you to wait. Right now you're going to go on a fun, virtual adventure that can offer you insight into who you truly are. This time is sacred. And if you've ever watched films like Inception, Avatar, or The Matrix, then you know it never ends well getting 'unplugged' in the middle of a virtual dive. Give yourself what you need to succeed.

Did you ever see The Quantum Leap television series of the early 90s? Or the Marvel film, 'Antman & The Wasp'? The basic gist is, that at the quantum level (which is really, really, really small!), the normal laws of physics break down. Time, space, and reality as we know them in the physical realm begin to behave differently. These stories are obviously science fiction, but believe it or not, the science is actually quite real. Multiple universes, changing outcomes just by observation, and even time-travel are all theoretically possible in the Quantum Realm. In the Quantum Leap series, the lead character, Sam Beckett, travels through time, arriving in a new body each time, compelled to right past wrongs, and in the process, is trying to find his way home. You're going to do the same.

There are FIVE virtual missions (should you choose to accept them). Each mission will be a 'quantum leap' – taking you to another time, place and possibly a new state of being. The missions are designed to be fun, to get you thinking differently, and ultimately, help you to understand your core self better. You can download a copy of your Mission Notebook at: www.thrivebydesignbook.com/resources

You are the hero in these stories.

Let's get started...

| 7 |

Your First Mission

You must go on adventures to find out where you truly belong.
SUE FITZMAURICE

MISSION 01

You hear the whir of the quantum generator and then a mechanical voice echoes in your earpiece – *"Get ready! 3, 2, 1, DIVE!"*

You wake up lying on a straw mattress, in a wood-lined attic room. A chilly autumn wind steals in with the morning light through gaps in the boards. The smoke from an open fire wafts up from the hearth in the large room below along with the delicious smell of frying eggs.

A pretty woman, dressed in a simple, linen dress, covered in a flour-dusted apron, busily fussing about downstairs calls up for you to come down for breakfast. "You don't want to be late for your big day, do you?" she chides.

Her accent lets you know you're probably somewhere in the British Isles. Your body is not your own. You can see that you're a young boy, about 12 years old and are dressed in brown linen pants and a loose green shirt. You make your way cautiously down the ladder that connects your loft-bedroom with the rest of the house, which is just one big room, more like a barn. The floor is made up of large stone pavers. The roof is held up by huge wooden posts and beams that look as though they've been pulled straight from the forest. A large, thick wooden table is in the centre of the room and as you come over, your breakfast, a slice of cold meat, 2 fried eggs, a handful of greens and a small dark brown baked loaf, all arranged on a piece of wooden board, is placed on the table. "There you go my Prince!" says the woman who you assume must be your mother.

She stands proudly near the table, waiting for you to try it. She has a kind and pretty face aged by hard work, which crinkles into a pleased smile as you tear off a piece of bread, put some egg on it and take a bite. It is like nothing you've ever tasted! Until that moment you didn't realise how hungry you were. It is clear from the woman's delight watching you that this is not a breakfast that happens every day. "Alrighty then, eat up. The cart will be here soon." She says, then busies herself again with her chores.

You finish your rustic meal that is surprisingly filling and wash up in a bowl near the one window on the south side of the house. About 10 minutes later a horse-drawn, wooden cart pulls up near your home. There are already about 4 children your age on the back of the cart.

"*Choosing Day!*" cries out an elderly man who is driving the cart and another boy and two other girls run out from nearby houses and jump on board. You stand looking at the cart unsure what you're supposed to do but feel a nudge from behind and a voice whispers, "Go on then." You turn and see your mother with her beautiful, kind face looking lovingly at you. A tear escapes the corner of her eye, and she pulls you tight for a parting hug. "Just follow your heart and you will make the right choice," she whispers. Then pushes you away, quickly brushing the tear from her eye, and motions for you to join the others. You feel reluctant to leave, but your mother has already turned and walked back inside. You jump on the cart and the driver cracks the reins and the cart lurches into motion.

You listen to the excited chatter of the other children and can gather that all are about to choose an apprenticeship. To be trained for a role within their village community.

You arrive about an hour later at a wide open, gently sloped grassed area. There are about 30 other boys and girls already there, all running about excitedly. There are also 5 different coloured tents set up. Each tent has a group of people gathered in and around it. Each group is clearly different. A horn blows and everyone assembles on the grassy hill and sits down.

A wise old looking man hobbles forward, introduces himself as 'Geralta' and says, "You have probably heard your parents speak of me as; *'The Elder'.* My job, among other things, is to help you make your choice today. Each of you will be choosing an apprenticeship that you will follow for the rest of your life." He pauses and looks around. Everyone is giving him their full attention. "I will shortly explain to you the 5 paths you may follow, but first let me remind you, that as you make your choice today, you must remember, it is not what you DO that is important, but rather WHO you are. The qualities that come from in here," he thumps on his chest with his fist, "are what make you of service to your village. As I explain the roles, I want you to listen carefully to the character of each before you make your choice. Do you understand?" he asked, and the whole assembly nodded solemnly. The Elder nodded back, satisfied the weight of his message had been received.

"First, there is the **BLACKSMITH**" the elder declared, and as he does a cheer goes up from one of the tents, which you now notice is surrounded by strong men and women all dressed in dark brown protective leather clothing. A roaring fire and bellows can be seen at the back of their tent and beautiful metal swords and fine jewellery can be seen hanging from display stands nearby. The Elder continues. "The Blacksmith are clever people. They are inventive. They can see ideas in their mind and can manage multiple projects all at once. They are strong minded and work hard. THAT is the Blacksmith." Another cheer goes up from the Blacksmith tent and all the children clap.

"Next, is the **WIZARD**" the elder says, and a flash of light and a puff of smoke leaps from a silver and white striped tent. Two tall, regal individuals, a man and women standing at the tent bow to the crowd. The Elder nods affirmingly in their direction and continues to speak. "The Wizards are kind and compassionate people, even if they don't always show it. They are studious. They help others by seeing what others don't see. They understand the roles we play and how all things work together for the good of God's will. That is the Wizards" the Elder declared, and the crowd clapped respectfully.

"Next, are the **JESTERS**" said the Elder, which was followed immediately by a screech and a bellow and out of the bright, multicoloured tent that was decorated with ribbons, steamers and bells tumbled 4 acrobatic performers. They bumped and tumbled over one another, the last one uncermoniously face-planting into the grass, which might have been an accident or just a part of the performance, it was hard to tell. Everyone laughed. The other 3 picked up their companion and half-walked, half-dragged him back into the tent. The crowd continued to giggle even after they had disappeared. That was the effect of the Jesters. The Elders shook his head but couldn't hide a smile at the corner of his mouth. He composed himself and the crowd settled. "The Jesters help us remember to have fun!" The crowd giggled again. "They are clever

– but irreverent! They do not take life too seriously. They might not admit it, but deep down they care for people. They are willing to humble themselves to make others smile." The Elder motioned toward the Jester tent and the crowd cheered and clapped again.

The Elder paused and took on a more serious tone before continuing. "Next, is the **WARRIOR**." Almost immediately, the clanging sound of 10 warriors stepping in unison from their olive-green tent echoed out across the grass field. They struck their armoured chests, then moved from attention to 'at ease' stance as though they were a single body. They looked fierce and formidable. Some of the children nearest their tent moved back from where they stood. These are our Warriors," said the Elder proudly. "The Warriors are courageous even in the face of terrible challenges. They believe in themselves and the best in others. They are fiercely loyal. They think strategically and have learned obedience through strict discipline and training. Children, we are very grateful to our Warriors" concluded the Elder and motioned to the troop who all responded with a stiff synchronised bow. The children all clapped respectfully.

"And finally, is the **BARD**" the Elder said. No sooner were the words out of his mouth, than an explosion of Celtic music, bagpipes, drums, and tambourines burst from a bright orange and yellow tent into a short rousing overture. The song ended as quickly as it began and the Elder turned back to face the crowd as everyone clapped, impressed by the show. "The Bards are kind and empathetic people. They are our story tellers. Our poets. Our musicians. Like the wizards they understand the deeper meanings of life. They delight in sharing positive messages and like the Jesters, they enjoy putting smiles on faces." As the Elder finished his description, one Bard with an accordion-type instrument leaned forward and played 'Ta-daaa!' and everyone laughed. The Elder smiled and nodded at the gang of Bards who were all obviously happy with themselves and their performance.

"And now," said the Elder, turning back to the crowd, "is your time to choose. Now is the time that you look deep within yourself and follow the path that life has for you." The Elder motioned to 5 wooden bowls that were set before him. Each bowl was filled with small, shiny stones. Charcoal, White, Red, Green, and Orange. "When you are called, come forward, take a stone, and then move to the tent to join your new tribe. In good time they will want to know more about your strengths and train you to be the best you can be. Choose well."

The voice of your mother rings in your ears. *"Just follow your heart and you will make the right choice."* You close your eyes and let the swirling ideas rushing through your head settle into one, clear vision of the future. You can hear the sounds of other children, the occasional laughter or cheer, but right now you are blocking it all out. It is all muffled and distant as you concentrate on your centre...

Then you are snapped to attention as you hear your name called. You stand up, walk to the Elder who looks down at you with kind, knowing eyes and motions to the 5 wooden bowls in front of him.

- Charcoal for the Blacksmiths
- White for the Wizards
- Red for the Jesters
- Green for the Warriors
- Orange for the Bards

You know what to do.
You reach forward and choose...

COMPLETE YOUR CHARACTER PROFILE

CIRCLE YOUR CHOICE:
BLACKSMITH - WIZARD - JESTER - WARRIOR - BARD

DESCRIBE REASONS FOR YOUR CHOICE:

YOUR NEW TRIBE WANTS TO KNOW MORE ABOUT YOU. CHOOSE PERSONAL QUALITIES/STRENGTH SCORES THAT ADDS UP TO A TOTAL OF 17 OR LESS:

	1	2	3	4	5
COMPASSION	☐	☐	☐	☐	☐
INNOVATION	☐	☐	☐	☐	☐
OPTIMISM	☐	☐	☐	☐	☐
VISIONARY THINKING	☐	☐	☐	☐	☐
DILIGENCE	☐	☐	☐	☐	☐

WHICH IS YOUR STANDOUT STRENGTH?

WHAT POSSIBILITIES IN YOUR NEW APPRENTICESHIP EXCITE YOU THE MOST?

| 8 |

More Adventures

A day of adventure is worth a thousand years of ease and comfort.

PAULO COELHO

MISSION 02

"Get ready - 3, 2, 1, DIVE!"

You wake up. At least you think you're awake. It's hard to know. You're surrounded by complete blackness. There is no sound, no smell, nothing. You're not even sure that you're in your own body anymore. You cannot feel anything. You're thinking, so you know you still exist, but that's all. You wait. Perhaps minutes, perhaps years, you can't really tell. Then you notice something. Out of the blackness, something is changing. It's like an impossibly low musical note, a deep, droning base note that you feel more than you hear. It's raw energy, saturated with emotion and intent. You feel like laughing, crying, celebrating, and weeping all at once. It is overwhelming and your mind and emotions are stretched to breaking point ...

There is a pause and for a short second there is silence again, as though the energy is drawing breath... Then, BOOM! The silence is shattered by an unbearable explosion of sound, light, and other forms of unseen energy. It is raw power, yet somehow there is a meaning behind it. You have no time to ponder this however because now there are shards of light being scattered in every direction like beautiful flying arrows. The magnificence is overwhelming. It's part light show, part song. A gorgeous symphony of sounds. Deafening but perfect. Magically woven together by an invisible master conductor. Even if you were given 1000 years to take it all in, you would only perceive an infinitesimally small fraction of the wonder of the moment.

Then, suddenly time slows down, almost frozen. Your position pans around. This is the first time you are actually aware of having a physical vantage point. As you pass through the waves of sound and light energy you understand that somehow you are witnessing the birth of the universe!

You realise that if you did have a physical body in this moment, it would be completely obliterated by the sheer force of the energy exploding outward in all directions, and yet, somehow you are not afraid. The overwhelming love that you sensed before the energy woke up fills you with an unshakable confidence. "If I die, I die grateful."

In a fraction of a millisecond the energy around you will create previously unimagined matter. Stars. Galaxies. Planets. Even light itself, but before it does, time stands still, and your attention is drawn to a small, single shard of light that is strangely familiar. Your memories all seem to come alive as you look at that beam, and you realise that you are looking at yourself. At least, at the idea of you, that existed at the moment of creation. This is the truth of your existence captured in pure, energetic form. The spirit-song that created you.

You don't have long to ponder this surreal idea because, at any instant now, the frozen sequence of time will begin again, and this moment will be gone. You don't know how long you have got. You know that when time resumes, memory will be a feeble vessel to try and captivate this kind of experience, but anything you can see, anything you can write down and remember will be a priceless treasure.

You have seconds left. And so, you grab your pen and write it down.

When you look at the purest part of yourself – what do you see? What do you know is true? What is the essence of your past, present and future? What makes you unique?

You don't have time to think, just trust your creative flow. Just start to speak out loud or write and keep writing until the moment is gone. Go!

REFLECTION

What words describe that 'energy' that is you...

MISSION 03

"Get ready! - 3, 2, 1, DIVE!"

You are standing in a wide, open carpark. People are still arriving, but it is now mostly full. After parking, people make their way slowly, almost reluctantly, from cars and small huddles to the large lone brick building at the edge of the car park. Most are couples and families. Many of these people look familiar. Most seem to know each other. They greet one another other with long, comforting embraces but no one acknowledges you. No one seems to notice that you are there. As you get closer, you recognise more and more people. In fact, there are not many here that you don't know, but all look older and a little weary.

You follow the crowd into the large building and there are solemn ushers standing in the foyer handing out small slips of paper to each person on their way in. The ushers ignore you, so you walk past them. Through the foyer area, through two large, wooden double doors and into a wide-open auditorium space. There is a lectern at the front. The seats are arranged in rows facing a raised platform. Banners with messages of hope and faith hang from the rafters. You recognise that this building is probably a place of worship on other days, but today the mood is much more sombre. You notice that most of the people, who are now all seated, are dressed in black. Even close friends do not notice that you're there. Somehow the quantum dive has made you invisible. You walk freely up the aisle, unseen.

A minister steps to the podium and greets the room, saying a few words before everyone starts to sing. You know the song. It's one that you remember from your childhood. A favourite. and it puts a smile on your face. You decide to take advantage of your invisibility and walk about the auditorium. People are passing tissues, consoling each other. And you realise that you are at a funeral. There is an open casket at the front of the room. You walk up to it and look inside. It is you. Older, peaceful, but gone...

The sight is shocking, and you gasp involuntarily. Stumbling backward, your head tries to make sense of it all. Just then you see an old dear friend, who is sitting towards the front, stand and walk to the lectern. They pull from their pocket a crumpled sheet of paper that is marked with scribbled notes, edits, and corrections. It's clear that they have spent considerable time thinking about what they were planning to say. They unfold the page and place it deliberately, carefully on the stand taking deep breaths to compose themselves. You can see 3 boxes on the page marked 'Connections'; 'Character'; and 'Accomplishments'. There is silence. The words stick in your dear friend's throat. You want to go to them and comfort them, but you know that you can't.

The minister gently places his hands hand on your friends back which gives them the strength they need to continue, and with a big deep breath, the eulogy begins...

Every word hits home in your heart. When you hear this speech, you KNOW that they knew you – the real you and all you stood for. Emotions well up. You feel so blessed that you got to hear this.

All of a sudden, a loud wind is rushing past you. The images of people blur and swirl. You blink, and instantly you're back in your own space and time. Some memories begin to fade almost instantly but the words spoken by your friend stay sharp and clear.

You look down, pen in hand, and see 3 boxes with the same 3 titles.

You smile as you write down the memories in each box. Your legacy.

EULOGY NOTES

Connections:

Character:

Accomplishments:

How Do You Want To Be Remembered?

MISSION 04

"Get ready - 3, 2, 1, DIVE!"

You look around the room. It looks like an office or medical facility. The room is white, except for the slightly tinted glass panels that act as petitions separating you from other similar white rooms. There is a white laminated benchtop along one wall and a similar floating bench in the middle of the room. There are vials of different coloured serums all marked with a confusing series of codes all along the wall bench. There are a row of tote trays and apart from a few printed computer pages scattered on the bench, everything else is neat and tidy.

A middle-aged man with long brown pants, a light blue shirt, and white lab coat is sitting on a stool and hunched over a microscope that is set up on the middle bench. You can see your reflection vaguely in the glass panel. You're also dressed neatly in brown pants with a blue-shirt, white lab coat, and you're holding a stainless-steel clipboard. On the clipboard are about 40 different icons. You notice the logo at the top of the document matches the logo on your associate's lab coat. You look down and see that it is the same on your lab coat too. It is made up of 2 intertwined pillars and reads: 'Stellar Genetics'.

There is a digital clock and calendar display showing on the wall. You can see that it is 4:30pm Friday, February 10th, 2136. You're in the future.

Just then, your colleague stops looking through the microscope and pushes back from the bench. His wheeled chair skates expertly across the white linoleum floor and he arrives at the other bench. You notice the glass panel behind the bench is also a large computer screen. Your colleague starts making grabbing and pushing motions in mid-air and you're confused for a minute, then realise that the objects on the screen are matching his motions. It's some form of advanced touchscreen – well, a *NON*-touchscreen.

You can see that the icons he is moving around on the screen are very similar to the ones on your clipboard. All of a sudden, he drops the last icon into the last empty space on the screen and the complex array of symbols all turns green. An animated combination lock icon appears and unlocks and the words "GENETIC CODE SEQUENCE COMPLETE" appears on the screen. A computer-generated woman's voice speaks calmly out of the screen: "*Your genetic design is now complete and has been forwarded for tissue generation. Estimated completion time – 38 weeks.*"

Your colleague pushes his wheeled chair back from the screen, cracks his knuckles and looks very proud of his work. "And THAT, Jent my friend, is how we make a baby in less than an hour!" You stare blankly back at him. He seems unaware of the potential awkwardness of his last statement, and he moves back to the middle bench and pulls what you can only guess is some form of tissue culture from a liquid nitrogen freezer at the back of the room. He slides it under the microscope and then looks up at the digital time display on the wall. "C'mon Jent, time to get one more done before we finish up for the week". (You guess that you're 'Jent') "Um. OK then!" you say, trying to sound keen and confident. You sneak a peek at your colleague's name badge. His name is Kayne.

"Pass the order, Jent," he calls out to you. You look down at the clipboard in your hands and then pass it to Kayne hesitantly. "No!" he says, sounding tired and annoyed. "That's the one we just finished! Where's the next one?" You look over at the tote trays on the bench, but the one marked 'orders' is empty, and so turning back to Kayne, you look dumbly at him and shrug your shoulders. "Um, I lost it?" you offer feebly.

"What!" Kayne explodes, looking up from the microscope. He slaps his forehead and looks back up at the digital time display. "Should I go get another one?" you offer, looking for any excuse to get out of there, but Kayne shakes his head and says "that'll take another hour and I want to get out of here *TODAY*" he complains, still shaking his head.

He pauses, considering the options. "Just make it up," he says quickly, glancing around as though someone might have heard him. You stare back blankly. "Just make it up!" he urges you again in an whispered urgent tone. You don't know what to do. You're pretty sure that you're not supposed *'make up'* a genetic baby order – that is, if you had the faintest idea of HOW to do that. But it's also clear that Kayne is keen to get out of the lab to whatever recreational pleasures awaits genetic scientists on a Friday evening in the year 2136.

"Um, how would you do that?" you ask casually, trying not to give away that you have no idea what is going on. Kayne looks up at you again from the microscope, a bewildered look on his face. Thankfully he doesn't berate you again, but just shakes his head as he pushes his chair back across to the tote tray bench. He mutters, "You're not with it today, Jent". He riffles through the tote trays looking for a new order sheet for a few minutes before throwing the papers messily back into the trays. "Darn it!" he says. "I wish Stellar would get with the 22nd century and stop using these paper forms!" He turns to you and says, "There's none of the code forms left. You'll have to use a text one instead, OK?" You nod enthusiastically – at least you might be able to read the text form. He clips a page to your stainless clipboard and passes it to you. It has a heading marked 'CORE VALUES' and 40 words below it which you instantly recognise. "Just base it on your own code" he says and slides back across the room and resumes his work at the microscope, leaving you to complete the form.

Kayne's advice, "Just base it on your own code" repeats in your mind as you look at the page. You ponder – if I was to replicate my own Core Values, what would I choose...

THRIVE BY DESIGN - 53

[Here is a copy of the code sheet]

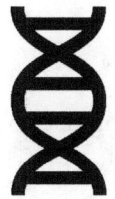

STELLAR GENETICS
Choose up to FIVE Core Values:

Independence	Freedom	Trust	Adventure	Achievement
Loyalty	Nature	Peace	Hope	Joy
Dignity	Curiosity	Structure	Wisdom	Beauty
Acceptance	Patience	Health	Courage	Leadership
Winning	Challenge	Honesty	Sensuality	Security
Fairness	Fun	Integrity	Power	Nurture
Learning	Wealth	Consistency	Family	Respect
Innovation	Compassion	Optimism	Organisation	Diligence

Or add your own…

1	2	3	4	5

MISSION 05

"Get ready - 3, 2, 1, DIVE!"

You look around and recognise the room around you. It is your room – but it feels strangely different. Something has changed. You're not sure what. You ponder for a while, trying to put your finger on it and then you realise... it's you! You are different! These quantum leaps, these adventures through time, have changed you. They have given you a new perspective and insight into who you are, but as you sit on the edge of your bed surrounded by the familiar and the normal, you begin to feel the memories slipping away. It's like awakening from a dream. Even now the clarity is starting to fade...

You look down and see that you still have your notes from each adventure and decide to record each mission outcome in your journal. You grab your notebook and reflect on your time as a young medieval village boy choosing your future path. You go back over what you chose, but more importantly, WHY did you choose it? What were the qualities or opportunities that attracted you to your apprenticeship? With all of these ideas/feelings/visions swirling around your head, you capture their essence with an ending to this simple sentence:

> "I am one who..."
>
> [Take your time. Write it down. Do this now.]

You then think back (or forward?) to your funeral. The crowds of friends and family and people whose lives you've touched. You reflect on the words that were spoken. All the things that they were glad you did and the person you grew to be. With all of those ideas/thoughts/feelings swirling around your head, you capture the essence of these memories with an end to another simple sentence:

> "My life matters because..."
>
> [Take your time. Write it down. Do this now.]

Now reflecting on one of the most epic experiences of your life, you blush as a warm sense of gratitude and honour washes over you. You were privileged to witness the birth of creation. You shake your head in awe, quietly confident that you will never fully understand the depth of thought and care that went into the creation of you... You take a deep breath, close your eyes again and feel the energy that still lives in you. The heartbeat pulsing through your veins. The spark of life that makes you special and unique. With the magnificence/wonder/awe swirling around your thoughts, you capture the truth of this moment by completing this simple phrase:

> "I have been created for a purpose. I am here to..."
>
> [Take your time. Write it down. Do this now.]

And finally, you reflect on your Core Values. Five qualities hardwired into your genetic code and shaped by your experience. Five words that epitomise what matters most to you. You capture these essential qualities with five simple statements.

> "My Core Values are... To me, this means..." (x5)
>
> [Take your time. Write them down. Do this now.]

It all fits on a page or two. It's simple but profound.

(You can download your printable Mission Notes journal from: www.thrivebydesignbook.com/resources)

After writing these sentences, you put down your pen and go to carefully file your journal in your top drawer. Instantly you are transported to another time and space. You're not sure if this is your imagination, another quantum dive, or perhaps just the aftereffects of too much time travel!

Whatever it is, you look around and see yourself. You immediately recognise this as one of the most difficult periods of your life. You are sitting, doubled over, your head in your hands, and that gut wrenching feeling of 'I don't know what to do' comes washing over you again. Tears fill your eyes, but then, just as suddenly as you went into this vision, you're out again. Back in your room, pen on the desk, your hands still on the journal in your top drawer.

You pause. You are filled with care and love and compassion for that lost and hurting version of yourself. You wonder... If it was possible to send a message back through the quantum realm – back to yourself at that moment – what would you say?

You pull out your journal one more time and write down one more sentence just in case. With all the hurt and fear and pain and uncertainty swirling around your heart and mind you finish this sentence:

> "You will be OK, just remember...
> (And you leave yourself a heartfelt word of wisdom and encouragement)
>
>
> [Take your time. Write it down. Do this now.]

<u>THE CALL</u>

You smile. Satisfied. Knowing that you have captured the essence of you in these simple statements. You're proud of who you are. You know that there is a very real 'calling' inside you. You know that realising your dreams are still a lifetime away, but you feel confident that you have unravelled the blueprint, and that is going to make all the difference. You put your journal with all its secrets back into your top drawer and walk out of the room thinking...

"I wonder where we are off to next?"

2

MAXIMISED MINDSET

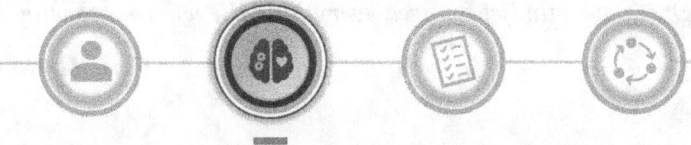

| 9 |

Welcome to the Dojo

Once your mindset changes, everything else will change with it.

STEVE MARABOLI

I am sure that you've realised by now, the adventures in Part 1 were not just for fun. Every journey you go on, every experience you have, real or imagined is a feedback loop shaping you into the person you were born to be. You've now tapped into the source code of your Maximised Life – your secret identity! Your Call. That's something no one can ever take away from you.

The Maximised Mindset is the next layer beyond Identity. It's the training you need to align your mind with the person you are called to be so that when challenges come your way, smart actions will come naturally.

These mindset training principles are all backed by cutting edge scientific research, and yet many of these principles echo ancient wisdom going back thousands of years. None of the ideas stand alone. They all overlap and work synergistically with each other to produce a holistic mental framework.

Mindset training is like walking in the forest. At first it makes sense to follow the trails you already know. When you are shown a new way, it can feel uncomfortable, unnatural, and even frustrating – but persevere! You are literally laying down a new pathway in your brain, and the more you use that path, the more well-worn it becomes, and the more that new path becomes a part of who you are. After weeks you will find these practices easy and habitual and wonder how you went so long without them!

Each of these chapters include a theoretical component and a practical exercise, so you can first understand, and then apply this understanding. **Do not skip the practical component!** I work with a lot of people who *know about* positive lifestyle habits but when I ask: "Are you doing them?" They shake their head, smile sheepishly, and say – "Um, not right now".

Confucius says, "to know and not to do, is to not yet know".

Your training includes the following Mastery Phases:

- Your Amazing Brain
- Neurochemistry Insights
- The Happy Mind
- The Growth-Focused Mind
- The Positioned Mind
- The Abundant Mind
- Mind Mapping
- Design Thinking

It is important to note here that many of the ideas included in these chapters are not my own. I have compiled the best brain-training techniques and strategies I have come across in my 20+ years as a designer, educator, and life-coach. In this section, there is no doubt that I am standing on the shoulders of giants. I will wherever possible share credit for the work that has gone before me, not just as a matter of due courtesy, but also so that you can pursue these other authors and thinkers to deepen your own understanding. You can also find additional mindset tools and resources at: www.thrivebydesignbook.com/resources

Now, let's begin your training...

| 10 |

Your Amazing Brain

> *If you are always trying to be normal,*
> *you will never know how amazing you can be.*
>
> **MAYA ANGELOU**

My wife and I bought a new dishwasher. When I went around to the loading bay there was a cheerful assistant waiting to help. His name was Craig. We chatted as we waited for the machine to be brought out. When I told Craig that I ran brain training programs he got visibly excited and began to tell me about what had happened to him a few years earlier.

Craig never thought of himself as intelligent. In fact, like many people he was told from a young age by teachers that he wasn't. He struggled with reading and left school at 14 to get a job. Walking home late one night he was attacked from behind and hit on the head. Medical records show that he died for a short time before being revived.

He suffered severe swelling on the brain. When he regained consciousness in hospital, he couldn't walk or talk. He struggled with memory even more than he did before and the doctors were unsure how much he would recover. He was in hospital for months with the left side of his brain 'offline' due to the injury, but the right side of Craig's brain, normally associated with creativity and spatial recognition, began to step up to make up for the missing skills. It was like the right-side, which had been side-lined for years, being told it wasn't useful or smart, now finally came into the spotlight and began to take on the work he once struggled with.

Everything seemed to make sense. He looked at a car engine and saw a big jigsaw puzzle. Motors, complex machinery all became clear and with this new clarity also came a renewed love of learning! Months later, when the swelling went down on the left side of his brain, he regained full function, but now with a synergistic boost of improved spatial and creative ability. His doctors estimate Craig uses 6% more of his brain than most other people and estimate his IQ rose more than 50% in a 12-month period. Once a self-professed "dummy" – Craig now asks his son's teacher for a full year's coursework so that he can read through it in the school holidays and be ready for when his son has questions.

Craig's story is amazing, but he's not alone. There are many other stories of how the human brain can adapt, redirect, and do incredible things in the face of adversity.

At 5 years old, Jim Kwik fell onto a metal heater when a chair was pulled from under him at his school. The head injury was life-threatening. A few years later, struggling with schoolwork, he heard one of his teachers refer to him as: "the boy with the broken brain" – an identity he carried through school and into college. Failing his courses and on the verge of dropping out, a chance meeting with a friend's father helped him discover his 'why' for learning and step into the relatively new world of personal development.

Desperate for a way forward but still struggling under the weight of academic pressures he asked himself, "what if there was a way I could *learn faster?*" His subsequent discoveries on how to learn faster and recall more has propelled him to the pinnacle of the brain-training world. 'The boy with the broken brain' has now become a memory and mindset coach for CEOs, celebrities and big companies including Virgin, SpaceX, Fox Studios, Nike, Zappos, and Harvard University. With more than a million followers on social media, his company Kwik Learning now helps learners in more than 100 countries around the world.[1]

Todd Sampson is an Australian media and marketing guru. On his quest for a better brain he underwent numerous assessments by a diverse panel of brain experts from around the world.

Their unanimous assessment of his brain? *'Ordinary'.*

And so begins Todd's arduous, but entertaining, 3-month brain training adventure. Guided by brain training expert, Michael Merzenich and others, he undertakes an array of training exercises and at the end of each season completes a body/mind challenge that puts his learning to the test. He climbs a 120m rock summit blindfolded. He escapes being bound by locks and heavy chains, submerged at the bottom of a swimming pool – again, blindfolded. He trains to remember the random order of a full deck of 52 playing cards and successfully competes in the world memory championships for Australia; and in the final episode, walks a tightrope strung between 2 high-rise buildings, 22 storeys above Sydney's CBD. Sampson says the series demonstrates how people can overcome obstacles in life like fear of failure by rewiring their brains.[2,3]

Jill Bolte Taylor grew up with a brother who lived detached from a normal understanding of reality through a brain disorder known as schizophrenia. She became a Harvard researcher and was studying the neurological distinguishers of this disorder when, at 37 she suffered a brain haemorrhage and over the course of 4 hours lost all ability to process information. On the morning of the haemorrhage she could not walk, talk, read, write, or recall any of her life. She describes it as becoming an infant in a woman's body. Following an 8-year recovery, Jill shares how her 'stroke of insight' has given her a rare understanding into the 2 different 'personalities' that exist within the hemispheres of our brain and how we can access the wonders of both.[4]

These stories of amazing brains show us what's possible. One of the most profound scientific revelations of the 21st century is that your mind's capacity is not fixed! This is known as *neuroplasticity*. The prevailing view of brain development up until the late 1990s was that you were born with inherent abilities, you stretched yourself through school, learning fundamental skills, but also revealing your limitations, and then you left, and made do with what you had.

Now the good news. Although your brain does undergo rapid learning and development in your early years, it continues to grow new neurons all throughout your life, which become a functional and an integral part of your mental capacity. The consistent repetition of new behaviours form new neural pathways, whilst knowledge and skills, that we ignore wither away. This is called 'synaptic pruning'; or in other words, 'if you don't use it, you lose it!' On the flip side, behaviours that are repeated consistently over years literally reshape who you are. The exciting part is – you get to choose!

YOUR SUPER-POWERS

Do you doubt your abilities? OK, let's learn how amazing you actually are!

Your brain weighs only about 2% of your overall body weight but it uses around 20% of your blood flow and oxygen.[5] Your brain is hungry for energy! You are constantly thinking. Your brain generates around 50,000 thoughts per day, even when you're asleep.

The harder you think, the more oxygen and glucose fuel your brain draws.[6]

When you're awake, your brain generates enough bioelectricity to power a small lightbulb. Messages travelling to and from your brain around your body via your neural network regularly reach speeds of over 400km/h. That's fast![6]

You have about 100 billion brain cells called neurons, which is about the same number of stars in our Milky Way Galaxy! Each of these neurons are connected to one another via trillions of neural connections called synapses. There's a lot going on in a very small space![7]

Your brain is the ultimate nanotechnology. A piece of your brain the size of a grain of sand has more than 100,000 neurons and more than a billion synapses all connected and communicating with one another![8]

There is a lot of talk about artificial intelligence and how computing power will soon outpace the human brain's capacity for thought. Let's examine that. Setting aside creativity and looking at pure data crunching capacity, Tony Buzan, a leading authority on Mind Mapping says if the power of the world's most advanced supercomputer in the year 2000 were represented by a 2-storey house, the human brain's processing power would be a 'heaven-scraper'![9] 10 blocks square at the base and reaching all the way from earth to the moon. This doesn't even account for the intricate nature of activities that the human brain performs effortlessly on a daily basis or the virtually unlimited creative potential that we embody. Most experts agree that, whilst we will continue to 'outsource' aspects of our thinking to technology (which can cause us to lose mental skills through synaptic pruning), computers will never surpass human intelligence and creative thought. Your mind is a miraculous thing.

BRAIN HEALTH

Your brain already performs amazing feats of strength, speed, and agility every day. It is an incredible machine – but you can make it better! You can optimise your brain to perform at its best. Although our mind is the tool we use to travel through time, conjure new realities, and explore supernatural realms, it also obviously resides in the very real physical space between our ears; and as a part of our body, it has some vital human needs.

1. **Water**. Just like the earth's surface, about 75% of your brain is water and it needs to keep this balance to function properly. A small drop, even as little as 1–2% in hydration levels can significantly impair cognitive function. Brain fog, loss of memory, low attention span could all simply be symptoms of not enough water. Most adults should be drinking about 10 glasses of water per day to maintain optimal health and brain function.[10]
2. **Fats**. You might be surprised to know that a fit and healthy brain is made up of 60% fat which it maintains through healthy fats and oils in your diet. Omega 3s and Omega 6s help to stabilise and rebuild brain cells. The brain also produces its own form of cholesterol which is important for learning and memory.[11]
3. **Sleep**. Sleep deprivation is not uncommon in our hectic, fast paced world. In the push for a competitive edge in business or education, sleep is often the first lifestyle habit to be sacrificed on the altar of achievement. (Some even wear their lack of sleep as a badge of honour!) Yet science shows that good rest is an essential step to maintaining optimal brain function.[12] During sleep your brain sorts and organises memories from the day. Your unconscious mind also goes to

work and can provide creative insights to real world problems as you dream. As you rest, blood flow reduces and your brain shrinks in size, which allows harmful stress chemicals to be flushed from your cells. Sleep deprivation raises brain temperature and prevents natural maintenance processes. It makes you angry, irritated, irrational, and eventually, kills brain cells. Maintaining a good sleep pattern is a long-term investment in brain health and an essential ingredient of your Maximised Life.

4. **Exercise.** Aerobic exercise has long been known to improve your cardio-vascular health. Good blood flow is the oxygen and fuel supply your brain needs to perform its best. It also releases endorphins – a cocktail of feel-good neurochemicals that boost feelings of wellbeing and give you a more positive outlook on life. People have described this mild euphoria that follows exercise as a 'runner's high'. Exercise boosts serotonin and norepinephrine levels which regulates sleep patterns, improves mood and creates an alert state that supports memory formation and retrieval. Exercise also promotes the production of neurotrophins; a protein that encourages brain growth. The resulting brain volume and density has been shown to buffer against the effects of dementia. Your body and your brain are a synergistic unit. When you have a healthy body, you are supporting the development of your mind and your mind is the control centre for your body to take smarter, more effective action in your life.[13]

BRAIN TRAINING ACTIVITY 1

Download the Brain Health Planner from www.thrivebydesign-book.com/resources

Print it out and stick it somewhere easily visible so you can track your progress.

1. Make a commitment to boost your heart health. Nominate 3 time slots each week. This can be any activity you choose. It just needs to raise your heart rate to 120 beats/minute and be fun! If it's enjoyable, you're much more likely to stick to your commitment.
2. Buy a 1 litre drink bottle. Fill it in the morning and drink from it often. Refill it as per the calendar.
3. When do you need to get up? Work back at least 8 hours from this time and set a time to turn in. Make sure that 1 hour before this, you're off any devices or screens, you've wrapped up any work activities. What else could you do instead? How about a relaxing bath or book? What about a conversation with your kids? How about some quality time with your partner? The more enriching and enjoyable the more likely you will be to make it happen – so choose wisely.

| 11 |

Neurochemistry Insights

How long must I sleep and wake,
with heavy heart about to break?
How long can an empty soul walk on,
before someone sees his life is gone?
Day by day I trudge the road,
with futile cause and heavy load.
If only I could just break free,
from the curse I've come to know as me.

This is the first part of a poem that I wrote in 2006. Re-reading the words takes me back there.

In 2003 we'd moved near the coast and bought a house. It was a great lifestyle and financial move, but it meant leaving my design teaching behind. The following year I had co-authored a series of books on the creative process, which was incredibly rewarding, but 2 years later, with 2 young children, another on the way, a mortgage, and renovation dreams we couldn't afford. The pressures of life were beginning to eat away at my normal *can-do* attitude.

Instead of design, I was teaching maths at the local high school to kids who had about as much interest in *'crocheting doilies'* as they did in learning mathematics. I tried everything I could to engage them. I drew comic strips to teach abstract concepts. We learned scale, measurement, area and volume through craft and building projects. We played games to learn statistics and probability. I organised survivor-style math challenge days out in the forest. I taught Pythagoras with ladders up against walls and stringlines set up all across the playground.

I wasn't a math teacher by training, but I enjoyed solving numeracy and logic puzzles and I thought I could share that joy with them. Despite other more experienced teachers telling me otherwise, I maintained the belief that learning could be fun and I was pouring myself out in the pursuit of that ideal.

I worked late each night, trying desperately to change the status quo but to no avail. Student interest piqued momentarily, like an animal munching grass that gets startled by a loud noise or unexpected event, but just as surely as the animal is compelled to return to its grazing, so too my students returned to their apathy about mathematics.

I felt out of my depth and out of place. I saw other more experienced teachers promoting obedience and conformity in their classrooms which seemed so natural for them, but so foreign to me. For them, the kids dutifully completed their work without enthusiasm or inspiration. They seemed content with the dull delivery and their own mediocre efforts. That cold, standardised method was so enticing, and yet so repulsive at the same time. I was trying to do things differently but I was physically and mentally exhausted.

Sleep was being interrupted by our young children and everyday my mood steadily declined. That familiar reality of 'I don't belong here' was looming like a storm cloud in the distance. I began to self-medicate with unhealthy lifestyle choices like more work, sugary-foods, and pornography. I was trying desperately to escape life and to numb the feelings of failure that were becoming more apparent every day.

I avoided exercise and conversation, some of the very things that could have helped me. I still found relief in nature and the wonder of my beautiful children. They could still somehow lift me up out of the mud, but each day joy was getting harder to come by. The days were getting bleaker and it seemed that there was nothing I could do about it. My journal was a place of solace but the themes, like my soul, were getting darker...

I have sat, bleeding heart.
I have sat, holding the knife.
I have sat, pondering my children's future.
I have sat, in grief and despair.

While one part of me was spiralling out of control, another part of me was detached and analytical. This part was curious about what was happening in me and why.

While all this was going on, my wife was growing bigger each day with our new baby. We were both reading books to prepare for the birth, and that was how I stumbled across the fascinating and intricate world of *neurochemistry*. Of course, I was learning about the wonders of birth, but the more I researched, the more I encountered unexpected insights into myself. Struggles began to make sense. This was before mental health had become the mainstream societal concern it is today, and it was the first time I'd given it any thought. I began to realise that I wasn't as trapped as I thought. Change *was* possible! I had found hope for the future. Here is some of what I learned...

OXYTOCIN - AKA THE LOVE HORMONE

Oxytocin initiates contractions in childbirth, and later stimulates milk production. It is also the hormone that helps us bond with our children. It increases romantic attachment, enhances orgasms, and plays a key role in reproduction for both men and women. It is stimulated by physical touch and is one of the '3 happy hormones'. It helps to foster empathy; solidify trust and social relationships. It helps regulate appetite; promotes restful sleep; and gives us those warm, fuzzy feelings we associate with feeling in love. [1]

CORTISOL - AKA THE STRESS HORMONE

Oxytocin has an inverse relationship to cortisol. There is evidence to suggest that oxytocin and cortisol compete for the same receptors in the brain – which means that you can feel connected, or feel stressed, but not both at the same time. One of the reasons we were electing for a home birth was that we had learned when you go to hospital, stress levels rise producing cortisol. This counteracts oxytocin and can slow or even stop contractions resulting in medical intervention. Staying in your own calm environment can help birth to flow more smoothly. Understanding cortisol helped me to understand how prolonged stress at work was affecting my mood and leading me to feel agitated and disconnected.

Cortisol is not all bad – in fact no neurochemical is *bad* in the right place, at the right time. The Hormone Health Network says: "Cortisol can help control blood sugar levels, regulate metabolism, help reduce inflammation, and assist with memory formulation. It has a controlling effect on salt and water balance and helps control blood pressure. In women, cortisol also supports the developing foetus during pregnancy. All of these functions make cortisol a crucial hormone to protect overall health and wellbeing."[2]

But it's a balancing act. If cortisol stays too high for too long, it starts to deteriorate health. This survival state shuts down less critical body functions. Skin health and digestion are two of the first areas to suffer.[3] It tells the body to seek out high-carb foods and stores this as fat. It keeps your body in a state of high alert, which can tip you into anxiety and prevent you from getting a good night's sleep. It narrows your arteries and increases your heart rate which can negatively impact your cardio-vascular health.

SEROTONIN – AKA THE HAPPY HORMONE

Initially, I thought managing cortisol was my problem. It was an issue for sure, but as I researched further, I learned it's just one piece of the puzzle. You don't get depressed because you have too much sad hormone. You feel flat because you're running low on happy hormones. The chief happy hormone is serotonin. It makes you feel upbeat and positive. It also regulates your sleeping patterns. It works in partnership with melatonin. Melatonin is stimulated by darkness, it causes you to unwind, relax and get ready for a deep, restful sleep. Serotonin is stimulated by light. It makes you feel energised, refreshed and ready to start the day. Working on the computer, looking at your phone, TV, and even bright lights at night can interrupt the natural seesawing of melatonin/serotonin and cheat you out of a fresh start to your day!

TESTOSTERONE – AKA THE MALE HORMONE

While oxytocin feels soft, warm, fuzzy, and friendly, testosterone brings strength and hard edges. It literally shapes the body by shedding fat, promoting lean muscle mass, and building stronger bones.[4] It correlates to better verbal memory, spatial abilities, mathematical reasoning, higher libido, confidence, and improved mood.⁵ Testosterone plays a key role in both men's and women's health. It is present in higher quantities and its effects are more discernible in men. Excessive testosterone is believed to be linked to aggression, dominating behaviours, and a lack of empathy,⁶ but perhaps testosterone is not the only culprit here? What happens when the strength of testosterone is combined with affectionate care of oxytocin? A study of male leaders showed that positions of high responsibility correlate directly with high levels of testosterone.⁷ Some handle these positions well. For others, the high responsibility equates to stress – enter cortisol. It might seem like cortisol and testosterone have a lot in common (alert, sharp focus, increased metabolism, etc), but they don't play well together in the long term. High testosterone brings confidence, strength, and the ability to act decisively under pressure, however, when cortisol shows up (and stays around), it takes over the wheel. It dulls the energy of testosterone the same way it does with oxytocin and the positive benefits are lost.

Studies have shown that raised testosterone and reduced cortisol is the ideal neuro-combo that makes the best leaders – strong, confident, decisive, but also more likely to maintain high empathetic accuracy, respect for others, and they avoid getting overwhelmed in positions of high responsibility.¹²

ESTROGEN – AKA THE FEMALE HORMONE

Estrogen is converted from testosterone thanks to an enzyme called aromatase and is present in both males and females.⁸ It plays different roles in both sexes. Estrogen rises in women during puberty and initiates the menstrual cycle. It helps regulates the rhythm of this cycle throughout a woman's reproductive years, until it ebbs in menopause. Estrogen in men helps to modulate sex drive and produce sperm. Surprisingly, estradiol (a specific type of estrogen) has been shown to improve libido for men with low testosterone. Estrogen spikes for women in the middle of their menstrual cycle, triggering ovulation and a series of other intricate flow-on effects including a rise in serotonin and other feel-good neurochemicals. When estrogen drops, mood, energy levels and libido can also take a dive. It is wise to be mindful of the ebb and flow of estrogen and how this might be playing into you or your partner's overall sense of wellbeing.

DOPAMINE – AKA THE 'FEEL-GOOD' HORMONE

Dopamine is a powerful neurotransmitter. It supports movement, memory, and attentiveness, but it is most commonly known for its role in desire. Dopamine inducing behaviours give us a rush, which reinforces those activities and makes us want to do them again. An experiment that gave rats a dopamine hit every time they poked their nose into a box led the rats to repeat this behaviour up to 800 times per hour! They quickly became addicted to the box.

In 1954 James Olds and Peter Milner made a breakthrough in neurological research with electrodes implanted in the brains of rats that allowed them to effectively turn off the dopamine receptors in the rat's brains. These rats lost all forms of desire. They didn't eat, didn't have sex, they didn't drink. The rats died of thirst in just a few days.[9] In follow up experiments, the scientists fed the rats a sugary substance and noted the rats had 'expressions of pleasure' on their faces. So, when dopamine was blocked, the rats were still able to sense pleasure, but their desire was gone, and without desire, action stopped.[10] In humans, dopamine typically rewards activities that would have kept our ancient ancestors alive. Eating high-energy foods, learning new things, completing challenging tasks, puzzles, or projects, having sex and regular exercise all give us a dopamine hit and therefore feel great! Dopamine can drive positive behaviours like these; OR it can result in unhealthy addictions such as over-eating, illicit sex, and drug use.

Low dopamine levels are mostly a flow on effect from other neurological imbalances.[11] For example, high cortisol can affect sleep patterns; which in turn affects serotonin levels; which in turn lowers mood and wellbeing; which in turn amplifies a craving for pleasure, and so we self-soothe with a dopamine hit. "Pass me the ice-cream please!"

While the ice-cream can provide some instant relief and is relatively harmless, other kinds of self-medication can be more insidious. Pornography, illicit drugs, gambling, self-harm, shop-lifting, and other addictive behaviours can spiral quickly out of control and cause irreparable damage. They spark a huge surge of pleasure on their first hit and so it is hard not to go back for more. The hunger for pleasure becomes unbearable and addiction gets locked in. What is worse, high spikes in dopamine also dull the sensitivity of dopamine receptors, which means that higher and higher dopamine levels are required to get the same effect. After sustained use, ordinary life feels grey, empty, and perpetually unsatisfying. Addictions are a pernicious counterfeit of the genuine Call on your life.

I had a healthy upbringing. My parents gave me a great start and yet, I've always had a hunger to learn, grow and have more – to be more. Perhaps they helped to cultivate that. I'm not sure. What I do know is that dopamine plays a core role in this desire. I've searched relentlessly and sometimes unwisely. I've made some big mistakes along the way. At times I've felt lost, alone, and stuck. A slave to my own ambition. I've had to spend a lot of years learning the secret of feeling content with less and unlearning unhealthy coping habits. I have made my peace with dopamine and now consider her an ally on my journey, but it's a never-ending quest in an ever-shifting landscape.

I'm guessing that you can relate to my story. Dopamine plays a fundamental role in our drive to succeed. In learning. Building habits, and ultimately shaping who we become. *Everyone* who hungers for more out of life has a healthy flow of dopamine coursing through their veins and their neural network. That's OK. Leveraging its powerful influence will be one of the key ingredients in your success story.

AN INTRICATE SYSTEM

The neurochemical world is multifaceted. It's a dynamic drama and every hormone is a complex character whose story is interwoven with the other. In the last chapter we learned about the trillions of neural connections in your brain. Now you can see that along these connections, there are several different languages and nuanced dialects being spoken! Science has still only scratched the surface of this incredibly intricate and complex world.

BRAIN TRAINING ACTIVITY 2

It might surprise you to know that our neurochemistry is not set. Just like we train our muscles through exercise, we also reshape our neurochemical profile with the actions that we take in our body. Elevating your testosterone and oxytocin, reducing your cortisol levels, and managing your dopamine to work for you and not against you is all possible with some easy-to-learn practices and mindfulness.

One simple exercise that has been shown to simultaneously raise testosterone and reduce cortisol levels is the '2-minute Power Pose' popularised in Amy Cuddy's 2012 TED talk.[12] You can watch

Amy's presentation and download my Power Posing Guide at: www.thrivebydesignbook.com/resources

Add this easy but powerful exercise to your Brain Training Calendar.

| 12 |

The Happy Mind

> *Most people are about as happy*
> *as they make up their minds to be.*
>
> **ABRAHAM LINCOLN**

On the 20th October, 2012, at just after 3:30 in the morning, Kate Gladdin received a phone call that would forever change her life. Kate's sister Nicole had been killed in a motorcycle accident and despite her broken-hearted pleas with the universe to change this reality, life was never going to be the same again. Her big sister Nicole was a bubbly, effervescent 24-year-old; a talented dancer, passionate football fan and up and coming TV sports journalist enjoying a getaway in Thailand at the end of the season when her life was tragically taken. Her death was devastating to everyone who knew her. In the weeks and months that followed Kate spent a lot of time lying on the bathroom floor. Weeping. Struggling to come to terms with the pain, the loss, and the overwhelming unfairness of it all.

Kate stumbled blindly through an emotional minefield of anger and despair. She felt hatred for the man who had taken her beloved sister, who was never charged and showed no remorse. She felt betrayed by life. How could such a horrible thing happen to such a beautiful person? As she sifted through these emotions and the pieces of her life that no longer seemed important or made sense, Kate came across other families who had gone through similar tragedy. Not only did Kate discover that she was not alone, but she also stumbled across the shocking truth that Australians are being killed in road trauma at a rate of **1 every 17 hours** in South-East Asia.[1]

From this startling realisation Kate made two big decisions.

1) She couldn't bring Nicole back, but she could decide NOT to be destroyed by the hurt and anger that she was feeling; and

2), in order to do that, she knew she needed to do something positive instead.

Kate resolved that Nicole's death was not going to be in vain and that she was going to make change where she could. She began a travel safety education campaign speaking in schools and anywhere else that would have her. Kate knew that if her message could prevent just one other family having to suffer like she had, then her work would be worthwhile.

With her family, she started the Nicole Fitzsimons Foundation which perpetuates Nicole's legacy through the travel safety message and also financially supports other up and coming athletes and artists as they pursue their dreams. Kate's mission became a huge success raising awareness for hundreds of *soon-to-graduate-and-travel* high school students. She also partnered with government agencies who supported her cause "to bring more Aussie tourists safely home to the arms of loved ones".

As this message grew, so too did Kate's impact as she began to also speak about resilience, sharing more about her own personal struggles from high school and the priceless life-lessons she has learned about getting back up, even when life knocks you down.

(You can hear my full interview with Kate at: https://www.blueprintlifecoaching.com.au/post/episode034)

Kate says: "if the unthinkable can happen in the worst way, then perhaps it can happen in the best way too!" Her story is a beautiful example of how shifting our perspective, and the stories we tell ourself and others can make all the difference in the life we end up living.

We're usually not aware of it, but our brains are always hard at work interpreting our circumstances and the events we experience in order to fit them into our worldview. These filters are what we're talking about when we're talking about mindset.

Cognitive Behavioural Therapy examines the interplay between Thoughts, Feelings and Behaviours and helps people to address chronically unhelpful thinking patterns such as anxiety, depression, and catastrophic thinking syndrome. The way our thinking shapes our belief systems is a big part of this theory. There are a lot of different interpretations of this model but in Life Coaching, the focus is on results, and so it goes something like this:

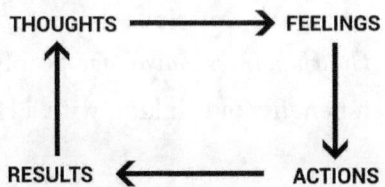

1. There is tension in your circumstances. Where you are is not where you want to be.
2. If you change your thinking/beliefs, then you change your feelings/emotions.
3. If your feelings, then you will change your actions
4. If you change your actions, then you will change your results.

A quote often credited to Albert Einstein is: "the definition of insanity is doing the same thing over and over again, expecting a different result".[2] Our brains are extremely efficient. They automate as much of life as they can, including our worldviews. It's human nature to repeat our mistakes but understanding this model can help us interrupt the cycle of insanity. This model is built on the very important idea that while we cannot always control our circumstances, we *do* have control over our own thoughts. Holocaust survivor and author Victor Frankl says, "Everything can be taken from man but one thing; the last of the human freedoms – to choose one's attitude in any given set of circumstances, to choose one's own way."[3]

So how do we change our mindset?

One way is by making the conscious choice for happiness. Shawn Achor, author of *The Happiness Advantage* points out some of the scientifically proven benefits of thinking with a Happy Mind.[4]

- Only 25% of job success can be predicted by IQ – the other 75% is determined by your optimism levels, social support, and your ability to see challenges as an opportunity for growth instead of a threat.

- Doctors are 19% faster and more accurate at diagnosing their patients when operating at positive instead of negative, neutral, or stressed.
- Retailers are 37% better at sales when operating at positive instead of negative, neutral, or stressed.
- We are all 31% more productive when operating at positive instead of negative, neutral, or stressed.
- Positive mindset can contribute to a 300% rise in innovation.

He also points out that our traditional formula for happiness is broken and backwards. It goes something like this. We set high goals, we work hard, we achieve our goals, and then we are happy – aren't we? This is the way we approach learning and productivity in our schools, universities, workplaces and even our family life; but here's the problem. Human beings are designed to grow. We are forever hoping, dreaming, and expanding our ideas of what's possible. So as soon as you reach your goal, you have a moment of celebration, but then set another higher goal. We keep moving the goalposts, therefore when happiness is connected to the goal, it is always being pushed forward into the future. It's the 'pursuit of happiness'. A state we perpetually strive for but never reach.

Achor proposes that we can unlock the key to reaching our true potential by reversing this formula. By finding ways to become happier in the present, you enjoy work and life more, therefore you work better, faster, and more productively. Consequently, you achieve your goals faster and with greater joy! That's not to say you won't face challenges along the way, but the conscious choice for happiness is a brilliant way of priming yourself to win when trials come.

BECOME MINDFUL OF MEANING

Every event, every circumstance, every experience is filtered through our previously established mindset and belief. As I've said, most of this happens on autopilot, which means that it happens without our conscious influence or control. The first step towards a happier mind is acknowledging that our thoughts ARE subject to our will, and therefore we can change the way we interpret these experiences. For example, let's say you're running late for an important client meeting. You're cutting it fine but if you push, you'll make it. You get halfway there, and traffic is backed up for 2 blocks. There's been a car accident up ahead and it doesn't look like moving for at least 20 minutes. You are going to be late. What are the possible meanings you can construct here?

- Typical. This ALWAYS happens to me!
- That's it. The client is definitely not going to sign with me now.
- God, why aren't you helping me? Why have you abandoned me?
- This is a lesson for me. I need to prepare better and get out the door on time.
- Wow – a few minutes earlier and it might have been me in that accident – someone upstairs is looking out for me.
- This is a great reason to explain why I'm late AND I have an extra 15 minutes to think through my pitch.
- The government needs to invest more in road safety.
- I bet it was a P-plater. Probably on their phone at the lights. Youth are wrecking society.
- I wonder how the emergency workers are going up there. That must be a tough job.

- It looks bad. I really hope that person is OK. I wonder if there is anything I can do?

How did you feel when you read each of these responses? Can you see how the shift in perspective immediately changes the meaning linked to the event and that meaning drastically changes the emotional response that follows? We are wired for story. Our brain will always construct a narrative to give meaning to and interpret life events. The great news is that you can control this story. You are the author of your thoughts. *You* get to decide how that story goes.

E-MOTION

Have you ever noticed that the word emotion is made up of 'e + motion'? The root meaning comes from Latin. 'E' is a variant of 'ex' meaning outward, and motion means 'to move'. Emotion is an outward-flowing excitement or agitation that drives action. We often think that our actions are driven by thought, and they are, but not directly. Emotion or feelings are a much more powerful motivator than rational thought.

Emotions are also an indicator of our internal state. Like a thermometer gauges the temperature of a room, our emotions let us know how aligned we are with our core beliefs. When there is conflict between our circumstances and our goals or values, we sense the tension through emotion. This drives us to take action. Action is designed to restore the balance. The trouble comes when we are telling ourselves unhelpful stories, which in turn creates a negative tension that moves us toward less productive and even unhealthy behaviours.

In the car accident example above, let's say the story you told yourself was: *"That's it. I'm done. There's no way that the client is going to sign with me now!"*

Imagine the emotions that follow. Resignation. Anger. Hopelessness. Now what actions follow? Do you bring your A-game to the meeting room? Do you show up with confidence to deliver your pitch? Do you even show up at all?

Now imagine your story is: *"Phew! That could have been me! This meeting is important, but boy there are bigger, more important things in life. I'm so grateful to be alive."*

What are the emotions that follow? Gratitude. Love. Purpose. How do you show up to the meeting now? You apologise respectfully to the client, explaining that there was a traffic accident that held you up, but inside you know that your value is not tied to this pitch. You give your best effort from a place of security, knowing that if this doesn't work out, that's OK. Opportunities come and go, but life's too short to not be grateful.

Same day. Same person. Same circumstance. Same client. Different mindset. Different response.

Which do you think gets the better results?

By becoming more mindful of emotions, we become more aware of the internal dialogue that is going on inside our head. If you have a negative emotional response – stop, pause, ask yourself, what is the situation that is provoking this response? What are some other ways I could interpret this?

REPROGRAMMING YOUR RAS

At the top of your spinal column, within the brainstem is a network of neurons known as the Reticular Activating System (RAS).[5]

The RAS automates certain life-sustaining bodily functions like heart rate, swallowing and breathing but also plays a key role in mindset. Every piece of information that comes into our brain from external stimuli – what we see, taste, hear, touch and smell comes in via this gateway.

Our senses take in about 11 million bits of information every second, but the conscious mind is only capable of handling about 50 bits of information per second,[6] or about 4 complex thoughts at any one time.[7] Without the RAS our conscious mind would be completely inundated with information and quickly overwhelmed. The RAS filters signals from the neural network and decides what's important and what's not.

Have you ever played the game Spotto? On a car trip you try to spot yellow cars before anyone else does. I'm terrible at it. I could be stopped at an intersection and a yellow bus could drive right past me and I wouldn't even notice. It wouldn't register. But my kids are another story. They are Spotto Ninjas. They can smell a yellow car from about a kilometre away. A yellow car can poke its bumper 2 centimetres past the edge of a building off to the far right, and like a backseat full of terminator robots, their heads will swivel in unison, all firing out the word "spotto" simultaneously. They then spend the next 10 minutes debating who saw it first. (Ah, the joys of car travel!)

Or maybe you've had the experience where you're in the market for a new car. You've browsed online for a few weeks and decided on a make and model, and then all of a sudden it seems like everyone has stolen your idea! Every fifth car on the road seems to be the same or similar to the car you've been looking to buy! How can that be?

What's going on here? Why does my brain seem oblivious to yellow vehicles and my kids seem to have a genetic disposition for coloured car spotting? Why, when you make a decision to buy a car, does it seem that everyone else around you has the same idea?

Well, firstly, it's got nothing to do with cars. Cars are just a good example because on the road they give us a regular stream of random information for our brain to sort. As we process this information, the majority of it hits our RAS and gets filtered out. Imagine millions of bits of stimuli are getting served up and the RAS is like the quality controller on a factory floor. Most information doesn't make the grade.

Not important...

    Not important...

        Not important...

            Wait! Yes! That's important!

Let it through!

The RAS is one of the largest dopamine producing areas in the brain, and while most information gets thrown out, when something does get the tick of approval, these little triggers of recognition send a cascade of positive reinforcement through our neural network to strengthen learning.

We can *switch on* our RAS to recognise certain stimuli, and when we do, those objects or situations become 'real' for us.

I once heard a story about a lady who worked with a life coach because she wanted to start her own business. As a part of her process, they established that she needed to find an office space and so her coach guided her through a visualisation exercise picturing her perfect office space. She described the light blue colour of the walls, the sheer curtains hanging near the window, the way the light and breeze came in and filled the room with a soft warm light. With her eyes closed, she brought every detail to mind. The session ended and she got in her car and drove home. On her way home she saw a handwritten sign stuck up in a shop window – 'room for lease'.

"Ooooh" she thought, and pulled over. She enquired with the shop owner who told her it was an upstairs space just above her shop and asked if she'd like to go up and take a look. "Sure!" the woman said, and they walked up the steps to the office space above. When she walked into the room, she gasped. A tear came into her eye as she looked at the colour of the wall, the curtains blowing gently in the breeze and the afternoon light pouring through the North facing window. "I love it" she managed to say.

What happened? Did this lady 'magically manifest' her new office space? Did she know a special 'secret' that others don't?

Not really. The kicker of this story is that the sign in the window had been stuck up over a month before, and this shop was on this lady's way to work. So twice a day, every day, she drove past the sign and if she looked, she would have even been able to see into the space through the North-facing window. She 'saw' it, but she didn't. Her RAS had filtered it from her conscious awareness but the information was still there. In her coaching session she tapped into her 'intuition' and described her dream office space. Then on her way home, she noticed the sign – the same sign she had driven past multiple times over the past 6 weeks – only this time, the RAS said: *"That's important – let it through!"*.

MAKING THE CHOICE FOR HAPPINESS

Have you ever had one of those performance reviews at work where your boss tells you the 4 or 5 things that you're doing really well and then gives you an 'opportunity for improvement'? And all you can think about is that one piece of negative feedback?

Why do we do that?

Unfortunately, our brains are more attuned to negative stimuli than to positive. The RAS has been trained over millennia to give greater credence to any form of physical, mental, or social threat, because in the past, noticing those things kept us alive. Scientists estimate that our brains prioritise negative information giving it about 5 – 6 times greater emphasis than positive information. (No wonder some days seem hard!) This is called 'negativity bias'.[8]

At the time of my writing this chapter, some of our major cities are in lockdown due to COVID-19. I hope that by the time of this book being published we will be looking back and saying "I'm glad that's over" but right now everyone is hyper vigilant. The media is doing what the media does best and taking advantage of the situation. Fear-based news stories are prioritised at about the same ratio as our negativity bias, further confirming our belief that the world is a tough, hard, horrible place to live, and that 'survival' is what life is all about. That's a sad way to live. You can retrain your RAS to lift the status of positive stimuli with these strategies:

BRAIN TRAINING ACTIVITY 3

Choose one of the actions below and add it to your Brain Health Calendar. Make it a regular part of your morning routine for the next week. Make yourself accountable to someone you trust by telling them that you're going to do it and ask them to check in with you in 7 days' time.

1. **Gratitude**. Writing down at least 3 things every day that you are grateful for is a scientifically proven way of switching your RAS to positive. Spending the time to write down these things forces your brain to slow down and recognise them as a part of your day. This in turn boosts your *feelings* of positivity, which in turn primes you for more positive action! And the positive benefits don't stop there. When you

know that every day you will be writing down good things that happened the day before, your RAS begins to place more significance on positive events. Your RAS begins to let more of these little wins through to your conscious awareness and your reality will begin to shift. Slowly but surely, it will seem as though your luck has changed for the better. This is the magic of perception. The evidence for gratitude was always there – you just had to tune in to see it.

2. **Vision**. Define success. This journaling exercise takes just a few minutes. Imagine I have just asked you, 'how would you describe success?' or 'how do you describe yourself when you think of yourself as successful'? You can go macro and describe big picture success – what does the Maximised Life look like to you? Or you can go micro – what does success look like today? Either way, you are defining the distinguishing features of success. This enacts your RAS to recognise information that reinforces this as true. Little by little you will gather evidence and you will begin to see opportunities that can reshape your future.

3. **Exercise**. Jim Kwik says: "when the body moves, the brain grooves!" Exercise teaches our RAS that action matters. It stimulates the production of positive neurotransmitters, endorphins, and sends oxygen-rich blood pulsing through your brain. Exercise is a celebration of bodily freedom and to whatever your capacity allows, you should shake it, stretch it, flex it, bend it, bounce it, and test it, in any way you can!

4. **Focus**. Make a list. Define what you will do today. If you're like me, then your to-do list is about a mile long and it will have twice as many things added to it today as you can possibly hope to tick off in a 24-hour period. I get it – but this is not about the to-do list. I'm asking you to define just

1, 2 or 3 things that you want to get done today. No more than 3. What 'big rocks' will you move that will make today a winning day? There are always a hundred little things to keep you busy, and if you let them, they will completely swallow up your time leaving you in a ground-hog day cycle of unproductivity. Narrowing your focus ensures that finishing projects becomes an important and rewarding part of your day.

5. **Positive messages**. I love this one. You cannot turn on the television, go on social media, or even walk down the street without your RAS being triggered to a potential threat. What we focus on grows. Take the positive message challenge! Whenever you hear a negative news story, grab your phone, and send someone a positive message, to praise them, encourage them, or just to let them know you're thinking about them. This will not only start a ripple of positivity in your circle of influence, but also make you more mindful of the type of information you are consuming. If every time you hear a negative news story, you have to write a positive message, you might even think twice before turning on the 6 o'clock news!

| 13 |

The Growth-Focused Mind

*You can choose comfort, or you can choose courage,
but you cannot have both.*

BRENÉ BROWN

At the end of 2007 I decided I wanted more than my teaching job could give me. I felt redundant in the institution and wanted to make a bigger difference in the world than twisting teenagers' arms to see the relevance of mathematics. I now know that every teacher feels this way sometimes, but back then I thought it was just me.

My wife Sofia and I combined our passions and we started 'Heartmade Gifts' – a gift business that bundled together beautifully handmade and organically produced products. We found people who loved what they did but didn't necessarily love sales. We positioned our gifts to customers who recognised their quality and value. I didn't realise it at the time, but the core mission of this business was helping others to thrive doing what they love – the same as it is today.

It felt great to be off on a new adventure together. Being creative. Full of hope and possibility. Mingling family life with the workday and building a community of people who thought like we did about health and authentic living. We compiled talented artisan's work together into amazing gift packages and sold them through a combination of party-plan, markets, and online sales.

It went pretty well for a while, but our network wasn't large enough to support us and we had to travel further and further to reach new markets. This cut into the family lifestyle we'd set out to create – and also our profit margins. 18 months later, after 3 months of consistent decline, the business was in trouble. After a disappointing Valentine's Day, we were now several thousand dollars in debt and with Easter holidays on the horizon, we figured this was our last chance to make a profit before we'd have to accept defeat and close up. I sourced some special organic chocolate Easter eggs and giant bunnies. They were premium products. Perfect for our target market. I bought several thousand dollars' worth of stock on credit.

We were pregnant again and expecting Number 4 which was adding to the pressure, but we decided to take a week away and rejuvenate, before the new baby came. We found a cheap holiday house an hour away in a quiet fishing village and enjoyed some much-needed reconnection time and rest. 3 days before the holiday ended, disaster struck.

After a beach walk, Sofia (heavily pregnant) slumped into a deck chair at another holiday house her sister was staying at. The chair had no traction on the slippery deck and Sofia slid backward, the tipped, toppling off the edge of the deck. The deck was about a metre off the ground and had no railing. She turned sideways as she fell and went shoulder first into the solid concrete driveway. I was away at the beach with the kids and by the time I got back, the ambulance had arrived. We drove together to the hospital. She was put in a cast and we were sent back to Port Macquarie for further scans. Sofia was unusually quiet and withdrawn putting all her focus into coping with the pain. She was avoiding pain medication due to any possible side-effects on the baby. An MRI revealed that the ball joint at the top of the humorous (where the arm joins the shoulder) was dislodged, completely snapped off the bone, and split down the middle into several pieces. Surgery was necessary if Sofia was going to heal with full use of her arm again. The surgical team consulted with obstetrics and planned to operate the next day. We had a few hours to ourselves. Sofia cried, releasing some of the fear and pain that she'd been enduring the past 24 hours.

Up until this point we had been planning a completely natural home birth. We had a midwife booked, Glen, who now came to join us at the hospital. When he arrived, Sofia matter-of-factly said. "I can't do this. I need a caesarean. My pain right now is at 99%. I just can't do birth now as well."

Glen knew how much this meant to her. How much thought and energy and prayers she had put into being ready for her lovely, natural home birth. He wisely responded; "we can get all that ready for you. It's your call. But you don't need to decide that right now. Let's see how you go."

A little later a pair of bubbly OT nurses came in and as well as lifting Sofia's spirits with their quirky antics, helped fit Sofia with a sling which held her arm in tight and freed her from the fear of sudden movements. This allowed her to relax a little. She had a chance to rest and pray. 24 hours went by, then another curveball came our way. Her waters broke.

Sofia was now in labour. There were mild contractions, possibly held at bay by the cortisol and adrenaline still coursing through her system. The surgeon came back to visit us. Mustering a wry smile, he said, "OK. New plan".

Operating before the birth was no longer an option. In a few hours the waves of birth began to take over. The pain of birth overshadowed the shoulder pain and Sofia later described it as 'a relief'. I'm not sure anyone has called childbirth a relief before! The shoulder pain was screaming at her, "Something's wrong! Something's wrong!" whereas the birth seemed 'right' and natural, and in it she found peace.

Our 4th baby girl was born in the afternoon of the 20th of March. Sofia did it all with a shattered shoulder and without pain meds. 2 days later Sofia went into surgery. A titanium plate and seven screws were added to her arm as well as a cast to immobilise her. I became her arms for everything. I had to learn how to attach a baby for breast-feeding. Some women make it look easy. It's not.

A few days later I travelled back to our holiday home and bundled up all our stuff into our van. The kids were shared among Sofia's family. I brought most of our chocolate stock to the hospital and gave it away to the doctors and nurses who were taking care of us. Heartmade Gifts was over.

It was a surreal time. We were broken and defeated in so many ways, and yet, so overwhelmingly grateful and happy in others. We called our daughter Christall-Star. Christall (spelt Christ+all) because it seemed that all we had left was our faith; and Star because amidst it all, she was a bright shining light. A beacon of joy and hope.

I am now genuinely grateful for that season of our life. It taught me a lot about business and about myself. It showed me that life rolls around in cycles and that every ending is also a new beginning.

It also shaped me as a coach. I know how it feels to go searching for your place in the world, only to be met with knock downs and defeat. I know what it takes to get back up and try again.

Heartmade Gifts is not my only failure. There have been many others and I'm sure there'll be more, but I no longer think of them as defeats. I am designed to thrive. And thriving is the result of persistent discipline forged in the fires of heartache, trials, and crisis. Henry David Thoreau says to "let your failures refine you, not define you". Robert Allen goes one step further and says, "there is no failure, only feedback". Thomas Edison, in the process of inventing the incandescent lightbulb said; "I haven't failed, I've just found 10,000 ways that don't work".

Brené Brown says, "If we are brave enough often enough, we will fall; this is the physics of vulnerability. When we commit to showing up and risking falling, we are actually committing to falling. Daring is not saying, 'I'm willing to risk failure.' Daring is saying, 'I know I will eventually fail and I'm still all in." Most of us don't think about courage this way. We don't plan to lose, but if we commit ourselves to growth, then getting knocked down, abandoned, betrayed or just plain old screwing up and falling short is inevitable.

Michael Jordan, arguably the greatest sportsperson of our time, was cut from his high school basketball team. He ran home and wept in his bedroom. Later, reflecting on his achievements, he said; "I've missed more than 9,000 shots in my career. I've lost almost 300 games. Twenty-six times I've been trusted to take the game-winning shot and missed. I've failed over and over and over again in my life. And that is why I succeed."

The Maximised Mindset requires 1) that we have the courage to show up and try – even when it looks risky and failure seems imminent; and 2) we find the courage to get back up and try after we've been knocked down.

In 2006 Stanford Professor Carol Dweck published a book called 'Mindset: The New Psychology of Success'. It's built upon more than 10 years of research and one simple idea. This idea distinguishes between 2 very different types of people with 2 very different mindsets. The first is a Fixed Mindset. A Fixed Mindset believes that intelligence, creativity, or almost any other ability that you can think of is 'fixed' – that is, it is based purely on your genetic disposition. It says, champions are *born,* not made.

On the other hand, the Growth Mindset believes that genetics are just your starting point. The real determinant of success is your willingness to learn and grow. That includes our response to setbacks. Research has shown that these different mindsets lead to very different behaviours and therefore very different results.

Let's compare:

When encountering difficulty...

- A fixed mindset says, "I've reached my limits".
- A growth mindset says, "If I learn and apply myself, I can overcome this".

When encountering other people's success...

- A fixed mindset feels threatened. Comparison leads to a sense of inadequacy. "I'm not as good as them".
- A growth mindset feels inspired. Achievement shows what's possible. "Wow, I wonder if I could do that? Or something great like that?"

When encountering feedback...

- A fixed mindset feels criticised and condemned. "You think I'm dumb".
- A growth mindset recognises the value of external contribution. "You see my potential"

- The fixed mindset takes it personally because identity is wrapped up in performance.
- The growth mindset understands the important distinction between work and identity.

When encountering a new task that requires a lot of thought or effort...

- The fixed mindset says, "Effort is for those who lack ability. If I was meant to do it, it would come naturally to me".
- A growth mindset says, "I've got some learning to do. Effort is how accomplished people make it *look* easy".

When success is delayed...

- A fixed mindset says, "Success follows gifting, opportunity and luck".
- The growth mindset understands "Success follows consistent effort and perseverance"

You can see again from these simple comparisons how mindset shapes behaviour, and behaviour shapes results. What is really exciting about Dweck's research is that she has shown how very simple interventions can very quickly shift students into a growth mindset and get almost immediate results.

In a study she did with Lisa Blackwell, she gave 7th grade students a set of puzzles to do, and when they completed them, they gave them 2 different types of praise. To one group they said, "Wow, you did well on these, you must be smart" (that's fixed mindset praise because it identifies a student's inherent level of ability). To the other group she said, "Wow, you did well on these, you must have tried really hard" (which is growth mindset praise, because it identifies the student's effort instead of ability).[1]

Then they gave both groups a hard puzzle to see how they would cope with the challenge. The growth mindset group significantly outperformed the group that had received the fixed mindset praise. The growth mindset group also demonstrated higher levels of confidence, higher motivation and they persevered with the problems for much longer than the group that had received the fixed mindset praise.

The final test was when they asked the 2 groups to report on their scores to the researchers. The fixed mindset group lied about their scores more than twice as often as the growth mindset group.

What was the difference between these 2 groups?

One short sentence.

Dweck says; "If parents want to give their children a gift, the best thing they can do is to teach their children to love challenges, be intrigued by mistakes, enjoy effort, and keep on learning. That way, their children don't have to be slaves of praise. They will have a lifelong way to build and repair their own confidence".[2]

TAKING CONTROL

What language are you using to prime your kids, your class, or your team? What language do you use when talking to yourself? The Growth-Focused mindset shifts our perspective. We are empowered by the belief that we can directly shape our own destiny. Chuck Swindoll says; "Life is made up of 10% what happens to you and 90% how you respond to it".[3] This is known as 'agency'; our ability to act independently and to make our own choices.

During my coaching training, one of my trainers introduced me to the 'Above the line/Below the line' framework.[4] Those who live 'above the line' are *OAR-some* – that is, they take **Ownership**, they make themselves **Accountable**, and they are **Response-able**. This combination contrasts with those living below the line, people who instead tell their *BED-time* story. They **Blame**; they make **Excuses**, and they **Deny** their agency.

You may have heard the old story of the 2 twins that grew up with an alcoholic father. One son followed his father's footsteps and became an alcoholic. "What choice do I have?" he said. "My father was an alcoholic." The other son never touched a drop of alcohol. "How could I?" he said. "Look what it did to my father."[5]

THINK LIKE A HERO

In 1949 Joseph Campbell published a book called *The Hero with a Thousand Faces*. In it he retells dozens of stories from traditional cultures from all around the world distilling an archetype known as 'the mono-myth' or 'hero's adventure'.[6]

What's your favourite book or movie? Star Wars? The Hobbit? Remember the Titans? Bambi? In almost every book or movie you will see Campbell's cycle of transformation. The Hero crosses the threshold and enters the unknown. He is supported by a mentor or a wise guide but eventually faces trials, heartbreak, and his ultimate crisis alone. He is transformed by the experience and on his return brings a treasure (often an internal change) to bestow upon his community or family.

No one likes pain, but challenges are a fact of life. They're also an essential ingredient in your success story. Stephen Pressfield says; "without the villain, you have no story."[7] Whether your demons are a result of external circumstances, or whether they rise up from within, the only way we stay motivated in the face of opposition is to understand the role adversity plays in growth. Hanging in there is key. Angela Duckworth, a researcher at the University of Pennsylvania, calls this 'grit'. Grit is the perseverance and passion to achieve long term goals.[8] Duckworth calls it 'sticking with your future' and her research shows it is a crucial attribute of high achievers. When you recognise that you are the hero in your own story, you know resistance is coming, but you also know how the story goes. Sooner or later, you will prevail. If you persevere, learn from your mistakes, and never give up hope. Eventually, you will win.

KNOWING (& BEATING) YOUR ENEMIES

You will face challenges. That's a given. Some are external. Some are internal. Most are both. Circumstance can be influenced by actions. That's easy. Internal battles are fought in the mind. Do you recognise any of these?

1. **False Humility**. You probably already bumped into this in Part 1. It arises whenever we dare to speak out the Call. A nagging sense of unworthiness that constantly interrupts your thoughts. Not smart enough, good-looking enough, creative enough, disciplined enough, lucky enough, resourced enough, or ____ enough (you fill in the blank). Its main weapon is comparison dripping with condescension. It sounds something like: "Ooooh, aren't we thinking big now! No one has done what you are thinking about, so why in hell do you think you're going to be able to do it? What makes you so special? Don't you think it's time to deflate that ego just a little bit? Come back down to earth! This is reality! You're no good to anyone with your head up in the clouds."

    Beating False Humility. False Humility is overcome with

True Humility. True Humility means accepting your innate value as a human being like a small child accepts the love of a parent. They don't doubt it. They don't question it. They didn't earn it, but they believe it without question. They draw confidence from their position, not from their performance. True Humility accepts that the Calling comes from above, and it is therefore immune to accusations of arrogance or pride. True Humility can rest, secure in the knowledge that we are just playing our part in a much bigger story.

2. **Second-guessing**. Is the bane of the creative mind. So many ideas, so little time. When things get hard, we wonder; "Maybe I made a mistake?" "Maybe I missed the mark?" "If this is the right path, it shouldn't be this hard!" New ideas lure our attention offtrack. Also known as 'Shiny Object Syndrome'. Second-guessing stops you from doing real work and instead, repeatedly loops you back around to the beginning to 'make sure you didn't make a mistake'. To re-explore options, do another plan, and start all over again.

    Beating second-guessing. It's OK to second-guess yourself. It's normal. It's OK to loop back around and revisit your notes, rediscover your why, reflect on the Call, and refine your plan. But once you've done that. It's time to do the work. Expect things to get hard! Don't expect a trouble-free journey. One or two recalibrations is fine. After that, second-guessing is beaten with grit and perseverance. This is self-belief in action.

3. **Perfectionism**. False humility and second-guessing can stop you starting. Once you overcome them, Perfectionism steps in to stop you finishing. Perfectionism leverages your desire to be your best and applies an insidious form of comparison that can be summed up in 3 crippling words: "Not good

enough." Winston Churchill said, "perfection is the enemy of progress".[9] Jon Acuff describes perfectionism as "a poison that pretends to be a vitamin".[10] It is the insistent voice of your inner critic.

Beating Perfectionism. Perfectionism is overcome with a Growth Mindset. A willingness to make and learn from mistakes is key. Focus on the process, not the outcome. We have to be vulnerable. Be willing to show up and submit our work. We must stay open to feedback. This takes courage. Willing to live *all-in* and be seen for who we are despite our shortcomings.

4. **Rejection.** "Nobody wants what you've got" quickly morphs into, "nobody wants YOU!" It provokes a deep, visceral fear that chokes momentum. You've spent time discovering your mission, you've designed a smart strategy and stepped out into the arena, only to hear… nothing. An awkward cough from the back of the room breaks the silence and shame swoops in. "You don't belong here". As human beings we're wired for connection and not belonging terrifies us.

   Beating Rejection. Beating rejection is very similar to overcoming false humility. You have to know your worth. You must accept the unalienable truth that you have value, not because of what you've done, but because of who you are. Also, it takes time to find your tribe. It's likely you'll get some knock-backs on the hunt. There ARE people out there who want and need what you've got. Be patient. Be brave. Keep looking.

THE FLOW STATE

All of these voices that come against us are different variations of the 'Inner Critic'. An internal nay-sayer that has evolved in us supposedly to keep us 'safe' from risk taking behaviours. Some of these inputs are helpful. They keep us alive. Unfortunately, these voices also can stop us taking healthy risks that could propel us closer to our full potential. If we are always 'playing it safe' we avoid risk, we avoid mistakes, and consequently miss out on the intrinsic lessons and growth that these can bring. We can get stuck, stunted, and dormant.

Mihaly Csikszentmihalyi, is considered one of the founding fathers of the modern positive psychology movement and was the first to identify and research the mental state of 'flow'.[11] Flow, also known as 'peak state' or 'runners high' or 'being in the zone' is a state in which that constant inner chatter from your inner critic goes away.

Dr Arne Dietrich coined the term *'transient hypo frontality'* to describe how the prefrontal neocortex of the brain disengages in flow.[12] 'Transient' (meaning temporary), 'hypo' (meaning decreased), and frontality' (referring to the frontal lobe in your brain). You might assume that in a peak state you use more of your brain, when, in actual fact, you are using less. The inner critic, that resides in that prefrontal cortex, finally steps aside and lets you do your Work!

Time disappears or becomes irrelevant. You are wrapped up in the moment. Action and awareness merge. You are completely absorbed in what you are doing to the point that what you do has become a part of who you are. You are not 'doing it' anymore, you are 'being it'.

Young children find this so much easier than adults because their prefrontal cortex is less developed and also less engaged because they trust their parents to take care of survival needs. Perhaps this is what Jesus meant when he said "the kingdom of heaven belongs to such as these";[13] and "unless you change and *become like little children, you will never enter the kingdom of heaven*".[14]

Studies have shown that this flow-state accelerates the path to mastery. It is not only the state of peak performance, it also directly correlates with rapid internal growth. In his book, The Rise of Superman: Decoding the Science of Ultimate Human Performance, Stephen Kotler examines how extreme sports athletes have been able to hack the pathway to flow and the subsequent rapid growth in performance that comes from constantly pushing the boundary of what's possible.[15] For them, it is quite literally a matter of life and death and therefore they have had to hack the pathway to learning faster and more efficiently.

Josh Waitzkin is an 8-time National Chess Champion in the USA, a 2-time World Champion in the Martial Art of Tai Chi Chuan, and the author of *The Art of Learning* in which he unpacks the state of flow. Waitzkin doesn't regard his mental or sporting achievements as extraordinary but rather examples of what can be achieved when we fall in love with the process of growth.[16]

Jamie Wheal, in his 2013 TED talk, 'Hacking the Genome of Flow', points out that we don't have to leave this state to chance.[16] He unpacks 4 phases that we move through as we approach, experience, and reflect on Flow. Struggle. Release. Flow. Recovery. These phases form a cyclic experience similar to the Hero's Journey we looked at earlier. Perhaps we are now just discovering and articulating through science this recipe for mindset that has been embedded in ancient mythology for thousands of years?

When interviewing Dave Florence, ambassador for 'The Flowcode' and SOMA breath instructor, I realised the ironic but obvious truth. It isn't struggle that we struggle with. It's the letting go.[17] That's not to say that struggle is not a part of the process. It is.

We discussed the importance of grit earlier, but there comes a time when we need to 'enter the rest'.

If you have ever embarked on any creative adventure, sought to improve yourself through education, started a new business or tried to break free from other people's expectations, then you are bound to have come up against the negative voices of your inner critic. You may also have stumbled across that magical state of productivity and performance, and its afterglow that embeds our learning we know as Flow. Imagine if you could get more of these moments...

BRAIN TRAINING ACTIVITY 4

Developing a Growth-Focused Mind in preparation for big life challenges is like honing your skills at a combat gym before stepping into the arena. Mental Toughness empowers you to take the hits. Perseverance equips you to go the distance.

True Humility. Self-Acceptance. Grit. Perseverance. Courage. Connection. Develop these in ever-increasing measure and you will overcome any challenge that life throws your way.

Right now, grab your Brain Health Planner. Block out a 30-minute block once a week and add the following activities to your training:

- **Review** your notes from Part 1. Remind yourself who you are and who you are called to be. Do this often.
- Make a journal note of a learning opportunity that you have in front of you right now. (Hint: any situation or struggle that is causing you pain or discomfort is an opportunity for Growth). **Reframe** it. How are you going to change yourself or your response to change your results?

- **Breathe**. Practice this. In for 5, hold for 2, out for 8. Slow and steady.

   As you do this, think about your breathing.
   In – absorbing life, oxygen, nourishment that will empower your blood, that in turn flows to your heart, your brain, your body.
   Hold – pausing, suspending the moment, halting the struggle. Trust. Reflect. This is a metaphor for this moment of contemplation right now.
   Out. Release. Freedom. Doing the Work. Living the Call. As the air flows out of your lungs you are releasing stress, toxins, unwanted ideas, disappointments, and the unhelpful words of the inner critic. You are not 'blocking it out', you are letting it go.
   This is a 15-second cycle. Repeat it 8 times, thoughtfully, consciously, and you have just spent two of the most valuable minutes of your day. This is a great way to start your day, but this 2-minute exercise is also practice. You can call on this breathing technique at any point in your day when stress levels rise, and you need to re-centre or let go.

- **Do more with less**. Another practical change that you can make to get more Flow in your life is to put less in your day. I know on the surface that sounds counter-productive or just downright impossible, but hear me out. Whenever you change from one activity to another, you have to 'break state' and start again. You do your best work when you are absorbed in it. In fact, studies have shown that learning can happen 230% faster when you're in this state.[16] Which means that if you can maximise your time in it, you are doing more with less time.

So, let's say you have 6 big jobs that need your attention. You could spend an hour on each of these each day, which means that if you have an hour off for lunch, that makes a typical 7-hour workday; but let's look at productivity. It usually takes at least 30 minutes to orient yourself with a task and to drop into Flow. So, in the example day I just gave, you are spending a total of 3 hours organising yourself and thinking about working, and another 3 hours actually working productively.

Now what if you could reorientate your week. What if you spent 3.5 hours working on ONE project? It still takes you 30 minutes to orientate yourself with the task and get into it, but for the next 3 hours you are absorbed in it. What if you took a lunch break and could come back and do that again? That's another 30 minutes to get into it, and another 3 hours focused, productive time. This means that at the end of an intense 8-hour workday, you have just completed DOUBLE the amount of productive work time that you would have achieved in a week if you were working the other way!

Imagine being twice as productive and then having 4 extra days to work on other things that are important to you? How would that change your life? Doesn't that make it *worth* trying to restructure your week?

I know that real-life wars against this kind of singular focus. Life is a cacophony of competing priorities. Noisy, demanding voices all vie for your attention. I know that the example I gave above is probably an over-simplification of the million different responsibilities that you deal with every day. I get it. *Oh boy, do I get it!* But what if you could make one small tweak to your weekly schedule that allowed you to spend some time in the zone? Not only will you feel more fulfilled, but ultimately you are also freeing up time that will compound for your benefit.

It's worth thinking about.

| 14 |

The Positioned Mind

It's not what you look at that matters, it's what you see.

HENRY DAVID THOREAU

The Positioned Mind is about how you perceive yourself, others, and your circumstances through different eyes. In relationships, it's about walking in another person's shoes if you can, and if you can't, then listening – *really listening* to what they're telling you.

People belong in relationships. In his research, Michael Fullan observes that 1) we're all wired for connection, and 2) we want to help others.[1] If you cannot master relationships, you will always struggle to reach your potential. Ralph Stacey says, "there is no 'I' without a 'we'. 'I' is the singular and 'we' is the plural of the same phenomena".[2]

Identity, Mission and Belonging are all inextricably linked.

A CHANGE OF PERSPECTIVE

After we'd wrapped up our gifts business and Sofia's arm and shoulder had begun to heal, we had another problem. We were broke and in debt. I needed to make some money, and fast. As much as I didn't want to face it, the local high school was my best option.

I cringed at the idea of relief teaching (aka babysitting). Not only was it a thankless job with little meaning, it also would mean walking into a different staffroom every day and being met with a well-meaning "Oh, you're back! How's the gifts business going?" But with a mortgage and 5 mouths to feed I didn't have a lot of choice.

Soon after registering with the school, I was offered a role as a tutor. I worked one-on-one helping students with literacy and numeracy. It was an awesome job. I didn't realise how much time was wasted in the classroom until those sessions. We got so much done and it was so rewarding seeing students make massive leaps ahead. Shortly after another funding channel opened up to help Indigenous students improve NAPLAN test results and because I already had the systems in place, I was given the role.

We worked in small groups. It seemed weird in that very personal setting to just jump straight into the content, so we started the session chatting about life outside school. This led to conversations about their hopes, dreams, and life aspirations.

I hate the emphasis on standardised testing in schools, but a year later these same students achieved such amazing growth in their NAPLAN results that the school celebrated with an awards ceremony, and I was nominated for a teaching award. My role grew and we began to involve the student's families in these aspirational conversations. Sometimes it was a struggle to get families who had experienced rejection and trauma at the hands of the school system to engage with me, but little by little, family by family, we made progress. Together we unloaded hurts and frustrations from the past, dreamed about what the future might hold, and made plans for action in the present. The community, the teachers and the parents all worked together, and I was simply the *relationship-broker* between them.

Together with that community, we authored a book sharing the stories of elders in the voices of children. We hosted events, we laughed, we danced, we sang – together. Success led to success. My work was rewarded with a number of education awards, and I landed an executive position at the school leading Aboriginal Student Engagement.

In a few short years I had found a way back to belonging by showing up as myself and listening to others. I was making a difference in the lives of young people and their families and at the heart of it all was empathy and connection.

The Positioned Mind empowers you to engage wholeheartedly with other people. To show up flexible and avoid getting stuck. With this mindset you cannot help but be grateful for the miracle of human diversity. The Positioned Mind is the foundation for effective leadership in every sphere of influence – your family, your work, your community.

Let's look at some mental positioning strategies.

THE PERCEPTUAL POSITIONS

There are, of course, infinite perspectives you can take in any given situation, but infinite options are unhelpful. The Perceptual Positions is a thinking model that provides 5 distinct points of view that can reframe the meaning of any situation. They are:

- P1 – Your Self-perspective. This is how YOU see the world. It is shaped by your own bias and pre-programmed filters. It is important to acknowledge your own perspective as it's the best way to recognise what you want. Having said that, you don't want to get stuck there. Anything of true value is co-created with others, therefore at some point you need to think beyond P1.

- P2 – The Other perspective. Thinking in P2 is usually described as 'empathy'. It's not just understanding from another's point of view, but really *feeling* what they feel. P2 requires us to ask good questions and then stop talking and listen. Not listening to respond, but listening to understand.
- P3 – The Fly on the Wall perspective. P3 floats above P1 and P2. P3 can read the body language of people who are engaged (or not) in a conversation. It notices who dominates and who withdraws and wonders why. P3 is focused on the culture of a relationship or group.
- P4 – The Organisational perspective. It understands the dynamics of bigger groups. P4 thinks about the 'common good'. It's not always in sync with P1, but can provide some useful perspective on governmental or organisational decisions.
- P5 – The Creator or Narrator perspective. Imagine you can look beyond time and space. You can see any situation and understand the purpose behind it. If you believe in a creator, then this perspective helps you to understand what God is saying to and for you. Alternatively, you might position yourself as the narrator of your life. Reflect on the hero's journey we covered in the last chapter and ponder what phase of the story you are in. Who are the other characters? What is their motivation? Are you in the trials phase or the crisis? Is your breakthrough just around the corner? If so, what are you meant to find that is going to get you through? P5 is a powerful perspective for reframing adversity.

BETTER CONVERSATIONS

Have you ever seen 2 people talking, but both are stuck in P1? It's common in politics, work meetings, even in marriage relationships! There's the polite nodding while the other person speaks, but the response is already loaded, only held back by social convention. As soon as the other draws breath, the respondent jumps in with their counterargument.

And it doesn't have to be an argument. Maybe you've done it yourself? It's a normal, everyday conversation, but you know that moment when you've stopped fully listening because you now have something to say? Your response has formed and now you're just waiting for the window to deliver it. You're no longer in P2.

Jim Knight, author of *Better Conversations* outlines 6 core beliefs that undergird authentic communication. These include being interested, balanced, non-judgemental, autonomous, reciprocal, and life-giving.[3] The first belief is seeing others as equal partners in conversations. This means not just listening to their opinion but valuing it as equal to your own. This can be difficult if you're in a position of authority – a parent, a teacher, a consultant, or an employer, but it is essential to develop your Positioned Mind.

The Stronger Smarter Leadership program outlines two main ways that organisations do business.[4] One is the Triangle. The other is the Circle. The Triangle is hierarchical. All knowledge, power, responsibility, and control is at the top and actions are delegated down. The triangle can be effective in situations that require a fast response to solve simple problems. The Triangle structure is used in the military, factories, companies, governments, hospitals, and schools. What the Triangle gains in efficiency, it loses in personal engagement. The Triangle is a dehumanising structure. In it the leader's P1 vision is the only one that matters. This disconnects them from the team. Eckhart Tolle says, "authentic human interactions become impossible when you lose yourself in a role".[5]

In the Circle, humanity is celebrated. All knowledge, power, responsibility, and control are shared. Each person has a part to play. Leaders still function in the Circle, but their role is less to direct and more to inspire, support and teach. Leadership is not limited by position. Anyone can be a leader in the Circle. The Triangle is based on our feudal heritage and has spread across western society through colonisation. Traditional cultures from all around the world have been using the Circle to do business for millennia. The Circle is the best structure for addressing complex social challenges.

Whenever I begin a new coaching workshop, I always spend time 'Setting the Circle'. I do this to acknowledge 2 things:

1. I have something to share, but I don't have all the answers. I need your engagement and participation if we hope to create meaningful changes together.
2. We're not machines. As humans we show up shaped by our stories. Sometimes we're not OK – and that IS OK. When someone has the courage to share their struggle, they bring a gift that brokers connection.

In the Circle, P2, P3, P4 and even P5 all become relevant and necessary.

Instructional coach Shane Safir has developed an archetype she believes is best positioned to facilitate change in schools. The Listening Leader.

> *The listening leader understands that school transformation is a long game: There are no quick fixes, turnarounds, or shortcuts. He or she leverages listening to grow a collaborative*

> culture and build the capacity of teachers and staff. Rather than declare a vision, the listening leader constructs one through a dynamic process in which dissenting perspectives are welcome. He or she also views student, staff, and parent voices as vital sources of data.[6]

The first step to developing a listening mindset is to become mindful of our own internal dialogue. Marshall Rosenburg calls this "showing empathy toward ourselves". Former United Nations Secretary General, Dag Hammarskjold once said, "the more faithfully you listen to the voices within you, the better you will hear what is sounding outside".[7]

Knight says, "once we demonstrate empathy to ourselves, we can demonstrate empathy to others".[3] Listening with curiosity to the voices within help us to know ourselves better. We can ask ourselves better questions and detect when our self-talk has become excessively critical or counterproductive.

Once you have acknowledged your own voice, you are free to listen more deeply to others. To listen whole-heartedly you must recognise that you need other people. Your dreams cannot exist in isolation. You are part of a bigger story. You must value what others bring – even when their ideas do not align with your own.

CEO of International Mission Ministries, Ross Nancarrow reminded me once, "we must appreciate the differences". Even our greatest strengths can over-correct and become weaknesses if not tempered and balanced by other voices. We need partners. We need mentors. We need coaches. We even need critics.

Do you remember the Cognitive Behaviour Cycle from The Happy Mind chapter? Relationship dynamics work in a similar way. Our conversations shape our beliefs and patterns of thinking. These internal stories shape our behaviour and responses. These collective behaviours accumulate to create the culture. And the culture, in turn, shapes the nature of conversations...

Ralph Stacey says, "we co-create power in every moment of every interaction".[2]

The Positioned Mind understands that our patterns of thinking are subjective and not limited to a single version of truth. If we can change our conversations, then we shift our focus and change the internal stories. When we change the stories, we change the culture – that is, we change the atmosphere and nature of the relationship and the tangible outcomes it produces.

In relationships we must distinguish between facts and feelings. Using 'I feel...' language infers ownership and acknowledges the subjectivity of your interpretation. It cannot be wrong because it is your feelings, and it promotes less confrontational conversations about where those feelings have come from. The Stronger Smarter Social Process suggests:

1. Take turns (P1)
2. Make turns (P2)
3. Monitor the themes of the conversation (P3)

THINKING DIFFERENTLY

Neuro Linguistic Programming (or NLP) is a method of reprogramming of your neurological nervous system through language to allow you to read people and communicate with them more effectively.[8] NLP is based on a set of 16 'presuppositions or assumptions about people. They are subjective and cannot be proved as true or untrue, but when adopted they provide an empowering perspective that is effective in reshaping actions and results.

My favourite NLP presupposition is: "people do the best they can with the resources that they have available". I had a hard time coming to terms with this idea when I first heard it. "That's crap!" I thought. "There's plenty of people I know who are NOT doing their best!" (At the time I was dealing with some challenging staff who were not interested in adapting their teaching style for students. As far as they were concerned, they were the experts. They liked their subject area, and if the students didn't feel the same way, then that was their problem.)

There are other NLP presuppositions that dovetail with the first one. These helped me to be more gracious. "There is no such thing as an unresourceful person, only an unresourceful state of mind"; and "everyone's behaviour has a positive intention – it is their best attempt to have their needs met".

All around us there is evidence to prove these true – or not. When you hold these as true, all of a sudden, your feelings toward other people begins to change. You recognise that not only is their perspective valid, but it is a necessary consideration if we hope to create a winning culture together. You can download a full list of the 16 presuppositions at www.thrivebydesignbook.com/resources

DIFFERENT HATS

We all get stuck in P1 sometimes. It's human nature. Flexing your creativity keeps your brain nimble and fit. It stops you from getting stuck in a single-minded train of thought and keeps the door open to exciting new possibilities. One popular framework for divergent thinking is Edward de Bono's 6 Hats.[9] A 'Hat' is symbolic of the different personas we take on in different situations. For example, a parent might say, "I'm putting my drill-sergeant hat on tonight!" if she feels that some tough love or extra discipline is required. The Hats acknowledge that better solutions are found by exploring multiple positions.

De Bono's 6 Thinking Hats are:

- **The Blue Hat** – takes the lead and facilitates the 6 Hats thinking process.
- **The White Hat** – symbolises paper. It calls for information and the facts.
- **The Yellow Hat**– symbolises brightness and optimism. Under this hat you explore the positives and probe for value and benefit.
- **The Green Hat** – symbolises nature and focuses on creative energy. It explores possibilities, new ideas, concepts, and alternatives.
- **The Red Hat** – is about feelings. It expresses emotions, hunches, and intuitive response.
- **The Black Hat** – symbolise a judge's robes and embodies critical thinking and judgement. It distinguishes risks, difficulties, and problems. It identifies what may go wrong and why. It is an important hat for decision making but must not be brought in too early otherwise it will squash the other perspectives.

The 6 Hats are a fun way to analyse a problem for yourself or spark dynamic conversation about a topic in small groups. Next time you're feeling stuck try using the 6 Hats – write down your challenge, then one by one, think about the problem using one of the 6 hats. Take breaks in between. You will be surprised at how different each one feels and what you can come up with.

DIVERGENT THINKING

Divergent Thinking is coming up with a large number of ideas to solve a problem. It's sometimes called lateral thinking. Process and logic take a backseat and quantity of ideas is more important than quality. Divergent ideas are often unusual – the quirkier and more original the better. They break traditional paradigms. That's the point. Divergent Thinking is super-powerful when you're stuck in a rut and your normal processes haven't achieved the results you were after. Clearly something needs to change. Divergent Thinking expands and explores the possibilities.

Divergent Thinking does not come naturally to the adult brain. Your brain is efficient. It likes to conserve resources when possible. This means finding the simplest, most predictable, most well-worn neural pathway – even when you're aware that this path is not getting you the results you're after. Most of our behaviour is habitualised. We stick with what's comfortable. Habits are great when they are aligned with your mission, but when we realise there is a mismatch between our habits and our end-goal, then we need to embrace a change. Challenging yourself to act in new ways stimulates new neural growth, which in turn primes you to think more creatively when life throws you a curveball.

BRAIN TRAINING ACTIVITY 5

Taking a pre-programmed habit and tweaking it slightly has been scientifically proven to improve your capacity for divergent thinking. These changes are uncomfortable – but that's the point. It's a type of flexibility and fitness. If you make it fun and keep a smile on your face – you'll not only improve your motivation but also optimise your neural development.

Choose one or two of these fun, easy 'anti-habits' to add to your Brain Training Planner.

- Brushing your teeth with your non-dominant hand
- Putting your underwear and/or pants on with your non-dominant leg first

- If you normally check your phone first thing in the morning, put it in a locked box until 9am
- Drive a new way to work every day this week
- Switch house jobs with your partner – e.g.: if you normally take out the rubbish and they clean the toilet, then swap for a week or two.

| 15 |

The Abundant Mind

As a man thinks in his heart, so is he.

PROVERBS 23:7

I'm standing outside the principal's office, shifting uncomfortably. There's a knot in my stomach and my throat is tight. I've been pushing a lot of boundaries lately and not everyone is happy.

It is two years since I was winning awards for my work integrated families into the learning experience and getting outstanding results. I had become a learning engagement expert and held numerous influential positions in the school. My work was celebrated because I was getting big results with students that had been previously written off, but I wasn't stopping there. The school I was in (like most schools) was stuck in a 100-year-old industrial model that was killing the joy of learning and it was time for a change.

I had some big visions for how to transform the school into a vibrant learning community pulsating with new energy and enthusiasm. What I've learned about people is, that we love the idea of change – just so long as we don't have to!

My proposals were making some teachers uncomfortable – including my supervisor. He was a weekend officer in the army cadets, and less than 5 years away from retirement. He had a firm belief in the hierarchical model of school and a vested interest in preserving the status quo. He saw my attempts to reform the school model as troublesome and mutinous. He didn't necessarily like how things were, but at least it was predictable. He knew how to play that game. He was frustrated with my pursuit of whole-school reform. He said my "focus was not with the faculty" and he made moves to have me terminated.

I could have avoided it. I went to my friend Matt for counsel, who was Deputy Principal at the time. He knew the system. He recognised the breakthroughs I was getting but told me, if I wanted to keep my job, I would have to come into line with the supervisor. "That's just how the system is", he said. It was sound advice – which I totally ignored.

I had come too far and believed too strongly that this school could be more than it had become. I believed in a place where young people could discover who they were and develop a vision for their life; and so, I stepped into the principal's office armed with ideals and a vision for something better…

The principal appreciated my passion and the work I was doing. She said my ideas had merit, but the system required her to support the Head Teacher. The Head Teacher was adamant and unflinching. "Either you stop, or you leave."

And just like that, I was done.

The past several years of hard work and success had led me here.

The others left the room, leaving me alone with Matt who'd come along for support. I started to say something, but the words stuck in my throat and an overwhelming flood of emotion drowned me in sorrow. I rarely cried and I was caught off guard by the profound sense of grief that consumed me in that moment. I buried my face in my hands and sobbed like a child. Abandoned. Unwanted. I had given my all and it wasn't enough. I had failed. Failed myself and my mission. Failed my students, my family and everyone else who believed that I was going to make a change.

Something died inside me that day.

THE MAGIC OF THINKING BIG

When I told Sofia what had happened, she convinced me to come away for a holiday. It had been pre-planned before my work-life came crashing down. I didn't want to go, but it was exactly what I needed. We swam. We played. We spent time with friends who all stated matter-of-factly that my supervisor was an idiot. They shrugged their shoulders and confidently declared; "You'll be fine. You've got so many talents. Whatever you decide to do will be amazing." Clearly, they had more faith in me than I did.

Rob Bell says that "despair is a spiritual condition that tells you that tomorrow will be exactly the same as today". Hope is the counterforce to that. Despair gives up, stands still, and eventually dies. Hope refuses to. Hope is the desire for more. It is the quintessential trait of humanity and the impetus for all great exploits. We don't have to strive for hope. Hope is already there. Like an ember that just needs a gentle breath to make it glow. Or like a seed in the ground that feels the warmth of the sun above. Anyone else looking on just sees dirt, but the gardener knows better. He knows what is hidden beneath the surface. The potential to produce an enormous tree. All it takes is time and care. Nature will do the rest.

We all reach a breaking point on our quest for true belonging, and at that point, even hope seems to disappear – but not for long.

In our holiday-home there was a shelf full of second-hand books. I looked them over and an interesting title caught my eye: "The Magic of Thinking Big" by David Schwartz. I started to read and I couldn't put it down. I was like a thirsty man in the desert who couldn't remember the last time he'd tasted water. The simple truth in this book can be summed up in a single sentence. "You win, because you believe you will". That's it. I didn't know it then, but Schwartz had just introduced me to the Abundant mindset. Summed up in *belief* is the motivation, the determination, the positive attitude, the willingness to learn, and an inherent need for connection with others. In the Abundant Mind all other mindsets coalesce and make sense.

I decided I wasn't going to just *guess* at life anymore. I knew I was meant for more than messy mediocrity and dumb luck. We refinanced the house. I took 10 weeks to enjoy time with my family and explore my options. I prayed. I waited. I wrote. And with a renewed assurance of divine goodwill pointed in my direction, and the call to think bigger echoing in my mind, I made a decision. I was going to purposefully *design* my life – and it was going to be incredible.

ART IS LIKE AIR

From then on, I was hooked on inspiration and looked for it everywhere. I read books, watched films, and took courses. I listened to podcasts, lectures and other people's stories. I became fascinated by anyone else I found who was also on the quest for abundant living.

The Abundant Mind is an inspired state. The word 'inspire' comes from Latin *in-spirare* and literally means 'to breathe life into'. It comes from the same root word as 'spirit' and can also mean an idea or purpose. Inspiration turns hope into belief.

Where does your inspiration come from? Books? Movies? Maybe an experience a friend has shared with you? Art inspires. Maybe this book has helped? Part 1: Maximised Identity, was written to inspire you with stories from your own inner world!

We're wired to cultivate this mindset collectively. Art is a collective celebration of who we are and the journey that we're on. Art is how we share our humanity. Art can turn the pain of life into something beautiful and together we learn from one another's stories. Art is about connection. When we are inspired our brain forms a neurological association with another person's courage or triumph and we make it our own. In the Abundant Mind, you have already made it. You are so connected, so consumed with belief, that your brain cannot tell the difference between your hero's victory and your own! From here you create your future with unshakeable confidence.

TAKE COURAGE

Inspiration gets you in the game, but holding onto these ideas, nurturing them, *believing* and acting on them, takes courage.

Faith is trust. Faith is believing what you cannot see. It doesn't require tangible evidence. It is dependent on your inner vision. True faith is *love-inspired*. It believes in goodness and focuses on the positive.

Fear is faith in reverse. Fear is believing the negative. We can fear events, circumstances, or people. Fear is not necessarily wrong. It is based on past experiences and can keep us alive in certain situations (like standing at the edge of a cliff), but it can also feed on its own self-perpetuating emotion, become irrational, and cripple our potential. Fear has the same creative force as faith to shape your reality because it motivates action.

On one of my programs there was a young boy about 14 years of age. Let's call him Michael. Michael had low self-esteem. During one of our 'Adventure Days' the group participated in a team challenge activity. The prize was a block of chocolate that the kids got to break up and share. After the challenge, when the crew had solved the puzzle and divided their spoils, I noticed Michael sitting off by himself NOT eating chocolate, and so I asked him, "Hey Michael, what's going on? You did it! You completed the challenge. Why aren't you eating the prize with your teammates?"

He replied sadly: "They didn't want to give me any!"

I thought, "That's strange. They're normally pretty good like that. They'd normally have no trouble sharing a prize. So, I talked to the group and said, "Hey guys, Michael said you didn't want to share any of the prize with him? I think that's a bit unfair because he participated, just like you did."

Then they said, "No, no. Zoe was joking at the beginning saying: 'It's all mine! Maw haw haw' and pretending she was going to eat it all, but we just laughed, then we counted everyone up and we divided the chocolate so EVERYONE would get an equal share – but when we offered it to Michael, he said, he didn't want any."

So, I went back to Michael and explained what the group had said. "They said they *offered* you the chocolate, but you didn't want it." And he replied, "yeah they offered it to me – but I KNEW they didn't really want to share it with me." And he went back to sulking about being left out by his friends.

Isn't it amazing what we do and say to maintain our current version of the world? We all have limiting beliefs that we've internalised to avoid pain. We choose our reality based on our experience, and we act according to those beliefs – even when it's a reality we don't like.

Fear amplifies negative memories, focusses on possible undesirable scenarios, and can lock us into a cycle of self-sabotage and disappointment.

The Abundant Mind is not without fear, but it has familiarised itself with the negative emotions associated with challenge and recognises this discomfort as a precursor to growth. It's like a Kung-fu master who has learned to redirect an enemy's attack back against him. The Abundant Mind *uses fear* to its advantage. That familiar discomfort becomes the signal to lean into the challenge, draw deep on courage, stay soft to the lesson, and emerge stronger than before.

LACK

The Abundant Mind is centred on wholeness. When we become aware of our *un-wholeness* through comparison, there is a break in coherence between our present reality and our call to the future. You desire what you do not have. Dr Joe Dispenza calls this the state of Lack.

This inner tension can be resolved in two ways. First, (and most obviously) you can go to work. You can get busy doing the things you need to do, to make more money or get a better relationship, or get healthier, etc. The trouble is, when you are operating from Lack, your focus is on the shortcoming and your subconscious mind tunes in to make more of what you're focussing on true.

Alternatively, you can resolve the tension by realigning your present state with the abundance of your future.

ALIGNMENT

Imagine you're holding a hose and trying to water your garden. It's not going well because the hose is kinked in several places, stopping the flow of water. You could add more pressure. You could turn the tap on, harder and harder until it's at full output. The pressure causes drips to leak out at the connections, but still, it makes little impact on the garden. Your plants are still only being dampened by a dribble.

Or you can turn the tap back to a regular level and spend time instead getting the kinks out of the hose. Then the water can flow easily and the garden gets watered quickly and effectively. When we apply this to our mindset, it's called Alignment.

Are your daily thoughts and behaviours aligned with your big dreams? Are you thinking and acting like the person you want to become? An Abundant Mind is regularly recalibrating. Thriving means working smarter, not harder. The Abundant Mind has a clarity of purpose that generates positive action. It is knowing your value, your identity, and the Mission you've been called to. The Abundant Mind stays locked onto this. It is keeping your eye on the prize. The Abundant Mind holds its ground. The Abundant Mind meditates on truth already uncovered. It embeds this. Internalised truth cannot be stolen.

BRAIN TRAINING ACTIVITY 6

Inspiration fans hope, which in turn becomes vision. Vision commands action, which in turn invites blessing. The first step is getting inspired.

1. Review your notes from Part 1. Does it still excite you? Make you a little nervous maybe? That's a good sign. Review it. Refine it. Believe in what you have already gained and add in new details that come to mind as you meditate on this vision.
2. Inspiring stories make our hope come alive. Art, Books, Movies, Podcasts – there are numerous places you can go to find inspiring media. Pick something. Add it to your week. I personally love sports films based on true stories. They capture the hero's journey so well and they help me

to believe that dreams can come true. To get a list of my top 10 favourite inspirational movie recommendations go to www.thrivebydesignbook.com/resources

| 16 |

Mind Mapping

*The best way to have a good idea
is to have a lot of ideas.*

LINUS PAULING

I've always loved learning about human potential. Ironically, it was outside the school system that I began to expand my conception of what 'learning' can look like. I came across a great book by *Tony Buzan – The Ultimate Book of Mind Maps: Unlock your Creativity, Boost your Memory, Change your Life*. This took what I knew about Mind Mapping to a whole new level.

Mind Mapping is a powerful tool that can help anyone to learn more about themselves, their passions, and unpack how to turn their inner convictions into living, breathing success stories.

You have the solution to your problem inside you. Lifestyle Design is about bringing that out. Mind Mapping can tease out the possible solutions to the problems you face or the area of life you would like to improve. You can use it to plan a holiday, start a podcast, create a course, or write a book! I have used it for all of these things and more!

Mind Mapping and the connected thinking it promotes is hard-wired into our biology. It directly mimics the physiological cell structure of our neurons.

Here is a neuron diagram from Wikipedia:

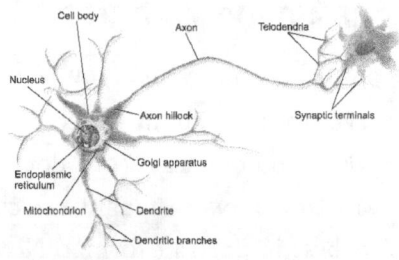

Multipolar Neuron
Bruce Blaus

And here is a Mind Map about Mind Mapping:

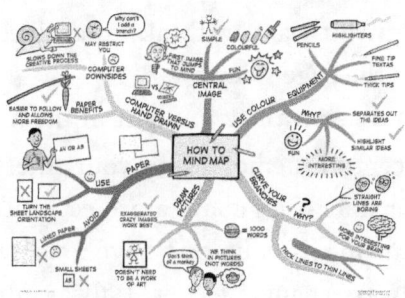

How to Mindmap
Dr Jane Genovese

Can you see it?

By imitating your physical brain structure, a Mind Map visually highlights the infinite possibilities of your mind. A Mind Map visually embodies the limitless potential inside you.

A good Mind Map also takes advantage of visual triggers to bring the whole brain into play. It is a feedback loop. It is a creative conversation that you are having with yourself, and a way of tapping into that hidden part of your consciousness that is unlimited by learned conventions.

THE PRINCIPLES OF A GOOD MIND MAP

1. **Turn the page sideways**. When you pick up a piece of paper have you ever thought about which is its default format? What about when you open a Word doc, which way is the page setup? Most of us were taught at school that a piece of paper works best in portrait format. Now, we rarely give it any thought. Consciously turning the page from portrait to landscape says, "OK Brain, today we're going lateral!" If you want to narrow your focus with a strict plan or to-do list, then sure, keep your page portrait – but if you're doing a Mind Map you want to think expansively, creatively, laterally. Turn the page sideways.
2. **Start with a central idea**. Right in the middle of the page goes your central theme. That's your title. If it's about you, write your name. If it's about a project you're starting, write the project name. If you don't have a name yet, give it one. You can always change it later. I always draw a little cloud bubble around my central idea. Firstly, because it makes a visual statement, "this is my central idea, other ideas will flow from here." And secondly, because I like to subconsciously remind myself, I am now tapping into the conceptual realm and a part of myself or the divine (or perhaps a little of both) that has the answers that I need.

3. **Use colour**. The brain loves colour. Research shows that people who study using coloured notes consistently outperform those who don't. Colour causes our brain to light up and engage with the page. Colour can also be used to convey emotional meaning in our ideas.
4. **Use curved lines**. Why? Again, because our brain likes it that way! We are all creative beings and curved, organic, flowing lines inspire us to think like this. Lines have momentum. A short, sharp, straight-line pushes one idea in a single direction. A flowing line that curves like a branch will turn as it needs to. The roots of a tree turn to find water and nutrients. A branch grows stretching toward the light of the sun. Your ideas will do the same. Your curved lines remind you that an idea is a living thing. It just needs some nurture to grow strong.
5. **Use images and icons**. A picture is worth a thousand words. A little icon or image conveys emotion and experience. It is a mini story. Imagine trying to use your phone and instead of icons, the home screen was covered with a word list of apps instead. How much slower (and less fun) would that be? Device designers know how our brain works. Images are easily interpreted by the right side of our brain, the side that usually gets sidelined in traditional schooling, and yet still finds a way to govern a lot of our decision making. It is the side we are trying to engage in this process because we value its connectedness and wisdom. I guarantee you, the extra minute it takes to draw a little image or icon is worth every second.
6. **Use a single word per branch**. One word per branch keeps your ideas concise and requires you to expand rapidly with sub-branches if you want to dig deeper into an idea. Let's say I was Mind Mapping ideas for recreation. One branch had

'sport'; the next sub-branch had 'basketball game'. By sticking 'basketball' and 'game' together I've summed up one concept, but if I had 'basketball' then branched off with 'game', I've now opened up a huge range of new possibilities! 'Game' could branch into 'board' (i.e.: board-games) and 'ball' (i.e.: ball games). The word 'basketball' now also has a range of new branch options – basketball + TV, basketball + cards, basketball + hoop, etc

7. **Use sub-branches to expand ideas**. As shown in the basketball example above, we use sub-branches to explore new ideas. It's easy to do the first level, but at that point, your Mind Map is still more like a description of elements. As you go multiple levels down, you start to unlock genuine creativity and 'what-if' thinking. Don't edit ideas as they come out. You may not like an idea at first, but that idea may connect you with another idea that you absolutely love but wouldn't have come across it unless you went down that path. Trust the process.

You might be thinking: "I'm ready. I know what I want. I just want to get stuff done! The last thing I need is more ideas!"

Trust me. Mind Mapping is a tool that can help you stop working harder and start working smarter! Finding the 'right action' for 'right now' is what smart Lifestyle Design is all about. Mind mapping will unlock your intuitive mind which knows the right path. If you want to learn more about Mind Maps, I recommend you check out some of Tony Buzan's short videos on YouTube.

To get my Mind Mapping Guide, go to: www.thrivebydesignbook.com/resources

BRAIN TRAINING ACTIVITY 7

Create a Mind Map of You, your life and your interests. Write your name in the middle of a page. Branch out with things like:

- Hobbies/Passions.
- Family/Community.
- Things that upset you.
- Things that you love.
- Experiences you've had.
- Work life.
- Dreams for the future.
- Or anything else you think is important about you.

Mind Map as though you were communicating to someone who didn't know you very well.

| 17 |

Design Thinking

Every great design begins with an even better story.

LORINDA MAMO

When I first decided that I was going to consciously redesign my life I knew nothing about life-coaching. What I did know well was design. I understood the creative process.

Design is about creating solutions for problems that people face. A common misconception is that design is just about styling or aesthetics. Sure, for products, environments or graphic media, visual appeal is important, but this is only one aspect of design. Good design is people-centred with a focus on how people interact with it. Design is art. It is a form of creative expression that evokes a response from other human beings. It is also a science; in that it follows a systematic method to produce a desired result. Good design is based on research and understanding. It requires connecting with a problem in the same way that an end user will experience it. It starts with empathy.

Design is smart. It lets you test an idea or concept before going to production and can save you pain, disappointment and millions of dollars; yet design also takes courage. You need to be willing to think outside the ordinary. To stretch the limits of convention. To challenge the status quo, break traditional boundaries and yet still stay relatable, and be able to communicate these ideas to others.

Design is at the core of all human endeavour. Design is about change, transformation, improvement, aspiration, and growth. Design has a lot in common with coaching and education. At the heart of good design is people. Who are they? What will their experience be? These are the key questions that drive Design Thinking. I have studied various models of change management, learning, personal coaching, the lifecycle of leaders, and numerous design thinking models. In all of these, I can see 4 distinct phases that consistently emerge.

These phases ebb and flow between the 2 realms we discovered back in Part 1. Do you remember?

There's the imaginary, conceptual realm. Let's call it the inner world. Then there is the tangible, physical realm. The outer world. What we normally refer to as *'reality'*.

conceptual realm

physical realm

Humans are the only creatures on the planet that straddle these 2 worlds simultaneously, and therefore the only beings capable of consciously creating our future. That is design. Every man-made object, every creative work, exists in the physical space because it was first conceived in the mind. We design our lives the same way.

The Stanford Design Thinking model involves 5 key stages that vacillates between the 2 worlds:

Empathise – Define – Ideate – Prototype – Test[1]

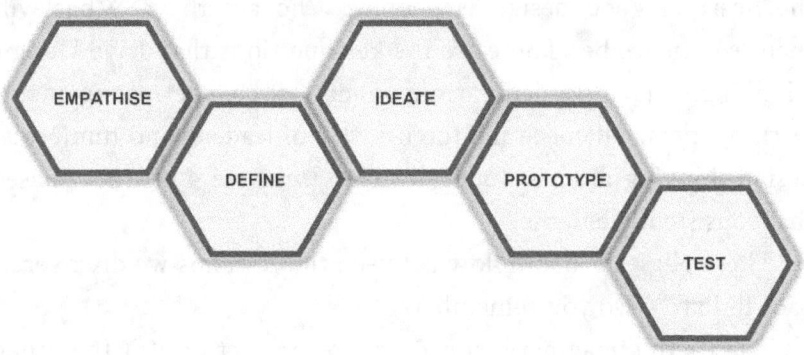

Stanford Design Thinking Model
Schwarz, Gordon, & Rohrbeck. (2019)

- To Empathise is conceptual. Reviewing the evidence, then internalising the experience.
- To Define is tangible. Expressing the problem in words and thereby grounding it in reality.
- To Ideate is conceptual. Creatively considering all the possibilities.
- Prototype is tangible. Building a one-off solution that can be Tested.
- Testing then offers a new tangible experience that can be Empathised, and the process begins all over again.

THE GROW MODEL

A popular life coaching model developed in the 1980s by Sir John Whitmore, Graham Alexander and Alan Fine is the GROW coaching model.[2] The phases are:

- Goal
- Reality
- Options
- Way Forward

They echo a similar pattern.

- Goal is conceptual. A hope, a dream or vision. It exists only in the realm of potentiality.
- Reality is now. The problem, issue or challenge that you're facing. It's grounded in present experience. There is then a tension between where you are now and where you want to be.
- This tension catapults you back into the realm of the conceptual where you explore with your coach all the possible courses of action and what the results of those actions might be. It is a creative space unlimited by time, finance, resources, knowledge or expectations. In the conceptual realm you can be unbridled by practical constraints and your intuitive response is much more likely to align with your core identity.
- The Way Forward brings ONE of these possibilities into reality with a simple commitment to action. This in turn will bring results and its own inertia.

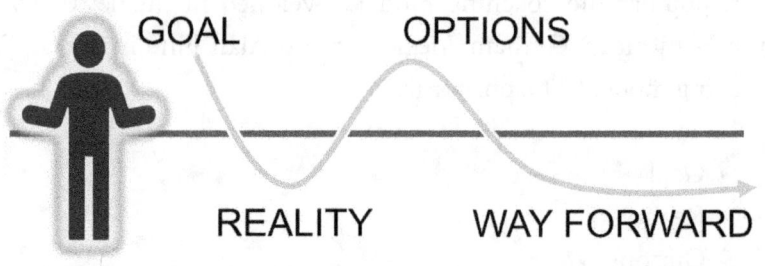

This is the natural creative process. Expansion into the world of imagination and possibilities, and then contraction into practical, focussed action.

The 2 realms give us 2 very different perspectives. Thinking of life as a journey, I like to call these:

1. The Hot Air Balloon Perspective – where you are floating high up above the forest, you can see the path clearly and the destination up ahead.
2. The Bashing Your Way Through the Trees Perspective – down in the forest, it's hard to know where you are, if you're heading in the right direction or just how far you have to go.

Our challenge is, it's really difficult to think in both perspectives simultaneously. Either you're up, out of the fight, aloof and looking down with clarity, but not actually doing anything toward the goal, OR you're down in the forest, bashing your way through the trees, doing the work, but clarity is low. You aren't sure if you're making progress or even if you're still on the right path.

Setting time aside to ponder 'above the trees' is vital if you want to stay on track. Sharing some of this time together with a wise mentor or coach will also increase your clarity and focus. Together you can discuss the best way forward. Identify some landmarks to help you to stay on track and sketch out a map with instructions to keep you on the path. THAT is what we're going to do together now.

In Part 3: Maximised Lifestyle, you're going to learn about the Anatomy of Strategy:

Vision – Goals – Milestones – Actions – Celebration

Then you're going to choose your path.

There was a time when my life was in limbo. I didn't know what to do or where to go next. We had recently renovated a bedroom and I stood in front of a large, unpainted, blank wall with a pencil in hand. I drew a huge Mind Map capturing my faith, my calling, my skills, learning opportunities, and where I believed I could have an impact; I also included lifestyle goals – what I wanted my family life to look like, what I wanted my romantic connection to feel like, what I wanted to achieve in business and finance, my goals for health and fitness, for fun and adventure and for the home we wanted to create and live in. Little did I know it then, but I had intuitively identified the 6 lifestyle domains and set goals for each.

- Fun & Adventure
- Health & Fitness
- Romantic Connection
- Family Life
- House & Garden
- Work, Business & Finance

In the next section I'm going to help you take strategic action in the area that matters most to you.

3

MAXIMISED LIFESTYLE

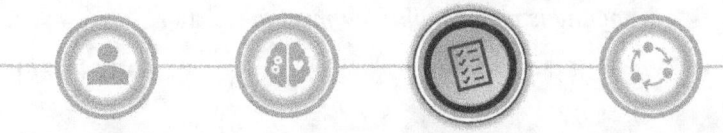

| 18 |

The 6 Lifestyle Domains

Knowing is not enough. You must take action.

TONY ROBBINS

Mindset Training is powerful, but action is what creates change. In this section you're going to step out of the Dojo and into your first assignment.

You are going to visit ONE of the six worlds, but don't worry, you've been there before.

Each world is one of your Lifestyle Domains. Each domain is a dimension of life that shapes your daily experience.

They include:

- Fun & Adventure
- Health & Fitness
- Romantic Connection
- Family Life
- House & Garden
- Work, Business & Finance

Some of these domains are fun. Some are easy. Some are uncomfortable. And others are downright painful. Some of them epitomise your failure and harbour demons you've faced before and lost.

Which path will you choose?

Which one is connected to your Call?

Which one does courage demand that you take on in order to complete your training?

Which one holds the treasure that you desire most of all?

In the next chapter I will brief you on the Anatomy of Strategy, the final tool for your journey – and then it's over to you.

I realise we will lose some people at this point. They picked up this book for information, not *transformation* – and now things are about to get real!

That's OK.

That's not you.

You embarked on this journey because you're called to thrive in life.

It's time to make that happen.

| 19 |

The Anatomy of Strategy

A vision without a strategy remains an illusion.

LEE BOLMAN

I'm sure you have some big ideas on the work you're going to do to make an impact in the world. That's exciting, but before we get to that, we must focus on You. What is the life you live around that mission going to look like?

Michael Gerber says "you need to begin living your life as though it were important... take your life seriously... create it intentionally... make your life into the life you wish it to be. Simple? Yes. Easy? No. But absolutely essential if your life is to have any meaning beyond work."[1] Gerber calls this Your Primary Aim. We're going to call it Vision.

What do you want your life to look like when all is said and done? This is the happy-hearted, P5, hero's story that your friends and family will share about you when you're gone. It's the story that embodies who you are and what you stand for.

A Vision is creative. It is a grappling hook we cast out into the conceptual realm. Into a multiverse of endless possibilities, locking onto the best version of you and then pulling yourself toward that reality. Part 1: Maximised Identity, was designed to help cast your Vision for the future. Now we're going to add even more clarity.

Who are you – and in 10 years' time...

- What does your family life look like, and feel like? Are you in a relationship? Describe the 'energy' you get from that relationship? What does your partner say about you to their friends? What do your kids say about you to each other?
- How do you enjoy your time outside work? Of course, family is a part of that, but beyond that – what adventurous experiences keep you feeling alive and inspired?
- How do you feel in your body? What sorts of food are you eating and enjoying? What are the culinary delights that get you excited? Describe the tastes? Describe the energy that flows from your physical health and vitality?
- What part of the country or the world are you living in? Are you travelling or have you settled down for a while? What does your residence look like? A house? A unit? A villa? A cabin? A resort? What about the garden? Do you grow your own food? Do you have beaches/forests/mountains/rivers/cities that you can explore nearby? How do those physical spaces make you feel?

Casting a Vision should be fun. In my coaching workshops we create 'Vision Boards' using images cut from books and magazines. I'm sure you've seen these. If not, Google it. You'll get some great ideas. Play with it.

Do you have a clear Vision? Your Vision is the inspiration behind your Lifestyle Design. It is the cornerstone of your Strategy. Before moving on you need to have a clearly articulated Vision Statement or a Vision Board. If you don't yet have clarity, pause, grab your journal, and do some work. You need to get this right. Your Vision is your North Star.

A Vision is broken down into smaller and smaller parts until the actions are easy and obvious. Vision is broken into Goals. Goals are broken into Milestones. Milestones are achieved through Smart Action steps. And, when you hit your Goal, it is important to recognise the win with a Celebration. Celebration closes the loop by reflecting on and recognising the breakthroughs and the opportunities for improvement. From here you recalibrate on your Vision and embark out again. That's the anatomy of Strategy.

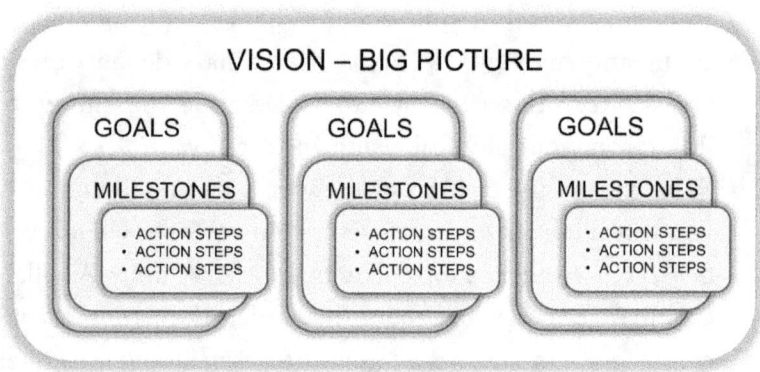

Let's unpack each one...

GOAL SETTING

A Vision is big by nature. It is holistic and it builds a feeling of excitement. Goals add a greater level of specificity and direction to your Vision. I'm a big fan of 90-day goals. Elite performance coach, Todd Herman, says that 90 days is the limit of most people's cognitive horizon.[2] The vague nature of Vision allows it to sit blissfully 5-years, 10-years, 20-years out in the future, but for clarity that generates action in the short term, 90 days is a great frame to work with. Also, four 90-day lifestyle design cycles fit neatly into a year.

I'm sure you've heard of SMART Goals – Specific, Measurable, Actionable, Realistic & Timebound. This is a good start. A goal statement should articulate clearly what you plan to achieve and by when. Jon Acuff, in his book *Finish* points out a few other key points to remember when setting goals.[3]

1. **They should be fun.** Your goal should inspire you to action. It should get you excited. If you smile when you think of your goal, then you're highly likely to get it done. If it makes you groan, success is much less likely. How can you make it joyful?
2. **Cut your goal in half.** This is counter-intuitive to a lot of goal-setting literature, but it's backed by research[3] and I've seen it work in my own coaching practice. If you aim high, work hard, and miss it (even by a little bit), then you get discouraged and you're less likely to try again. But if you halve that goal, work hard, and hit it – then you get a dopamine reward for your efforts. You close the feedback loop, embed the learning experience as positive and set yourself up for future success. Acuff also points out the human tendency to overestimate what you can achieve in a 90-day period. Cutting your goal in half gets you closer to realistic expectations.
3. **Choosing what to bomb.** Again, counter-intuitive, but smart. In order to get something new, something else has to go. What is it going to be? I chose to stop playing online

chess for 6 months while I completed post-grad studies in Educational Leadership. I've cut down on personal clients, reduced podcasting and watching movies in order to write this book. There are different seasons when different things will be important. The very real process of choosing what you're *not* going to do is a powerful way of deciding how committed you are to your goal.

Similarly, you also must choose what to focus on. If you try to change all 6 areas of your life at once, you're unlikely to be successful. If you focus on just one area at a time, you increase your chances of winning dramatically. For those of us with families, that's not always realistic or appropriate. For example, it's probably not appropriate to stop hanging out with your kids or neglect all household chores in order to read more or learn a language.

Pablo Picasso was arguably one of the most successful artists of the modern era, he was passionate and committed, but not to the women in his life. He had numerous wives and mistresses over the course of his life. Art was his true passion and women, it seems, were his hobby. The Maximised Life is not about winning in just one aspect of life but thriving in all of it. I'm hoping you already recognise the benefits of fostering happy relationships with the people you care about. If not, that is a great place to set a goal. Sure, this means that our other big goals are going to take longer, but ultimately it's worth the wait. Cut what you can but stay balanced and mindful of the bigger Vision.

WATCH YOUR LANGUAGE

When setting Goals, it is important to use positive language. Stating what you DON'T want is a poor way to articulate a goal.

Part of the power of goal setting is the triggering effect it has on the subconscious mind. The subconscious mind processes information sensually – that is, in images, sounds, smells, etc. So, if for example, you say, "My goal is to stop fighting with my partner." Then you are conjuring images and feelings of you fighting with your partner. Scenes of you having disagreements with your partner begin to play on the movie screen of your subconscious mind and then your RAS starts scanning for the evidence to make this reality true. Your subconscious mind doesn't discern this as what you *didn't want!*

So, frame your goals in the positive. For example, "I will spend 3 hours each week having fun together with my partner." Stating a goal with the words "I will..." instead of "I want..." also sets a more determined positive intention. It declares ownership of the outcome. "*I will...*" is a firm commitment. "*I want...*" is just wishful thinking.

MILESTONES ON THE JOURNEY

Big goals are made more achievable with Milestones. I love the term 'Milestones' because it reminds us we're on a journey. In Roman and Medieval times people would walk or ride to the next town and along the way there would be large rocks carved with a number indicating how many miles to the next town. On a long journey these were a form of encouragement. A single number on a rock implied; "Don't give up! You're getting closer!"

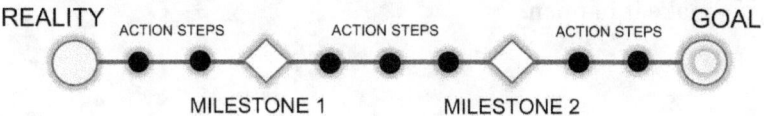

SMART ACTION STEPS

This is where the work gets done. Actions are what get results. Smart Actions are a clear set of regular steps you need to do to reach your Milestones on time. You decide these actions in advance so you can maintain focus when your 'adversaries' meet you in the forest. Stick to the plan even when doubt and anxiety and loneliness come flooding in. Believe. And get the job done.

All new action takes effort. Until repetition turns an action into habit you will encounter some resistance. Consistency builds habits which then frees your mind to go to the next level of productivity.

YOUR STRATEGY CHECKLIST

- Have you completed your Vision Statement or Vision Board?
- Have you chosen the Lifestyle Domain that you're going to take on first? If you're stuck you can take the Lifestyle Design Quiz, which will generate a free, personalised report outlining your unique strength profile, the area that matters to you most right now, and some personalised coaching questions digging deeper on how you can take some smart actions right away. You can find the quiz at www.lifestyledesignquiz.com
- **Have you written out a Goal statement that captures what you intend to achieve in the next 90 days?**
- Is it fun and inspiring?
- Is it achievable? Do you need to cut it down?
- Do you have time for this? If not, what will you give up to make it happen?

WHICH WAY NOW?

It's time to learn more about the Lifestyle Domains.
Skip ahead to the chapter that matches the goal you've chosen:

- Fun & Adventure – go to Chapter 20
- Health & Fitness – go to Chapter 21
- Romantic Connection – go to Chapter 22
- Family Life – go to Chapter 23
- House & Garden – go to Chapter 24
- Work, Business & Finance – go to Chapter 25

| 20 |

Fun & Adventure

You're off to great places. Today is your day.
Your mountain is waiting. So get on your way!

DR SEUESS

Welcome to Fun & Adventure! If you find yourself reading this chapter, then you have made an awesome choice. Fun is fundamental. ☺

Whenever I design a new learning program, one of the first questions I ask is; "Where's the fun?" If I can't answer that, then it's back to the drawing board, because I know there will be little or no engagement and therefore little or no learning. It's the same with you. If your life is all work and no play, then you're going to lose energy, motivation and focus. Eventually, you'll quit on your dreams because you have forgotten the point. A sense of fun and adventure helps you stay inspired and fresh.

I've been dropping clues to help you develop an adventurous perspective all through Part 1 & 2 – but if you're here, then I'm guessing we need to talk at a more practical level. To do this I've brought in 2 good friends of mine, Roy Simmons & Lloyd Godson to inspire you, and at the end of this chapter you will design your own simple success strategy to weave more fun and adventure into your life.

Roy is a Youth Coach. He helps me run Young Hero's Adventure Quest – an educational and personal development program for 10 to 15-year-olds. Roy is one of the recovery success stories for NSW Mid-North Coast Health after multiple surgeries on his spine. He was a guest on the 'Medical Miracle' episode of my podcast [Episode 3]. Roy is excited about life and always hungry for his next big adventure.

Lloyd is a professional Adventurer turned educator and knows better than most the infectious power of fun. His long list of achievements includes: the Guinness World record for most electricity generated by human power underwater, 2007 Australian Geographic Adventurer of the Year, and winner of the Australian Geographic $50,000 "Live your dream" Wildest Adventure Competition. He has been interviewed a number of times on national television and we've worked together on a bunch of different educational projects. He was also a guest on the podcast. [Episode 70]

MEET ROY SIMMONS

Hey guys, I'm Roy. I grew up in the UK. Back in 1985 I was playing soccer when a dog ran through my legs and turned me upside down. I landed on my neck and shoulder and dislocated my collarbone. The hospital didn't take an x-ray, they just put me in a sling, gave me a few Panadol and sent me home. I was in constant physical pain and mental anguish for many years. I did what I could to get through the days but became more and more incapacitated. I remember not being able to let my little girl come and sit on my lap because I couldn't handle the pain. I would have to push her away and see the look of disappointment and rejection on her face. In my early 30s I found out that 2 of my vertebrae had begun to dissolve and I found out that I had Hepatitis C. I know what you're thinking – I must have been an addict at some point. No, we suspect it came from a school dentist when I was a kid back in the UK. By the time the doctors realised what was wrong with my spine, they couldn't do anything. I was told by the doctors that my vertebrae had degenerated to that of an 80 or 90-year-old. There was no operation that could be done at that time. The doctors said to me, "Go home. Enjoy what you can, while you can. You are going to die."

15 years of hell followed. Muscle deterioration. Grand mal seizures. Choking. Dizziness. Falling over. Passing out. I couldn't raise my right arm. I had bedsores. I had no social life. The Hepatitis was poisoning my liver and slowly driving me mad. I was in pain all day, every day.

Every now and then I'd go searching for help. I met a one-legged doctor who told me of a revolutionary new operation being proposed by a world-famous neurosurgeon. She wasn't offering me a cure, just a chance at a better quality of life. I took it.

After surgery number 1, my neck was being held with a titanium rod, but shortly after I had internal bleeding in my neck that crushed my windpipe and all of a sudden, I couldn't breathe. The last thing I remember before passing out was the doctor grabbing a scalpel and slitting my throat to release the pressure and keep me alive. Surgery number 2 was to fix everything that had gone wrong the first time. I had several more operations after this to fix my shoulder which was calcified and immobile, and in between all this I had to start chemo treatment for the Hepatitis C. This part was the worst. The recovery was long and arduous, with several other operations to follow but mindset was key. During my years of sickness, I'd developed a mental disorder called 'catastrophic thinking syndrome' where, because I was always in pain, always hurting myself, I began to believe that 'life = injury', and 'injury = pain'. I believed that anything that could go wrong, would go wrong. My RAS was tuned into the negative. I lived believing that disaster lurked around every corner and it wasn't hard to find evidence in my life to validate that as true.

At the time I met Andrew, I was slowly recovering. The biggest accomplishment of my day was being able to walk to the Youth Hub, play a game of pool with some of the young people and then walk home. Afterward I was exhausted. I spent the rest of the day laid up on the lounge recovering – but also grinning from ear to ear. I had achieved something! The rush of exercise and helping those young people was amazing. My body was still quite broken, but in my head, I was saying *"I'm back!"*

Little by little my strength increased, and as it did my mindset improved too. Everything Andrew was teaching the kids at the Hub, backed up what the psychologists were telling me and what I was learning from my new life.

Having been to the 'dark side' now makes me appreciate every pain-free moment, every breath that I wasn't supposed to have. I live every day knowing that I am born to thrive. I delight in every opportunity that comes my way. My life is an adventure. I jump out of bed excited every morning about who I might meet and what the day might have in store for me! It's amazing the things I get to do. I live near the beach and train most days – that might sound ordinary but it's not – it's an adventure! I meet new people, I enjoy nature, and am getting fitter every day. Women half my age tell me how good I'm looking! I get to work as a Youth Mentor at the youth refuge and on Adventure Quest. We teach them about the hero's journey and how they can face their fears and start believing in themselves.

If I could give you just one piece of advice, I think I'd have to say, appreciate the little things. Life is amazing, and once you realise that, you'll never want to sit still again! I can see how coming through those years in pain has helped me to see things that I might have otherwise ignored – but the reality is, those things I get excited about everyday are just as real for you too! So go and find YOUR adventure!

MEET LLOYD GODSON

Hey guys, I'm Lloyd. My colleagues call me the nutty professor. It's not just the wild hairdo. I always have some new, crazy project on the go. I grew up in Albury, NSW. We were sometimes known as the 'barefoot-Godsons' because we never wore shoes. At university, they called me 'Crazy-Lloyd' for performing stunts like jumping off a three-story building through a flaming hoop of fire into a swimming pool wearing nothing but the husk of a watermelon!

I've lived, studied, and worked in Antarctica, Australia, Bahamas, Canada, Denmark, Germany, Greece, Indonesia, New Zealand, Panama, and the United States, and had a lot of fun along the way. I once stole a garden gnome from an elderly couple in New Zealand and took it with me to Antarctica for two weeks. In Canada somebody filmed me in the Toronto CBD trying to get people to drink their own urine after passing it through a makeshift filter I'd made. I turned up to my wedding in a full shark-wetsuit. I've spent 624 hours living underwater in a bio-sub that I helped to design and build. I teach science in schools, but I've never fitted into the traditional mould. I have an insatiable curiosity. I love coming up with wild ideas and putting them to test in the real world. My under-water projects are a way of raising awareness and tackling environmental issues in a fun way.

I think that adventure and learning new things is one of life's greatest gifts, and I don't intend to waste that. When I was a young boy, my dad used to put me to bed at night, listen to all my big ideas and then tell me, "If you can dream it, you can do it!" This is a message I want to pass onto as many people as possible. That's the message I want to share with you. Think back to when you were younger, what did you love to do? What's a funny story that others remember about you?

Wouldn't it be fun to do more of that?

STRATEGY SESSION

Now you've heard from 2 inspirational people living with Fun & Adventure in their life. Now it's time to create yours. Here's the steps.

1. Review your Goal Statement from Chapter 19. Is it still right or do you need to adjust it?
2. Now ask yourself, what do you get from that? For example, you may want to go on a travel holiday – but what do you get from that? Is it a sense of freedom? Is it the time and space to think? Is it joy? Is it making memories with your family? Whatever it is, write that down.
3. Now, think about what ISN'T going well. What is telling you that something's missing, that there's a problem. Write that down too.
4. Feel the tension between the two? That tension is evidence that YOU have the solution inside you! Your amazing body/brain/spirit is trying to communicate that to you. Write down a simple statement declaring that to be true. Something like: "*I was born to laugh, play and explore. I have the answers I need inside me right now.*"
5. Time to Mind Map the possibilities.

- Grab a new blank sheet of paper and turn it landscape. A4 is OK. A3 is better.
- In the middle of the page, write 1 or 2 words that sum up your goal and why it matters. Draw a bubble around that.
- Now branch out with curved, coloured lines including an idea on each branch
- Draw a little icon on the main ideas
- Branch out with sub-branches to include more of the details or other related ideas
- Let yourself get creative. You can go 2, 3, 4 levels down with your ideas. No idea is wrong or impossible. Don't let finances or time, other people's opinions or any other traditional limitations stop you from writing down an idea.

  Remember to make it colourful and include lots of little icons and images. For an example of a good Mind Map go to: www.thrivebydesignbook.com/resources

6. When you have finished your Mind Map, sit back, and look at it. What ideas are jumping out at you – either because they're really awesome OR because they're really do-able right now! Choose ONE idea that you love and use sub-branches to add what the next smart steps might be. What is the smallest, easiest action you can take right now?
7. Think about who you can talk to about achieving this goal. Who can keep you accountable along the way?
8. Download the Maximised Strategy Framework from www.thrivebydesignbook.com/resources and fill out the Goal, the Milestones, your Accountability Partner, your Smart Action Steps, and your Celebration.

Congratulations!

You have just designed your Strategy to get more Fun & Adventure in your life!

Now jump ahead to Chapter 26 – Mastering Your Calendar to get practical and ensure that you turn these good intentions into action.

| 21 |

Health & Fitness

Take care of your body. It's the only place you have to live.

JIM ROHN

Welcome to Health & Fitness. If you find yourself reading this chapter, then you have made an excellent choice. We've spent a lot of time so far focused on your inner world, but mastering your body is equally important. Your body is the vessel through which your abundant life takes form. It is the temple in which you honour the Call on your life. Your body is a weapon that is going to beat down all the fears, doubts and circumstantial adversities that stand in the way of your dreams. Your body is an artist's brush creating a masterpiece – your life!

I gave you a clue to the symbiotic relationship between your inner-world and your physical fitness back in Chapter 10 – Your Amazing Brain. I hope you're still using the Brain Health Planner and sticking to the 3 fundamentals? Water. Exercise. Sleep. If you are, you've laid an excellent foundation. If not, that's OK, you're in the right place.

I'm guessing that this not the first time you've had the thought: "I need to get my health and fitness on track". Health & Fitness is a game of delayed gratification. Usually, by the time that thought arrives, you've already gone months, or even years, making some poor choices and are now reaping the results. The good news is your body is an amazing machine. It is highly adaptable and responsive and small, consistent habits in the right direction can yield results.

Like any area of growth, you will get results faster if you connect with an expert in the field. A personal trainer, wellness coach or health practitioner can fast-track your path to success, so I thought I'd bring in a couple of my friends to help. Sarah and Terry are experts in the field of Health & Fitness.

Sarah Moss was one of my first ever podcast guests.[1] A busy wife, mumma and a passionate health and wellness coach for more than 16 years. She has an Advanced Diploma in Myotherapy, a Certificate IV in Fitness, and an Advanced Diploma in Dietetics for Personal Trainers. Through her programs she helps hundreds of busy men and women achieve their fitness and lifestyle goals.

Terry Power has been a kinesiologist, chiropractor, a Chinese acupuncturist and has been around wellness modalities for more than 50 years! He grew up doing his homework in the waiting room of his dad's clinic and he learned how to relate well to patients before he undertook his formal training. He now runs a successful health and wellness practice in partnership with his brother Leigh and has also been one of my guests on the podcast.[2]

MEET SARAH

Hi. I'm Sarah, and as Andrew said, I am a busy wife and mother to three beautiful girls. Like most busy mums, I struggle with the day-to-day challenge of finding balance between, motherhood, my own health, the family, housework, being present with the kids, working, running an online business. The never-ending do list, the self-inflicted pressures & expectations are endless and can become overwhelming. I get it. But I also know what a difference it makes being on top of my health. I know the difference it makes for me, and I've seen it in my clients, which is why I've made it my mission to inspire other busy parents to build a healthy body & mind that feels right for them.

I wish I could share some magic pill to fat loss, strength building & health but the truth is, there isn't one. My methods are very practical and realistic for building a healthy and strong body, but I also take a very personalised approach. I work with every individual and build a custom program around their goals, dreams, and desires.

The biggest lesson for me over the last 8 years is, like any other form of personal development, it doesn't happen overnight. It requires consistent effort every day. "Small steps lead to big results" It's putting in the small effort each day and learning new knowledge and skills. One day could be lifting weights, another day understanding more about gut health. There are thousands of health and fitness regimes out there and countless opinions about the merits of each. My clients hear me say ALL the time, "THERE IS NO RIGHT OR WRONG WAY TO EAT OR TRAIN," only the way that works for YOU and that makes YOU feel good! SIMPLE. Overcomplicating it is a recipe for inconsistency and in turn is unsustainable. It's about making mistakes, learning from them, and working out along the way what works for you and your lifestyle – most importantly, in a way that brings you pleasure & happiness!

Information overload leads to overwhelm and overwhelm leads to inertia. Inertia gets NO results. So, let's keep it simple.

NUTRITION

Knowing the fundamentals of nutrition is important for maintaining optimal health. Food is not only fuel, it is medicine. It impacts our gut health, hormone function, mood, and overall lifestyle. We all respond differently to different foods based on our lifestyle and genetic makeup. There is no single right diet for everyone but here is a basic guide:

- Fats (20 – 30%),
- Carbs (40 – 65%),
- and Protein (15 – 25%) with each meal, each day.

Knowing your calories and macros and tracking these can be very effective to create more awareness around portions and in turn will empower you to make optimal choices.

Eliminate decisions by having your meals planned and organised. It all STARTS with what food you have in the house. If you have access to processed biscuits, cakes, sweets then you're much more likely to mindlessly snack on these. A general rule when I am doing the groceries is to buy less packaged food and foods without numbers or ingredients I don't know about.

My shopping guide includes:

- FATS – butter, ghee, olive oil, avocado
- CARBS – basmati, jasmine rice, potatoes, gluten free pasta, homemade pasta, sour-dough, and an abundance of fruit and veggies
- PROTEIN – Seafood, chicken, turkey, beef, lamb, eggs, milk, yogurt, cheese.

I try to choose foods that are in season, locally grown and I have been learning how to grow my own food too. Choose free-range, organic, grass-fed meats and vegetables when you can.

I know Andrew has already talked to you about mindset but shifting your thinking about food from what you are *eliminating* to what you are *adding* is so important. Think abundantly. Don't say "I have to…" or "I can't have…" (because this makes you think about restrictions, limits, and deprival). Instead say, "I *get* to…" (and think about the opportunity, the freedom and exciting new ideas and flavours coming your way!) If you want to improve your health, and don't know where to start. My suggestion is instead of removing food, ADD food. MORE fruit, veg, and whole ingredients. MORE variety, which leads to more nutrients in your diet. Get familiar with what works for you, what makes you feel good, perform well, recover well. Check in with yourself and be aware of how different foods make you feel.

FITNESS & STRENGTH

We all have access to different locations and different equipment but as long as you are moving daily, enjoying yourself and your activity makes you feel good, it doesn't matter what you do! As I mentioned, balance is key. Overtraining is a common mistake that can lead to unsustainable results and injury. On your quest for improved fitness, surround yourself with the right people who are doing what you want to do, achieving what you want to achieve and looking how you want to look.

Personally, I love strength training. The benefits are endless. With a balance of the right cardiovascular fitness training and strength training you are safely improving your sleep, health, and your ability to deal with stress. Learning the fundamental lifts

(Squat, Bench-press, Deadlift, Shoulder-press) is the best place to start. Technique matters. Work with a trainer when you're getting started who can show you the right techniques, help you to get results faster and reduce overwhelm that comes from too many decisions.

The two most common things people struggle with is 1) lack of time and 2) lack of motivation. Andrew will help you address both of these challenges with structure and habits later in this book. For now, it's good to get familiar with your baseline health markers. When I train clients, I look at:

- heart rate,
- blood pressure,
- rate of recovery,
- stress levels,
- sleep patterns
- & digestion

If you'd like to learn more about how I can help you to reach your fitness goals, please check out my programs at: https://linktr.ee/sarahmoss or find me on Instagram @sarah_moss_pt or Facebook Sarah Moss – Fitness & Nutrition Coach.

MEET TERRY

Hi. I'm Terry. I help people live more balanced and healthy lifestyles with a focus on energy. We all know what energy feels like. When we lack energy we tire easily, we feel that we have to drag ourselves out of bed and through the day. When we have energy, we have a spring in our step and bounce from challenge to challenge. Nothing can hold us down.

So how do we get that?

Energy can be a simple concept to understand but it ebbs and flows through a complex web of systems in the human body. A simplistic scientific perspective might conclude that energy comes from the mitochondria. Mitochondria produce adenosine triphosphate (or ATP) which is the fuel source that our cells need to survive. However, when people lack that energetic sparkle, it is not necessarily a lack of ATP being generated in their mitochondria. It can be that, but usually its more complex.

For the mitochondria to function well it needs a healthy cell environment. If the cell is loaded up with toxins such as plastics or heavy metals or a virus or fungal infection, then the ability of the mitochondria to function is severely compromised. This can lead to a genuine lack of energy.

What else could be going on?

What if there is a blood clot or bruising in the lungs. Do you think your oxygenation will be 100%?

What if you're eating good foods but your absorption of nutrients in the gut is not 100%? Do you think that may impact your energy levels?

What about all the other minerals that are deficient in many of the soils used to grow plants? The thyroid releases a quarter of a teaspoon of thyroid hormones into the body every YEAR. They are very potent but Australian soils are known to be deficient in iodine. Plants cannot manufacture minerals. If it is not in the soil, then it can't be in the plant. If you're eating plants that have been grown on deficient soil, do you think that impact your nutrient levels and hence energy?

What if you caught the flu? Your lymphatic system is loaded with congestion. Your body feels terrible. We get sore and achy and have a headache. Again, this plays out at the energetic level. You lack energy and don't feel like doing much.

What if you're stressed? Not just at work but in your relationships too. You might feel that your partner is self-absorbed and being unfair? How do you think these emotional challenges play out in your cells?

Do you see how all these systems are connected?

You can see it's not as simple as, 'lack of energy = boost the mitochondria'. You need to discern each person's situation individually.

In my practice, I use kinesiology. In kinesiology, your energy is like a battery pack. We use muscle response testing to evaluate where the body is short circuiting. Where and how is the body short circuiting and loosing energy? In kinesiology we check the systems. The muscle will go weak when we challenge systems that are compromised and that gives us a clue. Then we work out what are the triggers in that system that are being attacked.

Not everybody accepts the validity of this method, but I have used it effectively to get powerful results for my clients for decades. I am confident science will catch up in the same way they have with acupuncture and chiropractic therapy.

A lot of our energy comes from the generator which is our nerves. If there is something impeding the nervous system, we can have pain or just a lacklustre feeling. Many different things can trigger this. People, animals, electromagnetic fields, toxins, insects, emotions, hormones, inhalants, ingestants, virus, bacteria, parasites, mould, fungus, yeast, nutrient imbalances, meridian imbalances, structural and biomechanical system issues in the muscles, joints, nerves, fascia, bones, etc. People can react to their houses where they work or live or even to parts of their own body in autoimmune sensitivities. Through kinesiology we can start to figure out what is truly short circuiting and compromising this person's system. People can react to pesticides, plastics, medications, vaccinations, even the food they have for breakfast!

Kinesiology is like asking the body what is happening, but that doesn't give us the remedy. The remedy is whatever tool or treatment you choose to rebalance the issue that is causing the short circuit. I use a range of different methods, but each method is personalised for the individual. In ancient Chinese medicine humans stand between heaven and earth. If a human's relationship with earth is compromised, then it affects their health and wellbeing. As spiritual creatures we also have a relationship with "heaven". What brings peace of mind and fulfillment to what we are as humans is our direct guidance and being provided by spirit. I understand Andrew has helped you to explore your inner world in Part 1 and 2. Acknowledging spirit is the single most important aspect of your health. Through it all other aspects of health and vitality unfold and are experienced in a very real way.

The quest to improve your Health & Fitness is an extremely personalised pursuit. That is why working with a good personal trainer or therapist is such a smart move. They can meet you where you're at and treat you specifically for your body, your circumstances, and your goals.

STRATEGY SESSION

Now you've heard from two experts with two very different approaches to health and fitness, and yet both of them agree; joy, a deeper connection with why it matters to you and a personalised approach that works for your lifestyle are all important points to consider. This chapter is not designed to replace the intensely rewarding experience of working with your own trainer or therapist, but it can help design a plan to get you started based on what you already know. It's time to create your own personalised Health and Fitness strategy.

1. Review your Goal Statement from Chapter 19. Is it still right or do you need to adjust it?
2. Now ask yourself, what do you get from that? For example, you may want to lose some weight – but what do you get from that? Is it a sense of confidence? Is it more energy to spend with your children? Is it feeling more attractive to your partner? Is it about longevity and wanting to grow old without the aches and pains getting worse? Whatever it is, write that down.
3. Now, think about what ISN'T going well. What is telling you that something's missing, that there's a problem. Write that down too.
4. Feel the tension between the two? That tension is evidence that YOU have the solution inside you! Your amazing body/brain/spirit is trying to communicate that to you right now! Write down a simple statement declaring that to be true. Something like: "*My body was designed to be enjoyed. I was born to run, jump, dance and express myself. My body is intelligent. I have the answers I need inside me right now.*"
5. Now it's time to Mind Map the possibilities.
    - Grab a new blank sheet of paper and turn it landscape. A4 is OK. A3 is better.
    - In the middle of the page, write 1 or 2 words that sum up your goal and why it matters. Draw a bubble around that.
    - Now branch out with curved, coloured lines including an idea on each branch
    - Draw a little icon on the main ideas
    - Branch out with sub-branches to include more of the details or other related ideas

- Let yourself get creative. You can go 2, 3, 4 levels down with your ideas. No idea is wrong or impossible. Don't let finances or time, other people's opinions or any other traditional limitations stop you from writing down an idea.

  Remember to make it colourful and include lots of little icons and images. For an example of a good Mind Map go to: www.thrivebydesignbook.com/resources

6. When you have finished your Mind Map, sit back, and look at it. What ideas are jumping out at you – either because they're really awesome OR because they're really do-able right now! Choose ONE idea that you love and use sub-branches to add what the next smart steps might be. What is the smallest, easiest action you can take right now?
7. Think about who you can talk to about achieving this goal. Who can keep you accountable along the way?
8. Download the Maximised Strategy Framework from: www.thrivebydesignbook.com/resources and fill out the Goal, the Milestones, your Accountability Partner, your Smart Action Steps, and your Celebration.

Congratulations!

You have just designed your Strategy to get more Health & Fitness in your life!

Now jump ahead to Chapter 26 – Mastering Your Calendar to get practical and ensure that you turn these good intentions into action.

| 22 |

Romantic Connection

> *Love is friendship that has caught fire. It is quiet understanding, mutual confidence, sharing and forgiving. It is loyalty through good and bad times. It settles for less than perfection and makes allowances for human weaknesses.*
>
> **ANN LANDERS**

Welcome to Romantic Connection. If you find yourself reading this chapter, then you clearly have wisdom about your priorities. A happy relationship is one of the greatest joys that life can bestow upon you. A miserable relationship is one of the most acute forms of pain imaginable. It can destroy you from the inside out.

I've tried it both ways.

A research paper by David Ribar of George Washington University points out that a healthy marriage is positively associated with a huge number of positive benefits, including improved cognitive, emotional and physical well-being for children, better mental and physical health for adults, and greater earnings and consumption for family members, but also, that it is not without its challenges.[1]

Ashton Kutcher laments that "marriage is one of the hardest things in the world".[2]

Sofia and I have been through a lot in our relationship. We've learned a lot. We have facilitated relationship groups but in no way consider ourselves relationship experts. At times we've felt like the opposite of experts! Frauds. Failures. There was a time when we both sat across from a relationship coach and heard him say; "If you two don't start prioritising your marriage, you're not going to have one!" It was a wake-up call that we both needed. In this chapter I'm going to share with you some of the insights that followed, and some reliable wisdom from people smarter than us that we've picked up along the way. I think you'll find it helpful.

So, what does it mean to 'prioritise' – a marriage, or anything else? Its root word is 'prior', meaning 'before'. It means to make a decision to put something first, ahead of everything else. Like you did when you picked this chapter. It means focusing on one thing, and saying 'No' (or at least, 'not now') to everything else. Prioritising is what smart, efficient people do.

At the time of the aforementioned relationship coaching session, we were being neither smart, nor efficient with the time we spent together (aside from the fact that we were getting help). Every conversation felt like a battle. Every careless comment like a knife-wound to the chest. Both of us were running on empty. We were out of ideas and all but out of motivation to keep trying.

With our coach's rebuke still ringing in my ears, I picked up my journal and wrote down my thoughts. I knew that there was some yet unheard truth to be discovered and I sensed the word 'prioritise' was a clue. A bible verse came to mind. "Seek *first*, the kingdom of God, and his righteousness, and all of these things will be given to you as well."[3] 'All these things' meant clothing, food, accommodation, and other fundamental physical human needs as mentioned in the previous verses. So, there was a directive to 'prioritise' the 'kingdom of God', and 'his righteousness'. What did that mean?

I pondered, if God is Love, then his kingdom is a place (or state) where love reigns. That sounds great, but it's not very helpful. It's too nebulous. Too airy-fairy. What about 'his righteousness'? I knew that meant being in 'right-standing' or 'right relationship'. Again, it was about a state of being, a state of 'oneness'. I was getting somewhere. It reminded me of the 'flow-state' we discussed in Chapter 13: The Growth-Focused Mind. I knew the gateway to Flow was mastering the art of letting go. Not giving up but learning to release and rest. Staying with the problem, but yielding to the solution that would exist, if only we could get ourselves out of the way.

I wondered, what if there was a way to find this state in relationship?

My thoughts wandered further, to Ken Robinson and his words about the ongoing quest for human potential. He points out that education is a *human-phenomenon*, which is why, when looking for education solutions, we need an organic metaphor, and not a mechanistic one. He says, "a great gardener knows that you cannot make a plant grow. We don't stick the roots on and paint the petals and attach the leaves. The plant grows itself. What you do is provide the [right] conditions for growth".[4] A marriage is the same. It's a human-phenomenon. If 'love winning' is the goal, and 'connectedness' is the peak-state that facilitates that goal, then the obvious next question is, how do you cultivate the 'right conditions' for this kind of growth?

In Chapter 13, we looked at the 4 stages of Flow. Struggle. Release. Flow. Recovery. In our relationship we certainly had the struggle part down pat. What we didn't have was 'release'. Our version of 'letting go' had become more like 'giving up' or 'not bothering'. Neither of these demonstrated true yielding. In fact, it was the opposite. We usually retreated to our positions of 'right' and set up camp there, hoping that the other one would come humbly to visit us there. They never did.

This is being stuck in P1. It dawned on me that this was 'self-righteousness', as opposed to 'God's righteousness'. These were opposites. Being 'right' is the opposite of being 'connected'. Being right puts you at the centre and stops you from entering the sacred state of connectedness with another.

The biggest obstacle to us achieving the flow-state in our individual lives is the Inner Critic. That egoic voice that claims to have your best interests at heart, but its constant badgering and fear-filled scenarios prevent you from entering the restful bliss of Flow. The same applies relationally. If we consistently articulate our ego, we stay firmly fixed in the judgement seat. Impervious to criticism, but impossible to connect with. When we do this, we sacrifice our quest for love on the altar of our own selfish-interest, and in so doing, give up ever finding the heavenly state that we once hoped our relationship would deliver. Instead, we find the opposite. Hell on Earth.

I wrote all of these thoughts down in my journal and drew a diagram, which you can see below:

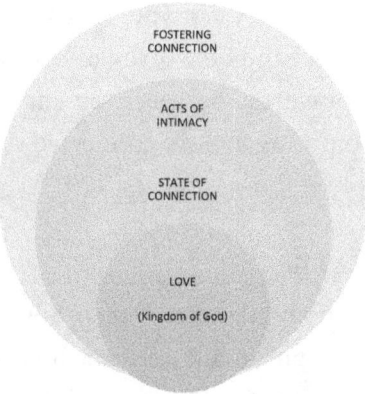

BEING RIGHT - THE ANTITHESIS OF CONNECTION.

You and your partner are two completely different people. You likely have very different definitions of success. Different expectations, different strengths and weaknesses, different backgrounds and beliefs, and different ways of going about solving problems. All of these differences have the potential to make you into an infallible team; they also have the potential to destroy your relationship from the inside out if they cannot be reconciled.

Start by saying what you think. As honestly, as simply and as forthrightly as you can. Listen to one another. But after you have stated your views, don't fight for them. Fighting for your own 'rightness' is the antithesis of connection. When you disagree, you have 3 choices. You can be clever and right, you can be silent and withdraw, or you can be respectful and foster connection. Choose the first option enough times in your relationship and you won't have one anymore. Being 'right' is hollow comfort in such circumstances. Choosing the second option seems noble on the surface. It is after all 'not fighting'; but withdrawing is refusing to show up. It is refusing to grapple with the challenge at hand because you're scared. Fear-based choices rarely produce good results. The right question to ask yourself is "how can I be honest and authentic and still foster connection?" How can you 'let go' and still stay present? How can you show trust and be worthy of trust at the same time?

Here are some powerful perspectives and tools that we have found helpful in promoting a more connected state...

2 POWERFUL PEOPLE

Relationship coach and speaker Danny Silk introduces the concept of '2 Powerful People' in any relationship.[4] A Powerful Person is someone who takes personal responsibility for their part in the relationship. They own their own stance and feelings. They do not blame the other for how they are choosing to respond. They refuse to become a victim. Powerful People is a relational version of the Growth Mindset. A Powerful Person aligns their behaviour with who they say they are. They show up with love and respect, even when others let them down. In the midst of adversity, they don't waste time with "why is this happening to me?", but instead ask questions like, "what can I do about this?"

LOVE LANGUAGES

Have you come across the 5 Love Languages by Gary Chapman?[5] We came across this simple concept early in our marriage and it has been a great tool to help us understand one another better. It's powerful because it reminds us of one of the most profound truths in marriage – that we are different people with different needs and wants. In his book and his online quiz, Chapman outlines 5 different Love Languages: Acts of Service, Quality Time, Gifts, Words of Affirmation, and Physical Touch. He also describes how the 'love-tank' that gets filled when others show us love and depleted when others disappoint us. The love tank can get filled quickly when we use the right love language, whereas a less valued love language barely gets a blip on the radar. The challenge obviously comes when we 'speak' in a different 'native language' than our partner.

Sofia is Words of Affirmation & Quality Time. I am Acts of Service & Physical Touch. Sofia might say to me, "Let's forget about work today! Let's just hang out and talk!" She may or may not be serious. It's often an expression of spontaneity and fun. At that moment she is trying to communicate 'I love you so much and I just want to spend time together with you' – but I don't hear that. Work matters to me. Getting stuff done is the primary way I show love to my family. To me, not working = not loving! So, hearing her suggestion, I get confused and hurt. "Why does she want to stop showing me love? Why does she want me to stop loving her? I don't think she understands what makes a relationship work." This miscommunication needs to be addressed otherwise it can spiral quickly out of control resulting in further pain and disappointment. The Love Languages is a wonderful framework for having these conversations and coming to a better understanding of one another.

What's YOUR Love Language? You can take the Love Language Quiz at: https://www.5lovelanguages.com/quizzes/love-language

CELEBRATE LOVE

Sofia and I have worked with mentors and coaches to help improve our relationship over the years. One great program was called 'Celebrate Love' and covered 5 important relational phases over a weekend. One of the most powerful concepts we covered on this weekend was right at the beginning as the facilitators outlined the 'rules of play'. This concept was: *No feeling is bad. No feeling is right or wrong. Feelings do not have any moral value. They are just an internal response to a person, place, or circumstance. How we respond to those feelings however, does have moral value.*[6]

Our feelings are our own and although we sometimes blame others, they belong wholly to us. It's essential to talk about feelings, both positive and negative, if we want to achieve deeper intimacy with our partner, but sometimes when we do, we take on an accusatory tone. We might say things like, "we never spend any time together! All you seem to want to do is hang out with your other friends!" You can imagine how well that conversation goes...

The framework we learned for expressing this better was golden. It communicates *ownership* of our feelings. It is called the L.I.F.E framework.[6] It is broken into 2 phases – the Reflect phase, which you do on your own, and the Exchange phase, which you do together.

- L stands for List – we scan the list and choose one or two words that capture most accurately how we are feeling (or you can use your own word/s) (for a copy of the Feelings list go to: www.thrivebydesignbook.com/resources
- I.F. stands for 'I Feel'. Write in your notepad about what's going on inside. Start with 'I feel' and in doing so you take ownership of those feelings. The feelings didn't come from the other person. They happened inside you.
- E stands for Embellish. Add more detail to your notes, getting as descriptive as you can. Use imagery, analogies, and similes to 1) help create a word-picture of how you really feel, and 2) draw attention away from any reference to the other person that could be perceived as blame. The feelings are the focus.

Once you have finished your notes, it's time to share them with your partner. It's a good idea to take turns. To have a Speaker and a Listener to be clear about whose feelings you're actually talking about. The Speaker needs to be mindful of using 'I language' to focus on their own thoughts and feelings.

Also, avoid using 'I language' as just another way to cast judgement and blame. We've all done it.

Sofia: "I feel like you don't really care about me"

Andrew: "Hmm. That's interesting. I feel like you have no idea what you're talking about!"

Don't do that.

The Listener needs to put aside their own agenda for the time being and be fully attentive to what's being said. Practice getting into P2. Active listening includes nods, visual feedback and asking clarifying questions like: "Do you mean…" Or, "Can you describe that part in more detail for me?" Or "Do you think it's like…" – being careful not to just filter what's being said through your own lens. If your partner gets frustrated with your questioning, it could be that he/she feels that you're trying to twist his/her story back into a version that suits your worldview better. If that happens – listen harder! True listening requires sidelining that inner chatter that is commentating every word being said. Connect with the feeling they are describing and step into their shoes. Our ability to connect with our partner is directly related to how well we can empathise. You need to tune in.

Once one person has shared their view, take a break. Do something different. The Listener may even want to write some notes while the comments are fresh in their mind. Fix a snack, take a shower, or just hug for a while. Whatever you find helpful to break state. Declutter for 10 minutes and allow the thoughts to digest a little.

Then switch places and repeat.

Intimacy is about knowing one another, appreciating the differences, and recognising your need for balance. Relationship is about humbly admitting your need for the other person to become the best of who you are. Intimacy is vulnerability.

STRATEGY SESSION

I hope some of this learning from the past 20+ years of our relationship have helped add a new perspective on yours. This chapter is not designed to replace the intensely rewarding experience of working with a relationship coach, but it can help you design a plan to foster conversation, connection, and a new level of intimacy in your relationship. Let's create your Romantic Connection strategy.

1. Review your Goal Statement from Chapter 19. Is it still right or do you need to adjust it?
2. Now ask yourself, what do you get from that? For example, you may want to get a deeper connection with your partner – but what do you get from that? Is it a sense of security? Is it a loving atmosphere to raise your children? Is it the confidence that comes from knowing you are attractive to your partner? Explore that. Write that down.
3. Now, think about what ISN'T going well. What is telling you that something's missing, that there's a problem. Write that down too.
4. Before discussing with each other, write down a simple statement acknowledging that you DO have the solutions inside you. It exists somewhere in that relational space between you; where right and wrong is irrelevant and all that matters is togetherness. Write something like: "I was designed to live in harmony with *another*. That person is _____. They are my friend, my confidant, the one who keeps me in balance.

They are my 'other'. Between us are the answers we need to become loving partners."
5. Then come together and discuss your goals and issues with each other. Remembering to use the techniques we've outlined above. Genuinely listen when it's your turn. Remember you're not trying to be the same, you're just trying to understand.
6. Once you understand the challenges, now it's time to Mind Map the possibilities.
    - Grab a new blank sheet of paper and turn it landscape. A4 is OK. A3 is better.
    - In the middle of the page, write the word "Connection". Draw a bubble around that.
    - Now branch out with curved, coloured lines including an idea on each branch on what you can do to foster connection.
    - Draw a little icon on the main ideas
    - Branch out with sub-branches to include more of the details or other related ideas
    - Let yourself get creative. You can go 2, 3, 4 levels down with your ideas. No idea is wrong or impossible. Don't let finances or time, other people's opinions or any other traditional limitations stop you from writing down an idea.

    Remember to make it colourful and include lots of little icons and images. For an example of a good Mind Map go to: www.thrivebydesignbook.com/resources
7. When you have finished your Mind Map, sit back, and look at it. What ideas are jumping out at you – either because they're really awesome OR because they're really do-able right now! Choose ONE idea that you love and use sub-branches to add

what the next smart steps might be. What is the smallest, easiest action you can take right now?
8. Think about who you can talk to about achieving this goal. Who can keep you accountable along the way? Is it each other, or will you include somebody else?
9. Download the Maximised Strategy Framework from: www.thrivebydesignbook.com/resources and fill out the Goal, the Milestones, your Accountability Partner, your Smart Action Steps, and your Celebration.

Congratulations!

You have just designed your Strategy to get more Romantic Connection in your life!

Now go to Chapter 26 – Mastering Your Calendar to get practical and ensure that you turn these good intentions into action.

| 23 |

Family Life

*Family and friendships are two of the
greatest facilitators of happiness.*

JOHN C. MAXWELL

Welcome to Family Life. If you find yourself reading this chapter, then you've made a smart choice. Having a vibrant and healthy support network around you is one our greatest predictors of happiness and wellbeing. Most people would agree that nothing matters more than family.

Family is bigger than just those who share the same genetic code as you. Family is about love and support. Family is about who you can go to in times of trouble, but also, how do you care, coach, and train the ones who have been entrusted to your care. Family is your inner circle. Families come in all different shapes, sizes, and styles – same as people do, but amidst all this diversity, family is still the key building block of our society. It is who we are together. Family means belonging.

If you have selected this path, I'm guessing that you're a parent, and as a leader in your home, you want to facilitate a positive, productive, and harmonious atmosphere for your partner and your children – right?

If you think the best place to start this family culture shift is with a more intimate connection with your partner, then Chapter 22 – Romantic Connection would be a better path for you – but if you already feel in-tune and connected with your partner and now you want to invest more into the culture of your home, then you're in the right place!

Sofia and I have raised 5 beautiful children of our own. We've home educated them through the majority of their formative years, and we've also played a role in coaching hundreds of other youth and families through the adventures of adolescence. We're happy to admit that we don't have all the answers. Sometimes we feel like we've got no idea what we're doing and some of our parenting moments we'd much rather forget, but we have learned a lot along the way, and I firmly believe that what we cover in this chapter will help you make smarter choices to create that happy family life that you yearn for.

THEY ARE NOT YOU

Parenting is leadership. Edgar Schein points out that leadership and culture are flip sides of the same coin. The way you lead (even when you think you're not leading) is what creates the culture that you will endure or enjoy.

At the time of writing this chapter, a new program has just aired on 9Now called 'Parental Guidance' which profiles different couples who adhere to particular 'parenting styles' and who assess one another as they take on a range of parenting challenges. There's Strict, Routine, Attachment, Nature, French, Tiger, Free-range,

Helicopter, and Disciplined.[1] I do like how all of these parents have been able to take a raw and honest look at who they are, what they stand for, and what is right for their family, but what I notice about these approaches is that they are all parent centred. The idea is that children are a blank canvas, completely mouldable, like dough or putty, and that the right inputs will give you the 'right' outcome. This is a hierarchical model built around the adults and leans on the ideas that children are an extension of our own identity. Shefali Tsabary, author of *The Conscious Parent* says, "When you parent, it's crucial you realise you aren't raising a 'mini me,' but a spirit throbbing with its own signature. For this reason, it's important to separate who you are from who each of your children is. Children aren't ours to possess or own in any way. When we know this in the depths of our soul, we tailor our raising of them to their needs, rather than moulding them to fit our needs."[2]

Cultivating a rich Family Life is about learning to be a coach. Not a dictator or an authoritarian, but a listening leader who fosters an atmosphere of learning and personal growth. A servant-leader who sets aside their own ego and facilitates an environment where their children can become all that they were born to be.

One of the most rewarding moments that I've had as a parent was going for coffee in a café that my daughter was working in. I sat at the table and watched her move about with confidence, smiling and interacting with other customers. She seemed completely at home, and she was shining in a way that only someone doing 'that thing' that they were born to do can. I was struck by a realisation; I didn't teach her that. Sure, there were hints of Sofia and I, the way she spoke to people, the way she wiped a table down. Simple disciplines that she learned with us at home but now she was using these to compose a completely new symphony of service that embodied her own unique flavour and personality. This was a magical moment. It dawned on me, probably much later than it should have, that my girl was not just 'my girl' she was also a free spirit with her own hopes, dreams and character and I needed to let her find her own way.

REALITY CHECK

There are some fundamental truths about being a parent that you would be wise to accept. The first is, at some point you're going to mess it up. Not completely because young people are generally incredibly forgiving, but you're going to make mistakes. People told me this when I had kids and I also knew that my parents certainly hadn't got it all 'right' – but I naïvely felt confident that I could do better. Looking at my beautiful, flawless baby girl sleeping peacefully and considering that somehow, I might stuff this up, was a horrible thought that I quickly pushed out of my mind. But sure enough, here I sit 20 years later, knowing that they were right. I don't say this to discourage you. I say it because perfectionism is a killer. It fuels the pride that can keep you holding onto your own ideas of what works long after wisdom would have told you to pivot and grow. Parenting is not about perfection, it's about people and it's about growth. Not just their growth, but yours as well.

CREATING CULTURE

When I teach about creating culture in my workshops, I always refer to the Triangle and Circle paradigms.[3] The Triangle culture is hierarchical. We are familiar with it because we see it in our schools, companies, hospitals, military, legal system, and governments. In the Triangle all knowledge, power, responsibility, and control resides at the top and is delegated downward. Nothing except unquestioning obedience is expected from the people at the bottom of the Triangle. The Triangle is a dehumanising structure. In the Triangle you are just a cog in the machine. It can be a very efficient structure. It is vital for rapid response in emergencies and great for dealing with simple problems with logical solutions.

The Circle is different. The Circle has been used by traditional cultures for millennia. In the Circle all knowledge, power and responsibility is shared. People can still hold roles, but these roles do not distinguish identity. In the Circle we are humans first. The Circle acknowledges that good ideas can come from anywhere. The Circle does not operate as efficiently or respond as quickly as the Triangle does, but the solutions it develops are more considered, richer in wisdom and experience. The Circle requires listening. The Circle requires patience. The Circle helps us to learn more about who we are. The Circle is how we foster genuine connection as a community and the only way to solve complex social problems.

There is a time and a place for both of these cultural modalities, however we are conditioned by society to lean more toward the Triangle most of the time. Triangle families are strict, uncompromising and tend toward punitive methods of discipline to maintain the status quo. Family Life needs more Circle time. Cultivating genuine connection is the essential foundation to build confidence, compassion and even for setting healthy boundaries that help our kids stay safe.

We often look at parenting styles the same way we look at management – on a 2-dimensional, linear spectrum with an easy-going, laissez-faire approach at one end, and strict authoritarian at the other. This is an unhelpful oversimplification and parents often feel that they have to choose one or the other. Some parents want to be 'besties' with their kids, whereas other parents see their role as the drill-sergeant, to help their child experience the best of life which only comes through strong discipline, success and achievement.

In my early years as a parent, I was more like the latter. Our first child was a gift. She was happy, content, she ate and slept well, and I secretly thought I'd done something special to deserve such an amazing young girl. I knew I was blessed, but I thought, "She's good. We can make her better." We took a child who was eager to please and set a high bar which she did her best to reach. This level of self-discipline helped her excel in her strengths. She won awards, business grants, and was a person everyone wanted to know. But she also faced significant struggles as well. Her fascination with diet and health danced into the realm of an eating disorder. Her empathic caring nature put her in the centre of numerous complex teen social dilemmas that she didn't yet have the skills to navigate, and she ended up anxious and overwhelmed. During her late teens she rebelled against it all and went on a mission to find fun. This was all very hard to watch. For me, it felt like an acute form of failure with the heartbreak to match, but it was where I finally began to learn that *my girl* was her own person whom I had been given the privilege to be a part of her story. I think I'm still learning this.

During some of those tumultuous years, Bella hung out with families who were very different to us. Many of these parents compromised healthy boundaries and even federal laws in order to preserve the 'friendship' status with their child. Whilst we have obviously made mistakes, I need to point out that these parents at the other end of the spectrum are not helping their children. When contrasted against the threat of losing a child to the myriad of temptations that the world has to offer, it may seem like wisdom to lower your standards, but abundant living is *never* achieved by compromising your values or who you are. Always strive to be the best of yourself, even when others may not agree with you. Even if that includes people you love. This takes courage. Gregg & Brett Harris, father-son co-authors of 'Raising Kids to Do Hard Things' says that your goal is not for you to like them now, your goal is for them to thank you when they're 30.[4]

So how do you be the best of you AND foster relationship with someone who needs to feel independent? Relationship expert, author and speaker Dr Justin Coulson says that parents should focus on giving our children 3 things – love, limits, and laughter.[5] The cornerstone of all of these is the same magic ingredient that builds any relationship...

Time.

Quality time where you are present, engaged, and happy because you get to be in the presence of an amazing human being. Do you remember in Part 1, when I asked you to think back to when your child was a baby sleeping, and how we marvelled at the infinite value and inconceivable potential? We sometimes forget that we're still looking at the same person today. The same amazing human being, and all they want from us is to connect...

There are a lot of competing priorities that take away from family time together but making this a priority is one of the best investments you can ever make.

FAMILY MEETING

In all the other lifestyle chapters, this section is called the 'Strategy Session' and that's what this is, but in this chapter, I've renamed it because it's important that 'Family' is the focus, not the strategy itself. Focus on the process and let the outcome take care of itself.

1. Set up a time and space with no distractions, no devices, no pressing appointments where each family member is going to be a willing participant in the meeting. You'll need to consult with one another, give people notice and reminders to get this right.

2. Before the meeting, review your Goal Statement from Chapter 19. Is it still right or do you need to adjust it?
3. Now ask yourself, what do you get from that? For example, you may want to get a better family life – but what do you get from that? Is it a sense of security? Is it peace? Is it a positive sense of identity? Is it happiness? Explore that. Write it down.
4. Now, think about what ISN'T going well. What is telling you that something's missing, that there's a problem. Write that down too.
5. When you come together for your meeting, it is wise to set the tone and get everyone in the right frame of mind for success. An easy way to do this is by going around the circle and asking each person to share some they are grateful for or a highlight from the week.
6. Then share the goal statement and ask the others – does that sound right? Does it need to be adjusted? Share with them your insights on why it matters to YOU – and then open it up (taking turns) why is that important for THEM? Let the conversation flow, but make sure that everyone gets a turn and that parents are not dominating the airspace. Be a listening leader.
7. Now gently bring up some of the shortcomings that you've noticed. Limit this to 1 or 2 issues per meeting. Use 'I' statements to avoid casting accusations, judgement or blame on certain people. Focus on situations and events and how these made you feel.
8. Feel the tension between the goal and the shortcomings and make a simple declaration – that we've got this. Cultivate belief through inspiration. Revisit times that you HAVE gelled together cohesively in the past and formed a formidable team.

Tell them that you trust them and you believe in them - that's why you're doing this.

9. Designing the solutions. There may be some practical steps that need to be put in place to address the issue/s, but inevitably the solution will include fostering connection. Sometimes just being listened to in the family meeting is all that's needed for a young person to feel empowered. Our kids love brainstorming connection experiences. We have a large sheet of paper, and all contribute ideas on fun adventures that we could do together.

10. Mind Map the possibilities. (15 – 30 minutes)
Try to get 15 – 20 ideas down.
    - Grab a new blank sheet of paper and turn it landscape. A4 is OK. A3 is better. A2 is better still!
    - In the middle of the page, write "Family Time" and why it matters, or some words that express your goal. Draw a bubble around that.
    - Now branch out with curved, coloured lines including an idea on each branch
    - Draw a little icon on the main ideas
    - Branch out with sub-branches to include more of the details or other related ideas
    - Let yourself get creative. You can go 2, 3, 4 levels down with your ideas. No idea is wrong or impossible. Don't let finances or time, other people's opinions or any other traditional limitations stop you from writing down an idea.

    Remember to make it colourful and include lots of little icons and images. For an example of a good Mind Map go to: www.thrivebydesignbook.com/resources

11. When you have finished your Mind Map, sit back, and look at it. What ideas are jumping out at you – either because they're

really awesome OR because they're really do-able right now! Choose FIVE achievable ideas that everyone agrees would be fun and use sub-branches to include details of any planning that needs to happen first. What is the smallest, easiest action you can take right now?
12. Agree to keep one another accountable to make these FIVE 'together times' happen in the next 10 weeks.
13. Download the Maximised Strategy Framework from: www.thrivebydesignbook.com/resources and fill out the Goal, the Milestones, your Smart Action Steps, and your Celebration. (You are the accountability partners for each other)

Congratulations!

You have just designed a Strategy to get more Quality Family Time in your life!

Now jump ahead to Chapter 26 – Mastering Your Calendar to get practical and ensure that you turn these good intentions into action.

| 24 |

House & Garden

*Beautiful surroundings make us happier,
more creative and more productive*

MELANIE FALVEY

Welcome to House & Garden. If you find yourself reading this chapter, then you are obviously an aesthetically and energetically inspired person. Like many creatives your external world is an extension of who you are and when one is in chaos so is the other. You know that beauty matters. Your home is not just the space that meets your physical needs, it is a sanctuary. It is a place to feel inspired and alive. This chapter is not about acquiring more 'stuff'. If you recognise that getting your physical space in order will release a flow of energy that takes your life to the next level, then you are in the right place!

Our physical environment is interwoven with who we are. It is a part of our life. Your home is a hub that facilitates fullness in many other areas of your life. It is where Family Life and Romantic Connection take place. It is a place that you can retreat from the challenging world of Work, Business & Finance and re-energise for tomorrow. Your home embodies rest. It is also a way that we share ourselves with others. We can invite others in and share a meal and fellowship together. Your home is a spiritual place.

In our life we have chosen homebirth, home-schooling, home-church, and a home-office to run our business. I love the sacred space that is our home, our garden, and the connected spaces of natural beauty around it. There is something about 'home' that captures a sense of belonging like nothing else can.

Working on your home is a creative process that can be incredibly rewarding. You get to make something that you can look at and appreciate every day. Home renovating has been a passion of mine for most of my adult life. It allowed me to channel my creative energies in an extremely practical way and justify spending significant amounts of money on one of my hobbies. It also gave me a great reason to make regular visits to the hardware store and own tools that would otherwise be an excessive spend.

Building or renovating a home and garden can be time-consuming, challenging, and expensive. It can be easy to lose focus on why this space matters. We need to make sure that our physical spaces are a source of joy and peace for us, not a reason for stress and anxiety.

STRATEGY SESSION

Designing and creating your physical space is an extremely personalised process. I cannot tell you what you should do, what to like or how to get it done. What I can show is how to design. Expect challenges along the way but enjoy the creative process, as well as the final product. Let's get started!

1. Review your Goal Statement from Chapter 19. If you share a home with your partner and family then they need to be on board with this goal. Ask them what they think and if it is not a high priority for them, find out why. Then refine it. Come up with a new goal together. This could be separate goals that you're going to work on individually and agree to support each other to reach, OR it could be a synthesis of both goals together.
2. As a part of this discussion, ask yourselves, 'what do you get from that?' For example, you may want to get a new kitchen or bathroom or vege garden – but what do you get from that? Is it a sense of peace knowing that everything works well? Is it reduced stress? Is it a feeling of accomplishment? Is it the confidence to invite others over? Is it that you just want to do a project with your partner or family? Explore that. Write it down. If necessary, refine the goal.
3. Now, think about what ISN'T going well. What is telling you that something's missing, that there's a problem. Write that down too.
4. Feel the tension between the goal and the shortcomings and make a simple declaration that is going to move you from Lack to Abundance. For example: *"My home is an extension of who I am. I am calm, confident, and caring. I will create a beautiful space because I want to express _____."*
5. Make a Mind Map of the things that matter most to you on this project.
    - Grab a new blank sheet of paper and turn it landscape. A4 is OK. A3 is better.
    - In the middle of the page, write "House & Garden" and why it matters. Draw a bubble or house or garden images around that.

- Now branch out with curved, coloured lines including an idea on each branch
- Draw a little icon on the main ideas
- Branch out with sub-branches to include more of the details or other related ideas
- Let yourself get creative. You can go 2, 3, 4 levels down with your ideas. No idea is wrong or impossible. Don't let finances or time, other people's opinions or any other traditional limitations stop you from writing down an idea.

Remember to make it colourful and include lots of little icons and images. For an example of a good Mind Map go to: www.thrivebydesignbook.com/resources

6. Is there a way you can make the goal smaller? For example, completely overhaul the vegetable garden, could become, re-plant one bed. Or renovate all the kids' bedrooms, could become, renovate one child's room. It might sound counter-intuitive, but a smaller, simpler goal will actually create more energy and momentum than a bigger one.
7. In your notebook, along with your goal, write down some of the key measures for success. How will you know that you have achieved what you set out to do? Write them down.
8. Start doing some research. You can look at magazines. Spend time in nature. Research on the internet. Create a Pinterest board. Browse the stores. Whatever inspires you.
9. Keep a sketchpad and draw your ideas. Use the drawing to help you solve problems on paper (it's a lot cheaper than making mistakes with building materials and there is a lot less time pressure on decisions at this stage)
10. Design the solutions. When you have LOTS of ideas to draw from, you need to create a final concept. If you've got the skills to draw that up yourself, great. If not, you'll need to get

a designer to help. A well resolved plan with all the details added is worth its weight in gold.
11. If you are using a builder or landscaper, talk through expectations around cost and timeframe. Ask him/her to give you some expected milestones. It's very important to know these early.
12. Download the Maximised Strategy Framework from: www.thrivebydesignbook.com/resources and fill out the Goal, the Milestones, your Smart Action Steps, and your Celebration. (You are going to keep your builder/landscaper accountable. If you are the builder/landscaper, then you need to nominate someone else to be your accountability partner.)

Congratulations!

You have just designed a Strategy to create a new and improved physical space!

Now go to Chapter 26 – Mastering Your Calendar to get practical and ensure that you turn these good intentions into action.

| 25 |

Work, Business & Finances

> *More important than the how we achieve financial freedom, is the why. Find your reasons why you want to be free and wealthy*
> **ROBERT KIYOSAKI**

Welcome to the world of Work, Business & Finances. If you find yourself reading this chapter, then you probably already realise 2 things:

1. money is the energy we use to fuel our lifestyle – without it, our impact is limited
2. a significant proportion of life is 'work' – if you don't find some level of satisfaction in what you do each day, then it is hard to feel that you are thriving in life.

In this chapter we're going to be looking at both of these elements. If you want to increase your income to reach other lifestyle goals AND find more joy and fulfillment in the work you do, then you are in the right place.

MONEY - THE ROOT OF EVIL?

We need to clear this one up pretty quickly. There is a mindset that says, 'money is the root of all evil'. That it causes pain, division, greed, and war. I disagree. The foundation of this belief is a misquoted bible verse that says, 'the *love of money* is the root of all evil'. The issue is internal. What you love shapes who you are. It's not about what's in your pocket, it's about what's in your heart.

I know some incredibly kind, loving, and generous wealthy people. I've also met some very nasty, angry, and selfish rich people too. I have watched with tears as people with next to nothing share everything they have. And, I have seen others, in similar circumstances, blame everyone around them for their misfortune, locking themselves up in a life of misery and despair.

The money these people had did not make them good or bad people. It didn't make them happy or sad people either. Money is a volume switch for your inner voice. If you have clear calling, a mission to make a positive difference in the world and you believe that you can do it. Financial resources enable that vision to become a reality. If you don't know who you are, if you're lost and unsure about what you're called to do, money won't help you. In fact, without purpose, money will cause you pain. It will turn up the volume on the emptiness inside.

I've heard people react with moral indignation when they hear someone's hourly rate? Someone says, "He charges $1000 an hour" and without knowing anything about the service they offer or the value they bring, a judgement statement follows. Something like, "How they can sleep at night!" Or, "I suppose if you can get away with it..." Or, "That's criminal!" These statements are rooted in the belief that people who are prosperous are greedy, manipulative, and unscrupulous. Sure, there are some people who make money like that, but one does not equal the other. Financial prosperity is not a sign of poor character, and while ever you equate the two, you will always subconsciously sabotage your efforts toward financial breakthrough. Have you got your mindset right? Maybe you need to pause this chapter and go back and review Chapter 15 – The Abundant Mindset. Apply the Abundant Mindset to your beliefs about finance.

Money is moral-neutral. It is not good or bad. It is a resource. It is like a battery that stores the energy that we create with our work. Or like a pile of wood that has captured the energy from the sun. The battery or the wood is not good or bad, it is just a resource in the hands of a creative person. Their intent, their purpose will determine what that stored energy gets used for. Good or evil.

Think of Bruce Wayne (aka Batman) and Lex Luthor. Both were inordinately rich. They had incredible resources available to them. One chose to serve the people and fight crime. The other felt threatened by someone else's power. Batman was all about the mission. Luthor was all about self.

PERSONAL FINANCES

If you are a creative, if you want to make an impact, or if you are in any way entrepreneurial, it is very likely that you have already ridden the highs and lows of personal finance.

I've been in situations where my wife would come home ecstatic because a local-church group was giving away day-old free bread to stretch our inadequate grocery budget far enough to feed the family. I've also earned a 6-figure income working just a few days a week. Ironically, back in those days, I knew little about mindset and I rarely appreciated the goodness of either circumstance, but when I think back now, I know I've been blessed. Sofia and I are polar opposites when it comes to spending and saving. We also both have very different interpretations of financial success. We've both made big financial blunders, but our differences have forced us to research, learn and develop strategies to communicate better. On our hunt for solutions we came across a book: The Barefoot Investor by Scott Pape.[1] We tried his 'buckets' concept, which helped, but for us, it wasn't enough. It did get us thinking though. We used his principles to develop our own strategy that completely shifted the way we manage our money together. It has made a huge difference for us and these are the principles I'd like to share with you.

PRINCIPLE 1 - YOU'VE GOT THIS

Scott Pape's Fire-Extinguisher[1] is a rapidly amassed sum that goes into an interest-bearing savings account to semi-insure yourself. You continue to build this with regular payments. Not only does it allow you to raise your excess on insurances and therefore reduce your premiums, as it grows, so too does your belief that if something happens, you will be OK. As Pape would say, "You've got this!"

I borrowed $10,000 from my mum and dad to help me build my business in the early days. I paid this back into an offset mortgage account to reduce the interest and term of our loan. In a year's time, when it was ready, I told my mum and dad to send me their bank details to pay it back. That was about 4 years ago and despite several requests, they keep 'forgetting' to give me the bank details. It is just like my dad. He won't tell me it's a gift, but he leaves the expectation lingering just so I won't spend it. He knows that keeping it there is a smart move for us. I agree.

This start-up has been an incredible blessing and we have continued to build this fund. It is still reducing our mortgage, but even better than that it now allows us to finance ourselves and avoid credit card debt which keeps other families locked up in a cycle of 'just-getting-by'.

PRINCIPLE 2 – THE ACCOUNTS

Pape's '3 bucket system'[1] wasn't enough for us. Being so different in our priorities we needed a better way to communicate our spending. I set up 8 accounts – all offsetting our mortgage. 7 of those are for different saving and spending categories.

- Housekeeping
- Car, Fuel and Maintenance
- Holidays
- House & garden
- Health & Fitness
- Education
- Hair & Beauty

(I'm sure you could think of more!)

A regular income goes into these accounts and as it accumulates it offsets our mortgage. The money in each extends that *'I've got this'* feeling to every aspect of our life, but the magic is in the 8th account. It is the lynchpin of our system. It's called the CLEARING account.

The Clearing Account is a separate account that we don't personally draw from.

Business income comes in waves, and in the high times, funds are siphoned off into the Clearing Account. The Clearing Account then in turn, drip feeds into the other 7 accounts every fortnight as though I was being paid a salary. It also covers other predictable expenses like mortgage, rates, electricity, etc. EVERYTHING is automated. The Clearing Account buffers the ever-tumultuous highs and lows of business income and takes out the points of conflict like how, when, and how-much gets spent on different things.

We only have 2 rules.

1. You can buy it IF the money is available in the right account, if not, wait till next fortnight
2. We don't touch the Clearing Account unless we've sat down, talked it over and agreed to make a change to the automation OR funnel one-off additional funds into another account

This simple system finally brought us peace after more than a decade of financial tension.

PRINCIPLE 3 – THE SPLURGE

It was always important to us to keep our personal finances linked. As hard as it got, we felt that dividing our money would be the start of living separate lives. A path we didn't want to go down.

Pape's idea of a 'Splurge Account'[1] is brilliant because we all need treats from time to time and unless you account for that it can bring any system undone. Unfortunately, this didn't work for us because we were using ONE Splurge account between us and we had very different ideas on what, when and how to splurge!

So, after we had set up our offset Clearing Account and 7 other spending accounts, we kept our original 4 accounts with a different bank that we'd set up when we were reading The Barefoot Investor. We renamed them 'Sofia Splurge', 'Sofia Smile', 'Andrew Splurge', and 'Andrew Smile'. Two fortnightly payments from the Clearing Account are paid into our Splurge accounts. This is for coffees, date nights, and any other treats that are a one-off splurge.

The Smile accounts are linked accounts that we can manage our own personal savings with. If I want to save up for a new hiking backpack (and dropping hints around my birthday or Father's Day doesn't work) then I have a way to steadily accumulate funds towards my goal. I can transfer whatever I want from my Splurge into my Smile and save as fast or as slowly as I see fit. If Sofia wants to buy a coffee each day and save up for giving to a charity, she can. It's extremely liberating. These accounts balance our personal financial freedom with our long-term financial security.

I highly recommend you take a look at The Barefoot Investor. Scott Pape has some other great ideas in there that you can make your own like we did.

ARE YOU READY TO SERVE?

Now to work. Once you've set up your system to manage your money, you're ready to 'turn on the tap!' There are hundreds of ways you can do this, but I'd like to help you find the way that works best for you.

Did you know that the root meaning of the word 'work' is the same as the word 'worship'? To work means to give your all. To take your 'worth' and offer it as an expression of reverence. It doesn't matter if you have your own business or company or if you work for someone else. Work is all about making a divine declaration about who you are. The way you work shows your honour and integrity. It reveals something about who you are.

Please note: work reveals character, but it does not define you. I have seen when someone loses their job; or when an athlete suffers a career ending injury; or a primary-income earner retires and thinks 'now what?'; or when the stay-home parent's last child is now ready to take care of themselves. It is a difficult transition. The 'who', the 'what' and the 'why', start to fall apart. All of a sudden, they can no longer be defined by what they 'do', and they must rediscover who they really are. Circumstances may change, people and jobs will come and go, but the Call inside remains. Often we just need to rediscover it in a new context. This is a good thing. This is growth. Work can help us learn more about who we are.

IS YOUR WORK ALIGNED?

I used to think that people in completely uncreative jobs like factory workers couldn't be happy because how could they possibly get *any* satisfaction from doing such unfulfilling work. To me that was like prostitution! Giving away your worth for something you didn't truly love, just for money. An extreme view, I know. I was wrong. I have met and now even coached a number of people who do menial work each day. They are happy to do it because their focus is on other things. For them, bringing in enough money to fund a lifestyle of fun, adventure and family time means way more than the intrinsic reward of work. In their mind, they are getting a great deal!

I also know a lot of people who draw a distinct line between their business and their mission. They are still making a positive difference in the world, but their work is the means to that end. Their business (or job) funds the mission. To be honest, I've envied people like that. I've wished that I could just punch the clock, keep my mouth shut and stop trying to make change. Life would be simpler that way, but whenever I've tried, I feel that a part of me is dying inside. I am driven to find and do the work that I'm called to. And I think if you are reading this chapter – so are you.

THE RISK

Doing work that you love is risky. It's much easier to make bottle-caps and get paid by the hour. If the quality controller points out a mistake, you know you need to lift your game, but it doesn't hurt your feelings. It doesn't shake your identity because you've severed the connection between who you are and the work you do. There is a clear distinction.

When your work is your mission, you make yourself vulnerable. You are taking a piece of your heart and soul and putting it out into the public arena for judgement and critique. Brené Brown says, "we need more people who are willing to demonstrate what it looks like to risk and endure failure, disappointment and regret... people willing to own their stories, live their values and to keep showing up".

Do you have this kind of courage?

Steven Pressfield in The Artist's Journey says that this kind of work is how human beings reconnect to the divine ground.[2] Through blood and sweat and tears, and an unrelenting pursuit of their work they are trying to find their way back to Eden.

In this chapter I've talked about work that invokes honour, integrity, joy, and love. Work aligned with the Call. But I want to be clear, that doesn't make it easy! Jack Delosa, founder of The Entourage business school says:

> People think that when you find something you love, something you're enthusiastic about, that working towards it is easy. Not so. Often the more you love something the more resistance you will feel progressing toward it. This idea of "if it's meant to be it should be effortless" or "if I'm in flow then it will feel good all the time" is a highly pernicious idea because it seduces the amateur into thinking they can produce something great without encountering the inevitable struggle of progress[3]

STRATEGY SESSION

The way I see it, you have FOUR options to improve your work/business/financial position:

1. You have a job that aligns well with your core identity. You develop a strategy to bring the very best of who you are to that work and trust that your efforts will be rewarded. There is a proverb that says, "A man's gift makes room for him"
2. You create and build your own business. I'm a huge fan of this model because you have complete control on the work you do, how you do it and the people you do it for. The trade-off is less control on cashflow. In a job you get paid an agreed amount and excepting extenuating circumstances, this is predictable and more or less guaranteed. In your own business it's up to you to weather the highs and lows of business-life. That's when a smart financial management system becomes so important. The rewards can be great, but so too the costs. It's a wonderful adventure and I think it holds amazing opportunities for you to 'hit the mark' with your work, but it's certainly not for everybody.
3. You become an investor. There are a myriad of things you can invest in, and all have their own combination of risks and rewards. You need to know what you're investing in or find somebody you trust who can advise you. To invest you need something to start with. I strongly advise against investing with credit, but if you do, understand that no investment is failproof and so you should have an exit and payoff strategy in place before you buy in.
4. Lastly, a combination of two or all three of the above. Maybe you have a job that pays well, you can do with relatively little input, and you want to pursue investment opportunities. Maybe your business makes solid, steady cashflow and you can do the same. Maybe you have a great business concept, but you want to supplement your cashflow, especially during the early days and so you combine part-time work with a

synergistic business. Any or all of these could be successful. Which one will you choose?

NEXT STEPS

1. Review your Goal Statement from Chapter 19. Is it still right or do you need to adjust it?
2. Now ask yourself, what do you get from that? For example, you may want to increase your job income by 10% – but what do you get from that? Is it a sense of freedom? Is it a sense of status? Is it a family holiday to make memories together? Think carefully about this. Remember money is just stored energy. What do you want to use it for? Whatever it is, write that down.
3. Now, think about what ISN'T going well. What is telling you that something's missing, that there's a problem. Write that down too.
4. Feel the tension between the two? Your amazing body/brain/spirit is communicating to you. Let's write down a simple statement that moves you from the tension of Lack, to the thriving state of Abundance. Something like: *"I am a blessing to the people around me. I was born to Thrive and I will not let hard work, doubts, or circumstances stand in my way."*
5. Time to Mind Map the possibilities.
    - Grab a new blank sheet of paper and turn it landscape. A4 is OK. A3 is better.
    - In the middle of the page, write 1 or 2 words that sum up your goal and why it matters. Draw a bubble around that.
    - Now branch out with curved, coloured lines including an idea on each branch

- Draw a little icon on the main ideas
- Branch out with sub-branches to include more of the details or other related ideas
- Let yourself get creative. You can go 2, 3, 4 levels down with your ideas. No idea is wrong or impossible. Don't let finances or time, other people's opinions or any other traditional limitations stop you from writing down an idea.

   Remember to make it colourful and include lots of little icons and images. For an example of a good Mind Map go to: www.thrivebydesignbook.com/resources
6. When you have finished your Mind Map, sit back, and look at it. What ideas are jumping out at you – either because they're really awesome OR because they're really do-able right now! Choose ONE idea that you love and use sub-branches to add what the next smart steps might be. What is the smallest, easiest action you can take right now?
7. Think about who you can talk to about achieving this goal. Who can keep you accountable along the way?
8. Download the Maximised Strategy Framework from: www.thrivebydesignbook.com/resources and fill out the Goal, Milestones, your Accountability Partner, your Smart Action Steps, and your Celebration.

Congratulations!

You have just designed a Strategy to improve your Work, Business and Financial life!

Now go to Chapter 26 – Mastering Your Calendar to get practical and ensure that you turn these good intentions into action.

| 26 |

Mastering Your Calendar

The bad news is time flies. The good news is you're the pilot.

MICHAEL ALTSHULER

Well done. Getting this far is an achievement. As you moved through your focus for growth and decided on some actions, I'm sure the sense of *'woah, this is getting real!'* would have begun to dawn on you. I'm sad to say, many people just give up at that point. They enjoy the wonder of the conceptual realm, where a business can be built in an hour and a happy family is just a conversation away, but nobody likes the rude shock of dropping down into actuality where decisions are complex, and results come slowly. Anyone can dream. Not everyone believes enough in their dream to make it happen. To act. That is the key distinguisher of success. People that 'do', and people that don't. Let's make sure you are one of the *'doers'*!

TIME MANAGEMENT

This is NOT about 'time-management'. There's no such thing as 'time-management'. No one can manage time. Time is a constant. Like gravity. It doesn't change. It cannot be sped up or slowed down, borrowed, or repaid. Everybody has roughly the same 650,000 hours on the planet, give or take, and after that, you're done. Onto the next adventure where time is less of an issue. 'Success' is determined by what we choose to do with the time we've been given. You have one life – just like Albert Einstein, or Mother Teresa, or Steve Jobs. We cannot manage time, but we can manage ourselves and the actions we choose to take. We can manage where we focus our energy and our effort. 'Time-management', more accurately, is 'Activity-management'.

OVERNIGHT SUCCESS

I'm sure you've heard the term 'an overnight success'. We love these stories, right? They give us the idea that the breakthrough we long for is possibly just moments away. We just need the wind to change or the penny to drop – for *something* to shift. This is the 'lucky break' where an unexpected turn of events endows you with resources (like winning the lottery) or thrusts you into the spotlight, and that sudden stardom is all you need to live happily ever after.

It isn't true. This is fatalism masquerading as hope. One study has shown that the happiness levels of people 3 months after winning the lottery, and the happiness levels of people 3 months after suffering a life-altering injury in a car accident, are virtually the same.[1] Sure, there is an initial high or an initial low in response to life events, but for the medium to long term, it makes little difference.

Happiness and success are never won or lost in any single life event. Happiness and success are built, moment by moment, hour by hour, day by day, week by week, season by season, and year by year. It is about doing the work – which, actually is great news! That puts your life right back in your hands where it belongs. That is your divine gift.

IN-TIME VERSUS THROUGH-TIME

I first heard these terms described by author and Master Neuro Strategist, Simone Leslie.[2] There are 2 main ways that people view time. Everyone has a tendency toward one modality or the other. She shared with me an interesting way to check which one you are. "Think about your past," she said. "Pause for a moment and see it in your mind's eye. Where is it? Point to it in relation to your body. OK." (She made a note of my response). Then she said, "think about your future." I did. "Where do you see it physically? Point to it." I did. She made a note of the response.

For people who are 'in-time', when they think of their past, (usually) it is behind them, and when they think of their future (usually) they think of it as 'out in front'.

For 'through-time' people, they see time laid out left to right like a timeline. The past is (usually) on the left, and the future (usually) is on the right.

'In-time' people live in the moment. They can drop into a peak state very quickly. They can lose themselves in what they are doing and waste less time fumbling about with 'how to'. They just are. They just do. This can be enhanced by training and habitual practices. This is the state we all need to find if we hope to follow the Call. The disadvantage of this kind of thinking is that they lose their big picture thinking. In-time means now, and so they're not thinking about tomorrow. In-time people struggle to plan for the future.

They often run late for meetings, and they tend to have a more P1 perspective of the world. Are you an 'in-time' thinker?

'Through-time' people see life laid out in front of them like a map or a timeline. Big picture thinking is what they do best! Through-time thinkers are great at planning. Project managers have to think through time. It's ironic that they are great at setting up the schedules required to train and develop habits, but if they stay 'through-time', they never actually set foot in the arena! Their disadvantage is actually doing the work. They can get stuck in the planning phase. They find it harder to get into the zone.

We need to learn to think from both perspectives. In the Design Thinking chapter, we learned about the 'Hot-Air Balloon perspective' and the 'Bashing Your Way Through the Trees perspective'. These are essentially 'in-time' and 'through-time' perspectives. To achieve any complex project, you need to start with that bigger picture view. You also need to get in, focus on the details and be absorbed in the work. One of the main benefits of working with a coach is helping you to transition between these 2 different worlds.

WHAT IS A CALENDAR?

Sounds like a silly question, but it's an important one. A calendar is a map to your day. When you're in planning-mode, you're wearing your manager's hat. You're through-time. You're laying it out in front of you and you can see how all the pieces fit together. By putting this on a calendar, you are freeing up your mind to then descend, down into the work and get stuff done. If you are constantly worrying about 'have I forgotten anything' or 'what's coming next', then you are cheating yourself out of genuine productivity. Your brain works best focussed on ONE activity at a time. It works best when it can become purely engaged in the activity at hand.

To achieve this, it is important to leave more space than you think you need. Research shows we usually overestimate what we can achieve in a period of time. Things always go more smoothly in our head, plus we forget to leave time for learning and making mistakes. This is called *'planning fallacy'*.[3] It's a common mistake. If we constantly cut short the amount of time we need or try to jam too many different activities into our day we rob ourselves of the joy of work.

A calendar is also a great tool to track how you are actually spending your time. Especially in business, this is a great way to go back and review where you are being productive and where you can improve.

LET'S BUILD IT

I have a weekly planner you can use at www.thrivebydesign-book.com/resources . It's a great tool but I prefer to use an online version. I like being able to easily move blocks around and schedule appointments that my clients and team can respond to. If you've never used a calendar (you're probably an in-time person!), I highly recommend you start. Like anything it takes a bit of practice, but I guarantee it's worth it in the newfound level of productivity you will gain.

STEP 1: Either print the weekly planner OR open your chosen online calendar app. I don't recommend doing this on your phone because 1) your phone is built to distract you from being productive, and 2) you want to see this bigger. You want to lay it out so you can see the flow.

STEP 2: Add in all the existing commitments you already know you have so you can see the spaces left over. Remember to include all the Brain Training activities here too. Don't stop doing these.

If there are no empty spaces, you need to make some. What's on your weekly planner that you could or should lose? What on your weekly planner is not taking you either directly or indirectly to your life-vision? If it has no purpose – cut it out.

STEP 3: Now you have some space in your week, it's time to float up even higher and look at a 90-day season. I've found that 90-days (3months) is a great timeframe for effective planning. Any further and it's more about the vision that the goal. It also fits neatly 4 times into a year. You can download my A2 90-day planner for free at www.thrivebydesignbook.com/resources but it's quite big, so you'll probably need to get it professionally printed. I always pay a little extra and get mine laminated so I can write dates and other details on the planner, then rub them off at the end of the 90-days ready for the next season.

STEP 4: The 90-day planner is broken into 13 weeks. 12 weeks of action and 1 week of reflection. I first came across this process working with Wez Hone from Business Greenhouse. It's an especially powerful tool if you're a visual person.

Use coloured sticky notes to add actions to the first 12 weeks. I like to colour code my actions in groups. I never use more than 4 colours otherwise I know that I'm trying to spread myself too thin. Four projects is *more than enough* to be working on within 90 days. Less is better. If you have more (or if an idea pops up during the 90days), put it on a sticky note and put it at the bottom of the planner to revisit at the end of this season. If it can't wait 90 days, then it's probably not worth pursuing.

STEP 5: In the last chapter you identified an action that was going to take you closer to your goal. That should be the first action that goes onto your planner, followed by the next, and the next, and the next. No more than 12 actions in a sequence. If you need to add more detail, create a separate action plan.

STEP 6: Now you need to find a space for each of the 'colours' in your week. Come back to your weekly planner. If you can't find a space, it isn't going to happen, and neither is your goal! If you want it, you have to pay for it. We pay for what we value with our time. How are you going to spend yours?

This is where many people realise they've been too optimistic with their 90-day plan. Remember *'planning fallacy*'? If necessary (and it probably is), pull some sticky notes off your planner. Put them on the reserve bench for now. You can always come back to them later.

STEP 7: Once you have your week planned out, you're ready to DO! Time to get off the 'through-time' Hot Air Balloon ride and get down into the forest and start bashing your way through the trees. Remember, if you ever get lost (and you will), or if you ever feel despondent and lack motivation (and you will), you now have these Planning Tools (as well as your Identity documents) to help keep you on track.

| 27 |

Habits & Systems

Every action you take is a vote for the type of person you wish to become.

JAMES CLEAR

In my office I have an inspiration wall. This began when I was studying life coaching. There are several quotes or sayings creatively illustrated in coloured chalk that have resonated with me in a profound way over the years. One of these comes from a presentation I heard by Shrikuma Rao, and reads, "invest in the process, not in the outcome". This is echoed by James Clear who says, "forget about goals, focus on your systems instead". Bruce Lee says, "a goal is not always meant to be reached; it often serves simply as something to aim at". I know this sounds contradictory since we've just built a lifestyle plan around your goal. Don't misunderstand me. Goals are great. A goal gets you started. It points your boat in the right direction; but your Systems and Habits are the paddles and the way you pull them. Efficient systems achieve predictable, consistent results with less effort.

Everybody loves talking about goals. Goals are exciting. They're sexy. A little scary at times, but they make us feel good. They tell a story of us winning in the future, and everybody loves that story!

Systems and Habits are less appealing. They conjure images of drill, and monotonous repetition. And when they're working properly, they are invisible. You don't even know they're there. We all like the image of the athlete stepping up, arms held high, onto the dais and receiving the gold medal, but the difference between winning and losing is made where nobody sees, in the gym and on the track. Day after day, hour after hour, rep after rep.

WHAT ARE HABITS & SYSTEMS?

A system is a pre-planned procedure that eliminates the need for critical thinking and complex decision making.

In business it could be a video that all new staff see before operating a piece of equipment, or a predetermined question that gets asked every time a customer places their order. ("Would you like fries with that?")

In family life it could be a chores roster or checklist for packing a school bag.

In health it could be a pre-planned gym routine.

In fun/adventure it could be an equipment list for camping.

Anything that has been done before, that you want to repeat again without deviation, can be systemised.

A habit is your brain's way of building this sort of efficiency into your life. Your conscious mind can only manage about 4 activities effectively at any one time and most behavioural specialists now agree that ONE activity at a time is best for optimal results. A habit is a *system-script* that has been programmed into your unconscious mind to free up thinking space for your conscious mind. Habits are learned behaviours. We all have helpful habits that align with the person that we want to become, but also not-so-helpful habits that detract from that. Lifestyle design is about consolidating and leveraging those good habits and diminishing the bad ones.

Last chapter we looked at planning tools. A calendar is a system. A 90-day planner is a system. Throughout this book you have been presented with different tools to add positive activity into your life. The ultimate goal is to turn these productive actions into habits. Smart actions that require little effort to initiate.

MORE HUMAN

Not all systems can or need to be turned into a habit. When people think of systems, a common question is, "doesn't that take out the human element?" For example, some people don't like using a recipe when cooking because they feel it takes out the intuitive element. This book is all about becoming our most authentic selves. Critical thinking and creative decision making is what makes us who we are, so it's natural to question the idea of systemising aspects of our lives. I interviewed Dave Jenyns, author of 'Systemology' and asked him the same question. He shared this story with me. [1]

Dave's first company was a digital agency that built and optimised websites. He was driving with his photographer to a site location to take some shots for a client. On the way there the conversation was predominantly comments like, "Oh, I hope I remembered to pack that second tripod…", and "Oh, do you think we can fit all three cameras into the one carry bag?" It occurred to Dave, they needed a system for packing the car before they headed out for location shoots. He developed one. It didn't take long. A simple packing checklist. About a month later, they were in the car together again, heading out to another job, but the conversation this time was completely different! Comments were more around "do you think that we should have the business owner in the foreground or standing behind the product?", and "what sort of lighting do you think will create the best effect for this shot?" It was a similar job to the one before, but the conversation was totally different. The system hadn't reduced or taken away from the photographer's creativity – it had enhanced it. The system had freed up his mind from the menial and the mundane aspects of packing the car correctly and allowed him to focus on his strength – taking amazing photos.

Systems take our game to the next level.

COMPOUNDING HABITS

Albert Einstein once described compound interest as "the most powerful force in the universe". He said that "it is the 8th wonder of the world"; and "he who understands it, earns it … he who doesn't … pays it."[2] If you have a mortgage on your home, it's likely that you know the effects of compound interest all too well. You start out making $1000 payments, only to find that at the end of the month you have been charged $999 in interest! So, you spent $1000, but your loan only decreased by $1.

This goes on month after month until eventually you start to make a significant dent in the principal and the interest begins to go down. Habits work in the same way. If you go to the gym today, you haven't got fit. If you save a dollar today, you're not financially free. If you speak a single kind word, you haven't formed a relationship. If you pull out a weed, you haven't created a garden. Single events make little impact on your life overall and so you'd be forgiven for thinking that big change comes from big events, but you'd be wrong.

Success doesn't happen overnight. Your Maximised Life is built moment by moment, hour by hour, day by day, week by week, season by season and year by year. Like a trickling brook that eventually carves a gorge, small, consistent actions over the long term can bring about momentous changes in you and your circumstances. We don't always see the change happening at first. The impacts are infinitesimally small. Impossible to measure. Which is why belief is so necessary, but eventually, change happens.

DOPAMINE – THE FUEL OF HABITS

Back in Neurochemistry Insights we learned about dopamine. Dopamine is a powerful elixir for learning and the fuel for forming and maintaining habits. Charles Duhigg, author of 'The Power of Habit' outlines the 3 steps in his Habit Loop: 'Cue', 'Routine', 'Reward'.[3]

- Cue is the trigger that initiates the motivation to act.
- Routine is the action itself.
- Reward is the payoff. The positive benefit of completing the action.

Dopamine is released when the cycle is completed, and the Cue becomes associated with the Reward. The Cue that triggers anticipation becomes the power behind the habit.

James Clear, in Atomic Habits,[4] clarifies the anticipation element by expounding Duhigg's 3 steps into 4 – Cue, Craving, Response, Reward and uses these to develop 4 laws of behaviour change:

1. Cue – Make it obvious.
2. Craving – Make it attractive.
3. Response – Make it easy.

4. Reward – Make it satisfying.

REVIEW YOUR CALENDAR AND 90-DAY PLANNER

When you look at your weekly calendar and 90-day planner are you going for the 'big win' – the one-off, life-changing event? Or are you playing the long game? Are you making small consistent investments into the person you want to be?

Are there other smaller, simpler ways you can make your actions more obvious? Perhaps putting your running shoes by the bed or setting your calendar as your homepage so it's the first thing you see when you access the internet. Make sure your planner is in a prominent place where you will see it often. Put 'check the calendar' onto your calendar to create a self-reinforcing feedback loop.

Are there ways you can make your actions easier? Think big but act small. Achievable, frequent, and consistent are the attributes that will turn your actions into a habit. What's the easiest, smallest step you can think of?

Are there ways to make your actions more compelling? How do you get your dopamine spikes? Regular recognition. Consistent celebrations. Think about your goal. What is it you want and *why* do you want it? Satisfy that craving. Can you bundle something you need to do together with something you want to do? Is there a way you can add more fun into the task you're trying to habitualise?

Are there simple systems you can put in place to make your work or life easier? Automatic email sequences, checklists, pre-planned menus and automated shopping lists. There are so many opportunities to save small portions of time. Imagine the compounding effect of adding a 20-minute time saving system to your week – every week! That grows into more than 17 hours of time back through automated activities each week by the end of the year! Imagine what else could you do with that time instead?

Now the refining is done. Time to do the work. Focus on the process, not on the outcome. Follow through. Finish this season. Then the next, and the next. Results will come as you faithfully stick to your plan. Trust the process. Enjoy the process. You are building a beautiful foundation for what comes next...

4

MAXIMISED IMPACT

| 28 |

Don't Settle

> *Many men die a good many years before the undertaker carts them away.*
>
> **W.E. BARTON**

I suppose the story could end there. You've done well. You've already been on quite an adventure! A deep dive into your Core discovering more than you knew about yourself. A suite of brain training activities that will stand you in good stead for the rest of your life. And your Lifestyle Design Strategy; planning documents to turn your dreams into tangible goals, exciting milestones, and powerful actions. Identity. Mindset. Lifestyle. You can come back to these again, and again, and again.

It could end there. No one would think less of you. Stable. Comfortable. Settled. These are all very reasonable goals… but I think you already know, there is more for you.

When you listen long enough, inevitably the Call will bring you to a place where it's no longer enough just to think about your own wellbeing. You are (or you will be) compelled to share what you know with others. To give. To teach. This is a natural progression. This is when your focus shifts from personal development to community development. It is still personal growth, but the reason gets bigger, and along with it, the weight of responsibility. If you are a parent, an educator, or the leader of a team, you get this already; and you know that this is rarely easy or straight forward.

It's in our nature to recoil from the unknown and crave comfort and security instead. Throughout history, when humans have tapped into the divine, we want to settle there. We build an altar. We think we've got it all figured out. We want to set up camp and stay comfortable. Our collective culture is littered with empty monuments marking revelatory encounters that have long since faded. Empty buildings. Hollow shrines. White-washed tombs.

The Maximised Life is also divinely inspired, but it's dynamic. It's unpredictable, uncontainable, and always on the move. It rarely gets comfortable or safe. You will need to keep moving, keep learning, keep growing if you want to keep up with it.

Human societies celebrate tradition. We love the old and the ordinary. You can see it in our laws, our governments, our religious traditions, and our schools. Especially our schools. Don't misunderstand me, there is much to be learned from our elders, and it is wise to listen well to their counsel, but sometimes conformity is not the most authentic course of action. If comfort replaces growth as the goal for the future, we lose our edge. We've been designed to thrive, and therefore we must not settle.

"Line up". "Come in". "Sit up straight". "Don't talk, listen". "Don't think, regurgitate". "Follow the rules". 'Study hard". "The answers are in the back". "Toe the line". "Comply". 'Don't be different". "Push it down". "Suck it up". "Fit in". "Have a drink. Take the edge of". "Let's not talk about it". "You've earned a rest".

You can live like that. Or more accurately, you can die like that; but I don't believe that will be your fate. There is still more for you. The final phase of your journey awaits.

If you have the courage to pursue it...

| 29 |

Brokenness before Breakthrough

> *Let me tell you something you already know. The world ain't all sunshine and rainbows. It's a very mean and nasty place and I don't care how tough you are, it will beat you to your knees and keep you there permanently if you let it. You, me, or nobody is gonna hit as hard as life. But it ain't about how hard you hit. It's about how hard you can get hit and keep moving forward. How much you can take and keep moving forward. That's how winning is done!*
>
> **ROCKY BALBOA**

The camera pans down. A close-up on my face as I turn around from the rugged rock wall behind me to face the audience. I smile warmly and launch into my enthusiastic introduction. "Welcome to the Dangerous Minds course! Over the next 40 days you're going to..."

My energetic tone conveys belief and passion. You cannot help but think, "this guy really knows what he's talking about!" A beautiful photo of the textured rock behind me becomes the background for professionally designed slides accenting my points and reinforcing my authority for the viewer. I am welcoming the learner in. Initiating them. Equipping them. Inspiring them with new-found self-belief and genuinely willing them to succeed!

As I finish the introduction, I offer a call to meet me in the next video as I turn and start climbing upward. An epic orchestral soundtrack builds. The drone-mounted camera pulls back away from the rock wall revealing that the rugged, mossy rock wall is a cliff face that I'm scaling hundreds of meters off the ground. The camera continues to pull back as I climb. The music reaches a climax. My tiny figure is lost in the trees, enveloped by the majestic mountain range of which I have now become a part. It is a fitting metaphor.

How did I get to this point? How did a multi-failed entrepreneur, misfit teacher, and an often-inadequate husband and father end up as a lifestyle design coach and educational leader on the side of a mountain speaking to hundreds of new parents and educators who had just signed up for his new course?

'Maximised Impact?'. *'Leadership?'*. I'd be lying if I didn't tell you that every time I have sat down to write these final chapters, a dark cloud of doubt has swarmed in to try and put a stop to it. It is as though a malevolent companion has been awakened by my intention. It hammers me with a barrage of not-so-subtle questions about my integrity and my worthiness to be holding a pen with such a cocky notion in mind.

Emboldened by my waning mental strength, my inner critic jumps to its feet and joins the tirade. It delivers a litany of scathing accusations, not least on the list is my apparent arrogance. The audacity that I would even consider writing about 'Impact' and 'Leadership' at all! "What do *you* have to offer?"

It's true. I concede that there are thousands more qualified, more experienced, and more accomplished men and women than me.

The ledger of my shortcomings piles high. The reasons *not* to write weigh heavily; and yet, here I am, together with you at the end. Just me and my story, hoping to inspire you to embark on life's biggest adventure of all – making a difference.

The roller coaster of recent years swirls through my mind. It's been a wild ride. And not in the *"weee-this-is-fun!"* kind of way. More like the *"let-me-off-I-think-I'm-going-to-die"* kind of way. I think back to that moment of profound rejection, sobbing in the principal's office and my work-life turned completely upside down. It was a crushing blow, but I'd bounced back pretty quickly. I shifted my mindset, stepped out into the unknown, full of hope, the confidence of my friends spurring me on, and armed with a firm (although slightly naïve) conviction that I could redesign my life, and that it was going to be awesome. The only problem was, I didn't have the faintest idea on how I was going to make that happen.

BIG HITS

Fast forward a year later. I was back on my feet. Connected as a family. Sofia was pregnant again. Life was good and I was now running my own mini school. It was auspiced under the local high school, but it was off-site, and I was calling the shots. I was making a difference for at-risk kids. I had a steady 5-day income and still had the capacity to look for other passive income streams. I started to learn day-trading (at night) and was making some small but steady gains on the trading platform.

I loved that it was automated. I could make money while I slept! Automations included a 'Take Profits Order' (TPO) and a 'Stop Loss' – an automatic trade-out at the lower end to limit the loss on any trade. Some of my trades were hitting their TPO and I made money, but others went the other way, hit the stop loss, and I lost. I was learning but overall, I wasn't going anywhere. It was like taking 2 steps forward, 2 steps backward. I started to get frustrated. To make matters worse, when I reviewed the trade, usually I could see that the prices had often jumped down, hit my stop loss, and traded out; then immediately jumped back up again near my Take profit goal! It was like the market had a mind of its own and it was playing this game just to aggravate me!

I decided to put a trade on with no Stop Loss. The prices never went too far down before they recovered and so I figured taking out the Stop Loss would just take out all those annoying 'jump-down, tradeout, jump-straight-back' scenarios. And it worked. I made money. I tried it again the next week and made money again! I thought, "I've cracked it! I've hacked the secret to day-trading! Small consistent goals and no Stop Loss. This is great!"

This went on for weeks. When prices went up, I made money. When prices went down, I let my original trade hover in deficit, opened another trade, and set the new take profit at the original price. Then when it recovered, I made money, but still had the original trade open if it climbed further. That was my system, and it was working.

One day I had a gold trade open. A reasonably small take profit goal and no stop loss. The price went down and hovered there. I watched it for a few days and there was no change. So, I opened another trade. I set the take profit goal at the original price. I watched for about a week, but it also didn't recover. The price dropped again. So, I opened another trade. Take profit was set at the last trades starting point and no stop loss. Prices danced about but not enough to close any of the trades. Then it dropped again. So, I opened *another* trade! Same system, but now I was getting nervous. A few more weeks went by and eventually I had 6 trades open. The first trade was in significant deficit, but I reasoned it was OK because it was just like borrowing on an interest free loan. I didn't have a time limit to pay it back and, so long as I was patient, the gold price would eventually recover, and I would settle the debt. It was nerve wracking. I didn't like hovering in such an uncomfortable place. Watching. Waiting.

Sofia didn't really know what was going on. She knew that I was spending a lot of time learning about day-trading and we were growing a little distant. She didn't like me spending late nights on the computer, but she trusted I knew what I was doing.

One day I was driving home to join Sofia for an antenatal appointment at the doctors. She'd been having some bleeding and we were a bit concerned. We wanted to get it checked out. I left work with a half hour drive ahead. A 'ping' on my phone let me know I had a notification, but I was just pulling out and so I thought, I'll check it when I get home. When I got to the doctors' I quickly checked my phone before Sofia arrived and saw that one of my trades had traded out. *I had lost a thousand dollars!* "Oh my Gosh!" I thought. How did that happen! I didn't have a Stop Loss set so it shouldn't have traded out. It must have been a mistake, but I didn't have time to investigate. Sofia arrived and we went in. I didn't want to say anything to her about the trade. She was already visibly anxious about the appointment. We were sitting in the waiting room. 'Ping!' My stomach sunk. Another trade out. TWO thousand dollars. I felt sick. Sofia went into the doctor and I anxiously scanned my trading app trying to figure out what was happening. I learned later that the price of gold had taken a big dive. Some world event (I can't even remember what it was now) had sent a shockwave of falls cascading through the market, breaking support level after support level until my trade deficit hit the limit of my credit card. I lost FIFTEEN thousand dollars that day. Money we didn't have. Now a debt. On a credit card.

Next hit. Sofia came out, and I found out that we had lost the baby. We cried together in the car. I felt terrible. A cloud of guilt swarmed over me as I recalled how unenthusiastic I'd been about the news of the baby. I wondered if I had somehow radiated rejection and damaged this tiny, delicate soul? I was a father who had un-wanted his own child. I begged heaven for forgiveness. I was so sorry.

Next hit. That evening I told Sofia what had happened on the trading platform. She was heartbroken. She was already resentful from lost hours together while I tried to learn this platform. Now, raw and broken from the news of our lost little one, I had come in and taken the one thing she thought we still had. Trust. She had always stood by me and believed in me when others didn't, and I had let her down. She felt robbed and betrayed. She didn't yell. I wish that she did. She just sobbed alone in her room. She said she didn't want to talk to me. After a time, she drew comfort from time with her friends, not me. Nothing I could say could repair the damage.

It seemed as though, despite my best efforts, in a single day, I'd destroyed everything I held dear. Grief, shame, sorrow, and disappointment swirled in like a dark cloud, choking me for breath and slamming me against the floor when I dared to look up for a glimmer of hope.

For the next few days, I lived on autopilot. Going through the motions. Numb.

Like an imposter, I had to keep showing up at work to help young people and on weekends continue my life-coaching training. The irony of these endeavours was not lost on me. I was a fraud. A failure. A fool. How did I possibly think that I had anything of value to offer? I didn't belong in education. I didn't belong in business. I didn't belong in investing. I didn't even belong in my own family – at least that is how it felt to me. I was a disappointment. I was striving for more, but my life was a lie. I had failed at everything. I wanted to give up. I wanted it to end.

| 30 |

The Wilderness

Everyone fails at who they're supposed to be...
The measure of a person, of a hero, is how well they succeed
at being who they are.

FRIGGA, AVENGERS ENDGAME

I was in the Wilderness.

The Wilderness is hard. The Wilderness is a place we all must go in order to learn some necessary truths about ourselves, the world, and our place in it. Poets and script writers for years have described the Wilderness as a place we go *through*; but in reality, we never truly leave the Wilderness – or more accurately, it never leaves us. The Wilderness becomes a part of who we are.

The first thing you realise when you're in the Wilderness is that you can't go back. You long for comfort but that door is now closed. You had the option to settle, and you didn't. You choose to keep going. Keep growing. Now you've seen too much. Dug too deeply. You have peeked inside that Pandora's box we know as 'The Call', and now you can't *unknow* it. As attractive and secure as 'being ordinary' looks right now, you know that you cannot go back. Going back would drive you mad and mean giving up on truth, courage, and everything else you hold dear. It would mean giving up on yourself. No, in the Wilderness, the only way out is onward. You are going to live (or die) at the hands of your fate.

Eventually, you realise that you are at peace with either outcome. To live fully, in service to the Call, or to die trying. As Theodore Roosevelt once said, "to dare greatly... so that your place will not be with those cold and timid souls who know neither victory, nor defeat". In the Wilderness you put one foot in front of another and hold onto the belief that the path is taking you somewhere. Somewhere is OK. You're OK with 'somewhere'. Somewhere is better than nowhere.

In the Wilderness you realise that in some strange way you belong here. You are wild at heart. In the Wilderness you are alone. No one truly understands you. Not really. Your partner, your family, your friends will all question you. "Is this what you really want?" "Are you sure you've made the right choice?" And you cannot explain that of course you don't know! And, of course you're not sure. But you don't have any other choice.

To walk in the Wilderness is to be misunderstood. And yet, in the Wilderness, you *cannot* not-belong. You belong to the Call. You ARE the Call! And the Call connects us all. The Call is God's voice. The Call is poetry that binds us together. It flows through us as art. Our Real Work. And to do that Work, often we must stand alone. This takes great courage. It takes sacrifice. But when we do it, we find our place. Our place is here, out on the edge. Where 'making a difference' can happen. It is scary, it is lonely, but it is where the wild at heart belong.

In the Wilderness your brokenness reveals a beautiful gift. In the Wilderness you learn that you did not come here for yourself.

You may have picked up this book and embarked on this adventure for what it could do for you. 'Thriving By Design' – sounds pretty good doesn't it? Sounds like where you want to be. And it is. But in the process, you have discovered a treasure. Something very special. A prize to share with the ones you love. A gift for the people.

That gift is you.

| 31 |

Bigger Than You

Coming together is a beginning, staying together is progress, working together is success.

HENRY FORD

You know that mission we've talked about? You know how it makes you want to laugh, and cry, and throw up a little, all at the same time? The reason for that is because it's bigger than you.

'Bigger than you', meaning: 1) You can't do this as you are. The mission demands personal growth in knowledge, in character, and in skills; and 2) You can't do it alone. Impact cannot exist in a vacuum. Impact, by definition, is a transfer of energy, and as such needs a medium through which to travel. In society, that medium is people. Impact happens in and through people. Therefore, you need to work in communion with others to become all that you can be.

I know this is a big twist to the story so far. We've talked a lot about having the courage to walk alone, being misunderstood, embarking into the Wilderness and feeling that you don't belong anywhere. That's still true; painfully so. But the paradox, (or perhaps the magic) of venturing out on your own to follow the Call is that, when you do, other people start to pay attention. The old are left behind, but *new people* are attracted to the mission. These are the right people. These are *your* people. They love what you do and many of them want to be a part of it.

One of my most popular youth programs is the Young Hero's Adventure Quest. We take a small group of 10 – 15-year-olds into the bush, or beach (or some other wild space) and we run learning activities designed first and foremost to be fun, but also mentally and physically demanding. Learning is an adventure, and we want our participants to face 'trials' on their own hero's journey. Embedded within those experiences, is traditional curriculum content (i.e.: Maths, English, History, Geography, etc), and overlaid on this is a suite of mindset training methods. They build positivity, perseverance, teamwork, creative problem-solving, communication and decision-making skills – all the so-called 'soft-skills' that they are going to need to thrive in the dynamic world of the 21st century. When people who have heard about Adventure Quest meet me and find out that I'm the designer of the program, they tell me how amazing it is. They wonder why every kid in school is not being given the same opportunity. (I often wonder the same thing). These are *my* people. I don't have to convince them that their child is going to benefit from the experience. They know intuitively it's going to work for them. Marketing this kind of program has become easy. My clients are my best advocates. To them it just makes sense.

GETTING BIGGER

As more and more people heard about and wanted to participate in Adventure Quest, we began look into starting another group, and consequently, I needed help. I faced the same challenge that many entrepreneurs face, how do you expand your reach without losing the essence of what you do?

I started out using systems. I wrote carefully scripted program notes, I trained apprentice leaders in the hero's journey, curriculum content, and all the different nuances of program delivery. At first I thought I needed a 'business in a box'. Something like a franchise that I could sell to others and say, 'do what I did'. My model was to use traditional hierarchical education and management techniques to scale a very personalised form of impact. It didn't work.

What I eventually realised was that in order for my work to become 'bigger than me' – I had to think bigger than me. I knew I couldn't do this alone, but creating more 'mini-mes' was not only egocentric, it was also undermining the very people I was trying to empower! *My mission* is to co-create success stories. My Call is to help others step into and thrive in theirs. I have no business telling others how to be me! My job is to empower other leaders. Showing other parents, educators and entrepreneurs who want to make a difference, how to share the best of *themselves*.

I had to find the balance between showing my team how to run the program, but also how to bring their own unique qualities to the experience. This isn't easy. It's a paradox – be like me; but do it like you. Therein lies the art of good leadership. This is why teaching (and many other human-to-human professions) are described as both an art, and a science. There are methods that work, systems you can use, but ultimately, the real work comes from the heart.

Josh Waitzkin in 'The Art of Learning' describes his journey becoming a master in both Chess and Martial Arts. He explains the importance of training to turn fundamentals into instinct so that your intuition can then operate at a higher level. A master can see further and further into the future. They can see things that others cannot see and for people looking on, it looks like magic. Pure genius – built upon hours and hours of disciplined training.

CREATING CULTURE

Adventure Quest will never be a franchise. It will always be shaped by the natural environment we play in, and the unique qualities of the Mentors who are delivering it. Moreover, every group of young people brings with them a unique set of skills, challenges, hopes, dreams, and expectations to each adventure. As this grows, so too does the richness of the program. This is culture. It's how we are together. Cultures, like the people who make them up, are infinitely diverse. They are a living entity of their own. They are dynamic and vibrant. Good cultures foster growth. Bad cultures breed decay and eventually destroy themselves. Good team cultures happen when you have a group of mutually respectful individuals who can see and appreciate the differences of the people around them, and yet don't feel compelled to fundamentally change who they are in order to fit in.

Brené Brown says, "Fitting in is about assessing a situation and becoming who you need to be to be accepted. Belonging, on the other hand, doesn't require us to change who we are; it requires us to *be* who we are." Healthy team cultures recognise that we all need one another. That we are a part of a bigger whole, and that supporting one another is as important, probably more so, than having our own voice heard. A good leader is someone who can cultivate this sort of culture.

| 32 |

Stepping Up

> *Leadership is not about titles, positions, or flowcharts.*
> *It is about one life influencing another.*
>
> **JOHN MAXWELL**

I make an Impact. Each week I connect with hundreds and work personally with dozens of families, young people and adults, helping them to unlock their potential and live more abundantly. I'm grateful for the privilege of sharing life with these amazing men and women.

You also have a Call, and as you pursue it, eventually you will find yourself in a position to positively impact the lives of others. It's a natural part of growth. Your journey will take you to a place where your setbacks, and breakthroughs, your disappointments and your delights, have all wrought in you a story worth telling. That story can inspire others. Think of Martin Luther King Jr.

Think of Malala Yousafzai. Think of Mahatma Gandhi. Think of J.K. Rowling. All men and women, who were moved by an idea greater than themselves. All have faced more than their fair share of adversity, and yet grew into leaders as they followed the Call. You may not lead social movements or shape government policies. You may not become a great athlete or speaker. To you, your work may not seem significant or newsworthy. To you, it's just doing what you do, and occasionally getting the shit kicked out of you in the process. But your stories from the Wilderness position you to impact the lives of others. They qualify you as a leader in 2 ways:

1. They tell me you've got courage. In the face of adversity, criticism and overwhelming odds you don't give up. When the giants loom large, you don't run, at least, not for long. A leader keeps showing up. They risk defeat and in doing so tap into their greatness.
2. And secondly, if you're bold enough to be out on the edge, then you must have a good reason. You have purpose. People see that. A leader has a vision for the future, and someone with a clear vision is someone that people will want to follow.

WHAT IS LEADERSHIP?

Leadership is a grand and lofty word that has come to mean different things to different people. More work, sometimes more money, always more responsibility; but at its core, leadership is the process of cultivating meaningful change. Leadership is making a difference. Leadership is what makes the Mission happen. A leader stands in the gap between the stories of the past and the hopes we hold for the future. Leadership is something that we're all called to do in our own unique way.

Are you a parent? Then you are a leader. Are you a man or woman of faith? Then you are a leader. Do you have a network, a circle of friends that benefit from your company and influence?

Then you are a leader. Do you run a business or look after a team at work? Then yes, of course, that too, is leadership.

There are copious books on the subject of leadership. I have included a list of some in my 'Books for Leaders Guide' you can find at: www.thrivebydesignbook.com/resources I don't pretend that these next few chapters will hold a candle to the wisdom offered by these great authors, but I do hope to inspire you with the belief that you have the capacity to stand between what is, and what could be.

LEADERSHIP STYLES

There are several different styles of leadership. Shane Saffir, a writer and coach whose work focuses on education, describes 4 leadership archetypes that sit at the extremes of two continuums; Facilitative versus Top-down, and Change-agent versus Status quo.[1] Two of these archetypes, the 'Driver' and the 'Manager' fit the stereotypical views of what it means to be a leader.

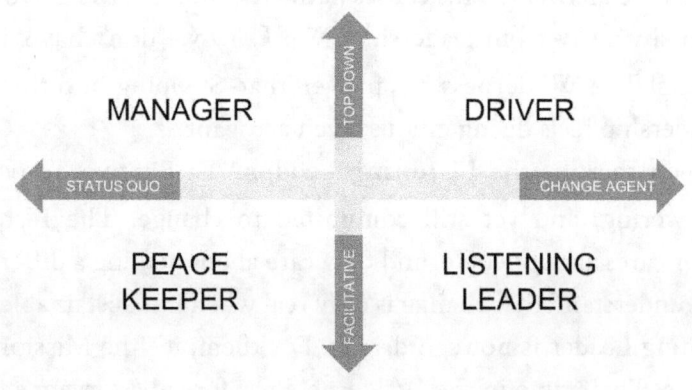

Leadership Styles
(Safir, 2017)

The **Driver** raises the bar. They have high standards for themselves and for everyone around them. They are not always pleasant to be around, but they get results. They are the Michael Jordans, the Steve Jobs, and the Elon Musks. They are autocratic, dictatorial. It's my way or the highway kind of people. This leadership style usually does not empower others and therefore cannot be sustained without the leader continually driving change. This suits the Driver because they are egocentric. They like to know they are indispensable.

Then there is the **Manager**. Management has become synonymous with leadership in organisations but in its purest form, it is not really leadership at all. Leadership is about change. Management is about staying the same. Preserving the status quo. Management is about control. Managers are a function of the Triangle. They derive their power from the system and are primarily concerned with preserving its order. Think of our health-system, our governments, our legal and our education systems. These are all hierarchical models designed to operate on delegated responsibility with little or no power resting with the individual. Not only do they disempower the individual, they also reinforce that erroneous belief that 'leaders have all the answers'. This causes authentic individuals like you and me to shy away from leadership. We *know* we don't have all the answers! The Wilderness has proven that. Stepping into that kind of leadership feels disingenuous, even arrogant.

Then there is the **Listening Leader**.[1] Facilitative, respectful, empowering, and yet still committed to change. The Listening Leader cares about people, and they care about making a difference. They understand that change is only real when it is sustainable. The Listening Leader is not ego driven. For them, it's the Mission that matters. Their time in the Wilderness has forged a servant's heart. The Listening Leader is courageous and vulnerable. They recognise that change usually needs to start internally and they are willing to learn and grow as necessary. They understand the essential function of education, not as a means to control, but to uplift and empower others.

MAKING TOUGH DECISIONS

If the Listening Leader has a weakness, it is that they deliberate too long. They want to make the right choice by all, but in so doing hold back when a decision needs to be made. All leaders need to get comfortable with making imperfect decisions.

Colin Powell served as the United States Secretary of State from 2001 to 2005 under President George W. Bush. He developed what he calls the 40/70 rule; and that is, if you don't have at least 40% of the information you need to make a decision, you're just guessing; but then, if you have more than 70% of the information you need to make a decision, and you still haven't moved yet, then you're probably just stalling. You know enough. It's time to trust yourself. It's time to move.[2]

Where are you right now?

I'm guessing that you're getting close to the 70 mark? The arrow is on the string, the bow is pulled taught. Pause. Breathe. Then…

I have learnt a lot as I've tried to grow my business, support my family, and have a positive impact in an arena that is traditionally dominated by hierarchical systems and that promote uniformity and conformity as their main managerial methods. One of my favourite speakers of all time, Sir Ken Robinson, who sadly passed away while I was writing this book, once said, "we need to move away from an industrial metaphor of education and back to an agricultural one" and "every great gardener knows that you can't make a plant grow, the plant grows itself, but what you do is to create *the right conditions for growth*".[3]

He was talking about shifting our paradigm for schools, but this equally applies to a business, a social enterprise, or a family. I have now adopted an 'empowering-people' philosophy to all my scale-up endeavours. As I help others to be better, to find their special something and combine this with my training tools and frameworks, growth is inevitable. I am not the 'boss' trying to drive my workers along; instead, we've become co-creators in a joint mission. A mission we both believe in, and therefore willingly and passionately work towards.

The obvious question is, how do you do that? How do you create these 'right conditions for growth'?

In the next chapter we will look at the key ingredients as part of an overall process.

| 33 |

Impact is a Process

Success takes an investment of time, dedication, and sacrifice. This is true education. It is a process.

ROBERT T. KIYOSAKI

As we discussed in 'Habits & Systems', success is not a phenomenon that happens in any single moment of time. It is not an instant revelation or a single critical decision that makes or breaks your future. Ask any 'overnight success' and they will tell you that their 'recent good fortune' is built on their last 20+ years of hard work! For them, their big breakthrough is just the natural next step in an evolution on their quest to fulfil their Mission. They are following the Call.

Similarly, 'Impact' is not one momentous event that shakes society to its core and changes all lives thereafter. It may get remembered that way, but it's not. Impact is a process. It happens in the doing; often slowly. Impact is what happens when you determine that you are going to become the person that you were born to be, and as a consequence, change lives for the better for the people around you. Howard Thurman says, "don't ask yourself what the world needs, ask yourself what makes you come alive, and go do *that*. Because what the world needs is men and women who have come alive." I would also add that what the world needs is men and women who *keep* doing this, who refuse to give up, even when the going gets hard.

GREAT LEADERS KEEP GOING

Albert Einstein didn't speak for the first three years of his life. Many of his teachers thought he was lazy and had little academic potential because he was often distracted by abstract concepts. His childhood education was constantly disrupted by his father's business failures. He was sent to a boarding house in Munich and was destined to join the military at 16. Feeling alone, abandoned, and miserable he ran away and 6 months later returned to his parents. He had a strong notion of spirituality as a child and yet was compelled by scientific understanding to explain the nature of the universe. He struggled to reconcile these two worldviews. He constantly felt out of place in a Prussian-style educational system that stifled originality and creativity. Very few adults in his life believed in his capacity to make an impact. One teacher told him that he would never amount to anything. However, he rose above this negativity and developed a body of work including the Theory of Relativity, one of the most profound scientific discoveries of the modern era. 25 years after graduating his troubled school years he won the Nobel prize for Physics. He is now generally considered the most influential physicist of the 20th century.[1]

Oprah Winfrey has been dubbed the most influential woman in the world.[2] For a time, she was the only African American billionaire and has been described as one of the greatest philanthropists in

American history. She is, of course, the host of the wildly popular, multi award-winning talk show, "The Oprah Winfrey Show" which during the early 90s would average 12 – 13 million viewers on any given day; yet life has not all been smooth sailing for Oprah. She was born into poverty in rural Mississippi. She was molested and raped as a child, sent to a juvenile detention home at 13, and later fell pregnant at 14. Her son was born prematurely and died in infancy. Oprah's talk show became number one in 1986 and remained so for more than a decade. It has won 34 Emmy Awards. Oprah launched O-Magazine in 2000 and Super Soul Sunday in 2011. She continues to innovate her influence and remains a role-model for women wanting to live impactful lives.

Nelson Mandela is considered the father of Modern South Africa.[3] His own father died when he was just 12 and he was sent away to school. As a young man he was expelled after just one year of university, but later re-enrolled and completed his education. He became one of South Africa's first black lawyers and a political activist in the late 40s and 50s. In 1962 he was arrested for treason and spent the following 27 years in prison. He was released in 1990, unbroken, but shaped and matured by his time in the Wilderness. In 1993 he received the Nobel Peace Prize for peacefully dismantling South Africa's racist Apartheid regime. In 1994 he voted for the first time in his life and was elected the first black president of South Africa. As a leader he went to great lengths build the nation as a whole, not just for the previously oppressed black South Africans. Despite facing extraordinary oppression throughout his life, he says; "We must strive to be moved by a generosity of spirit that will enable us to outgrow the hatred and conflicts of the past." And later, "You will achieve more in this world through acts of mercy than you will through acts of retribution." At age 76, in his first book, *Long Walk to Freedom*, Mandela says, "No one is born hating another person because of the colour of his skin, or his background, or his religion. They must learn to hate, and if they can learn to hate, they can be taught to love, for love comes more naturally to the human heart than its opposite."[4]

WHAT CAN WE LEARN FROM THEM?

These great leaders and others like them demonstrate the power of perseverance, but also how to love, to hope, to believe, to think and to take smart action. There is no point persevering when what we're doing is counterproductive, but if we can distil the effectual phases of Impact, then we too can be successful on our own quest.

- Compassion
- Innovation
- Optimism
- Faith
- Diligence

These are the 5 virtues of leadership we will explore in this final phase. Each are powerful on their own, but when synthesised together, form an effective sequence to bring about change.

COMPASSION

Every story of Impact begins with a person who cares. Often this caring is forged in the fires of personal adversity or tragedy. As the darkness swoops in, they are not twisted or broken by the blows that life has dealt them. They hold onto hope instead of hurt or hate. The word 'Compassion' is made of two words. 'Co' or 'Com' meaning 'together'. And 'Passion' which comes from the Latin 'pati', which means to suffer and/or endure. Therefore 'Compassion' means to 'suffer together'. Compassion is empathy. Compassion says, "I get it. I've been there. And I'm here with you now." Compassion knows pain but it doesn't run. It stays. It waits. Compassion is courageous. Compassion is the birthplace for human connection. In the modern era of personal development, the goal of life is often identified as 'happiness'. This is a beautiful goal. There's nothing wrong with happiness; except that at times it can be short-sighted. Decisions for happiness may point you in the wrong direction. Leaders must play a bigger game. Compassion is willing to embrace the discomfort of suffering in order to better understand and affect change. Compassion is a much more reliable guide. Caring leads to connection, connection to fulfilment, and fulfilment leads to a deeper and more lasting happiness than you could ever imagine. Love is our guide.

INNOVATION (AKA WORDS OF TRUTH)

To create is to be human. That is what we were born to do. Some people insist that they are not creative. If that's you, I would suggest that you've simply 'switched it off'. You *can* get it back. You *need* to get it back! Within the pain of Compassion is also a call to salvation. This is the motivation to grow. You *can* change. You *can* improve. You *can* be better. "How are you going to do it?" is the question that triggers Innovation.

What comes next are your *ideas*. These are a gift. The word 'idea' is from the ancient Greeks. It refers to the perfection and purity of the spirit but literally means 'a pattern' or 'to take form'. The ancient Greeks believed that true ideas came from the gods, and these ideas are expected to take form in the physical world. One of the simplest, yet profound ways that an idea can take form is through words. Untold it is incomplete. Unheard it is like the morning mist.

Unless an idea is shared with someone it is nothing more than a vague passing thought.

A Psalm of David, later quoted by the Apostle Paul says, "I believe; therefore, I speak." These five simple words sums up the potent nature of creative intent. We're told in the Book of Genesis that the universe was once formless and empty, and then God spoke. Words are how we give substance to ideas. Words are powerful. They carry energy and purpose. I think if we truly understood the creative potency of our words, we would probably use them more carefully.

Our words define us. Think of our 3 examples of impact/leadership. Einstein, we know by his theories. Oprah, we know by her stories, both hers and others. Mandela, we know by the policies he penned, the speeches he gave, and the books he wrote. To have a Voice is to have an Identity. To speak-out is to give substance to the Call. We believe; therefore, we speak. The words we speak are our ideas. They flow from, and ultimately define who we are.

OPTIMISM

Martin Seligman's theory of 'Learned Helplessness' states that when people fail repeatedly, they sever the mental link between actions and outcomes and eventually stop trying altogether. Many years after his original research Seligman published 'Learned Optimism' arguing that the opposite also holds true. That we can cultivate a more positive perspective, and that people who do so are primed to be more successful with higher levels of personal well-being. Seligman is regarded as the founding father of the modern positive psychology movement which has shown with almost endless examples over the past 30 years how those with an optimistic outlook consistently outperform and outlast their negative counterparts. It makes sense. Our brains are wired to find what we're looking for and to make it true. Our focus magnifies our reality. Optimists expect, attract, and inevitably multiply the good things in their life, whereas those with a negative mindset do the opposite.

Optimism and Ideas are the Yin and Yang of creative endeavour. Two complementary phenomena that give rise to life and achievement. Ideas and the Words of Truth that articulate them give form and substance to the Call of heaven. This is the potent Yang dynamic. The masculine energy. The seed of the future. Optimism is the Yin. The feminine energy. Not its opposite, but its counterpart. Full of hope and possibility. When Optimism says 'yes', ideas become possible.

A hopeful heart is the fallow ground that an inspired idea needs to take root and grow into anything significant. Bitterness, cynicism, distrust and despondency are mental weeds that will choke ideas before they have a chance to even be properly considered.

FAITH (AKA VISION)

When a divine idea takes root in the fertile ground of the human heart, and then is expressed outwardly, with words or otherwise, it has been made real. That's faith. It is the substance of things hoped for. "I believe, therefore I speak".

Faith is when we are captivated by an idea bigger than ourselves, and we trust that this idea holds the potential to make life better. Everyone believes in something. Even those who claim otherwise. Faith is inextricably connected to our identity. It's how we see the world and our place in it. This in turn forms our values, which in turn shapes our actions. People live and die by their faith.

Faith is as unique as individuals themselves and therefore it's wise to stay respectful and reverent when discussing what you believe. Beliefs are deeply rooted in what each of us know as 'truth'.

To challenge another's belief is to pinch a nerve at the deepest level. Don't expect a passive response.

Faith is vision. It tells you clearly what the future could be and is infused an inherent trust that there are forces for good at work in your favour. It has been moved by Compassion, inspired by an Idea, imbued with Hope, and now it rests in the confidence that all will work out for the best in the end. From faith, aligned actions are compelling and inevitable.

As cute and naïve as it might sound, Faith is one of the most powerful forces in the universe. Faith moves mountains. It changes who we are and is the necessary precursor for all great deeds. There is no impact without faith. It is a defining quality of any leader. A *must-have* trait to be able to stand in that lonely space between what is, and what could be.

It's worth noting, that the opposite of faith is fear. These two phenomena work in the same way. They are both a source code that shape our actions; except that faith is inspired by the good, whereas fear is fixated on the negative. Faith is the dream of a better tomorrow. It is not always clear on the details of *how*, but it knows enough. Faith declares, 'God is good' and rests confidently on that. Fear on the other hand has latched onto a crippling premonition of failure. Death without purpose. Life without impact. The ultimate unhappy ending. Faith is a fountain of youthful energy. Fear is cancer to the soul. Both, of course, see what's possible. Both are scripts that will inevitably outwork themselves if given the chance. Ultimately, it will be decided by the story we play most in the cinema of our mind. Your life will be shaped by one or the other. You get to choose. Choose Faith.

DILIGENCE

And finally, belief turns into action. 'Diligence' is defined as "careful and persistent work or effort".[5] It comes from the Latin, *diligere*, which means, "to value highly, to take delight in". Diligence is work of love and joy. Diligence is passion put into effect. Note that it is 'careful' (full of care), and persistent (ongoing, unfailing). Diligence flows from Faith. You might rightly describe a diligent person as '*faithfully* carrying out the *trust* that they have been given'. They are faithful to the Call.

Diligence is the farmer with his hand to the plough'; it is the student with her head in the books; it is the writer with a pen in hand; it is the tradesman who shows up, smiles warmly and does good work, day after day; it is the athlete who spends countless lonely hours out on the track and in the gym while no one is watching. Diligence is hope-fuelled, inspired effort. Diligence is how winning is done.

Can you see how these phenomena all flow together? We are moved by Compassion; we eagerly expect tomorrow to be better which opens us up to new possibilities. Ideas are triggered and we speak them out. Good ideas stick. They take form. Divine ideas take on a life of their own, and we believe in their power to change lives; so much so, we act. We work. We give our lives, happily and consistently with more thought of the mission than of the reward. But make no mistake, there are rewards. Maximised living invites a blessing.

Compassion, Innovation, Optimism, Faith, and Diligence. Each powerful and life-shaping on their own, but when connected together, are unstoppable. This is the process of Impact.

Of these qualities, what's *your* greatest strength? What areas do you still need to work on?

If you haven't yet done so, you can take the Lifestyle Design Quiz at www.lifestyledesignquiz.com and get your own strength profile as a part of your Lifestyle Design report.

| 34 |

You Will Face Resistance [But You've Got This!]

I want to live my life in such a way that when I get out of bed in the morning, the devil says, "aw shit, he's up!"

STEVE MARABOLI

Your Call might be to raise inspired kids? Your Call might be to help the homeless? Your Call might be to support health and vitality in yourself or in others? You could be called to initiate fun, adventure, or social connection? There are billions of different ways that humanity can be made better, and infinite different expressions of how these visions might be realised. This is the noble pursuit of impact. But you need to know (in case it wasn't obvious already), that deciding to be better, deciding to do something great, deciding to take a step toward positive impact, is also stepping into the arena. You're asking for trouble. Sparks are going to fly.

In leadership, with judgement, criticism, scoffing and disapproval swirling around you, it would be easy to make the mistaken conclusion that people are your problem. That is a mistake. Your real enemies are ethereal and internal.

As you boldly commit to make a positive change, in the conceptual realm, coming out from across the battlefield is your adversary. A very real and ruthless enemy seething angrily at the audacity you've shown, by thinking you could make a difference. This dark malevolent force plots your destruction, intent on shutting you down before you can gain any traction.

Collective wisdom from thousands of tales, from mythology, ancient philosophies, and different faith systems from around the world, have all found value in personifying this dark force. Angra-Mainyu, Erlik, Satan, Ruha, Jinn, or The Enemy. No matter the expression, one of the great revelations to be gleaned from these stories is that our battle is not against flesh and blood, and therefore, the weapons we wield are not forged with, or fought by the skill of our hands. They are shaped by the positive intentions of our heart, and fortified by the convictions of our mind.

Your enemy's real goal is to undermine, decay, and diminish the best of who you are or might become. A primary strategy he will use is to blind you from the reality that we are all connected and that our interactions with each other, even the unpleasant ones, can be for our benefit when combined with humility.

Humility is the characteristic that allows us to remain in a perpetual state of growth. It's opposite, let's call it 'egoism' (because the word 'pride' has positive connotations linked to the qualities and achievements of people we love), is the notion that you are already complete. It's the idea that you have all the answers, and that others cannot contribute to your growth. When one person (or a group of people) think that they have reality resolved, they disconnect themselves from dissenting views that might undermine their dogma. Jordan Peterson goes so far as describing this sort of rigid belief system as 'murderous'.[1] He describes how Egoism is exemplified by totalitarian ideologies which have led to the mass genocides of the 20th century.[1] Exploring the epic poetic works of John Milton, Peterson distils a definition of Evil, "as the force that believes that its knowledge is complete, and that it can do without the transcendent, and as soon as it makes this claim it instantly exists in a place that is indistinguishable from hell".[2]

THE BATTLE OF BALANCE

One of the first lessons you learn in martial arts is 'being grounded'. A strength that comes from balance and that allows you to redirect the force pitted against you to your advantage. In the last chapter we unpacked the phases for making meaningful change. Compassion, Innovation, Optimism, Vision, and Diligence. These are balanced states. Your adversary will try to knock you off course by pushing and pulling your mind in different directions with either an over-emphasis on self, or an over-emphasis on the world and its multitude of problems. Both of these over-corrections are sneaky because they both contain truth. You *need* to focus on yourself at times. Without this you lose sight of who you are, and the work you're called to do. You also *need* to feel deeply and care about the hurts of others. Without this you become cold and calloused; uncompassionate and unmotivated to serve. Your challenge is to stay centred, not being drawn off course by either of these noble-sounding over-corrections.

Let's examine how your adversary can twist and distort these virtues, so that you will be less likely to fall prey to his schemes.

TOO INWARD *An over-focus on self*	CENTRED *A balanced focus on purpose and tribe.*	TOO OUTWARD *An over-focus on the world's problems*
Self-interest	Compassion	Overwhelm
Greed	Innovation	Inertia
Fake-positivity	Optimism/Hope	Negativity/Despair
Dogma	Vision	Confusion
Driver	Diligence	In-activity

The spectrums – 5 phases of impact and 10 ways you can be knocked off course

BALANCED COMPASSION

Compassion is a state of consciousness that links us with others. Gustave Gilbert, the consulting prison psychologist at the Nuremberg Trials concluded that evil is a lack of empathy. When we use '*Us versus Them*' dichotomies in our thinking and speech, we are already well on the road to disconnection. The Us/Them dualism is a tempting cheat for impact. Hitler did it. Stalin did it. So too did Mao and Pol Pot. Politics is an arena that seems to find this destructive language and behaviour acceptable. Whether you agree with their political stance or not, it's likely that (to a lesser degree) your current national leader has used the same type of polarising language in their rise to power.

You can motivate people by painting another group as the enemy, but ultimately it leads to suffering. Abraham Lincoln had the opportunity to win the American Civil war more quickly and with less hardship by using propaganda to cast the people of the South as 'evil', but knew that if he did, reconciliation and diplomacy would make rebuilding the nation impossible thereafter. He chose instead to characterise 'oppression' and 'slavery' as the demons that must be defeated. His troops were moved by the ultimate goal of freedom.

Compassion is undermined by Selfish Interests. It is easier to do nothing when the focus shifts from what might be gained as an individual as part of a community, to an individual who is responsible for making one's own life as trouble-free and as comfortable as possible. It is an easy lie to sell considering that we all have responsibilities to take care of our own families. Family should be at the centre of our mission. So, we must carefully balance the needs at home alongside the needs of our community. The truth is that we are stronger together as a community and that when we serve others, we are richer for it.

At the other end of the spectrum, Compassion can also be tipped off-balance by Overwhelm. Stretching yourself so thin that you neglect yourself, your family and eventually are of little use to anyone. You cannot serve everyone. This error is often motivated by a sense of inadequacy and a failure to properly understand your inherent value apart from the work you do. When your identity is caught up in the service you give to others, you are susceptible to this kind of fall.

BALANCED INNOVATION

Innovation is the creative expression of Compassion. Its antithesis is Inertia. Just as anti-compassion is apathetic and has lost the desire to love, anti-innovation shrinks back from anything different, bold, or unusual. It is fear of the unknown and produces impotence in a person's daily life.

At the other end of the spectrum is Greed. Too many ideas, all of them self-generated with zero divine input. These can be ideas on the quest for Selfish Interest, or more deceptively, take the form of too many ideas, for other people. This is a recipe for overwhelm; the distorted form of compassion we identified above.

BALANCED OPTIMISM

Optimism (aka Hope) is the internal positive perspective that makes us resilient in the face of adversity. Its opposite is Negativity, ultimately leading to despair. The inertia caused by too many ideas produces a sense of hopelessness because any efforts you make are ineffectual or unappreciated. As the proverb says, "hope deferred makes the heart sick".[3]

Another twisted form of Optimism is what we might call 'fake-positivity. I'm sure you've come across it before. The immature 'name-it-and-claim-it' kind of hope. People who have heard or read a little about the power of positive psychology and decide they're going to hack it for themselves, channel their selfish interest into a wish-list. This sooner or later leads to disappointment (which is the appropriate response), yet many months or years can go by before questioning their approach, because fake-positivity stakes its claims on the paradoxical caveat of 'never giving up'. They have set themselves up to fail.

This exaggerated positivity linked to a specific outcome became known as the Stockdale Paradox, after Admiral Jim Stockdale, who was tortured twenty times in a Vietnamese prisoner-of-war camp during his eight-year imprisonment from 1965 to 1973. Stockdale was interviewed by Jim Collins and shared the importance of never losing faith *"I never doubted not only that I would get out, but also that I would prevail in the end and turn the experience into the defining event of my life, which, in retrospect, I would not trade."* [4] However, when asked, what was the counter-belief? Who didn't make it and why? He replied "That's easy. The Optimists". This sounds contradictory, but Stockdale clarified. "The Optimists were the ones who said; 'We'll be out by Christmas!' And Christmas came and went. Then they'd say, 'We're going to be out by Easter.' And Easter would come, and Easter would go." They were constantly being undermined by their own optimism. "[Eventually] …they died of a broken heart."

Whilst 'never losing faith' and this other sort of 'positivity' appear to be of the same root mindset, Stockdale points out how they are fundamentally different: "This is a very important lesson. You must never confuse faith that you will prevail in the end—which you can never afford to lose—with the discipline to confront the most brutal facts of your current reality, whatever they might be." [4]

Do not fall into the trap of inevitable heartbreak that comes from overly optimistic predictions.

BALANCED VISION

This leads us to Vision, a clear, big-picture view of what you want to achieve, and as much as possible, details on how you're going to do it. The counterforce of Vision is Confusion. It feels like having no-ideas, but usually it comes from having *too many* ideas and being pulled simultaneously in multiple different directions. Confusion is an internal storm that saps your energy and motivation faster than anything else can. Those who know this will resist new ideas, however they then become susceptible to the other form of distorted Vision known as Dogma. We all know people and organisations that operate like this. Dogma is a firm, immoveable set of principles that are usually well-past their use-by date. How we continue to run the traditional school system is a classic example.

This kind of inflexibility prevents us from adapting to the nuances that life continually throws our way.

BALANCED DILIGENCE

The joy of your Work can be robbed when these mistakes listed above have run their course. Diligence is the final character trait leading to impact, but when overwhelmed, inert, confused and despairing, the end result is in-activity. This is the enemy's preferred outcome; but if he cannot achieve this, then he will push for an over-correction in the opposite direction. Pushing ahead with self-centred ideas, false-hope and Dogma, the 'Driver' emerges.

Driving is deceptive, because sometimes we need to push. Impact has a cost. That's life. But constant, blind, unyielding ambition can leave a trail of misunderstanding, hurt and disappointment in its wake. This is Driving — not Thriving. Some would call it 'the cost of winning', and therefore it becomes ammunition against future change-makers, should they dare take on the quest for impact.

TAKE YOUR STAND

Your enemy is real. On your quest to make the world a better place, you *will* face resistance. You should not be surprised or caught off-guard by this. We trained for this in the Growth Focussed Mindset chapter.

Remember, without an adversary, there's no battle; and with no battle, there's no victory – no story. You are designed to face struggles and win. That is the nature of abundant living.

The enemy gains unauthorised access to your life with subtle doubts, overwhelm, frustration, misdirection, distraction, and a myriad of other strategies to kill your dreams, steal your hope and destroy your future. You picked a fight with him when you decide to strive for *'better'*.

The devil undermines all that is good, but don't be too quick to attribute blame (or credit) for all your misfortunes on this malevolent force. It's natural to want to explain away suffering, and it's easy to think in dualistic terms. Black and white, good and evil, but life, people, relationships, different perspectives, and circumstances are all much more intricate and complex than that. Sometimes, the twisted fact is that the enemy we face is ourselves, and our struggles are necessary to reveal our own shortcomings.

So don't hate your enemy. Anger and aggression just make you easier to knock off-balance. It doesn't bring about the amazing life that you are striving for. Instead, think of your adversary as the counterforce to balanced truth. His mission is to ensure that you 'miss the mark'. To prevent you from heeding the Call. When there is the truth of the Call, then there are also a multitude of possible inaccuracies. He will attempt to push and pull you off the path. Either urging you to consider yourself more highly than you ought, or weighing you down with fear of failure or the heavy burdens of the world.

Biblical scholars tell us that the devil is a fallen angel who once enjoyed his place in the light of God's glory. After foolishly abdicating this privileged position, it would make sense then, that this deposed demon now devotes all its/his/her resources to stopping anyone else from discovering the light that lives in them.

Everyone needs to come to terms with the reality of resistance in their own way. If it helps to personify your enemy, then do that. If it doesn't, don't; but make no mistake, there *is* a counterforce to impact. It's not another person. It's a force that can – no, *will* bring you down if you're naïve, unaware and unprepared. Ignore that at your own peril.

But no matter hard things get, whatever forces rail against you, the Call that lives inside you is more powerful than any enemy or circumstance that tries to stand in your way.

Trust me. You've got this!

| 35 |

Who Are You Going to Serve?

> *The only really happy people are those who have learned how to serve.*
>
> **RICK WARREN**

A leader who *cares* is primed to make powerful and significant change. However, a big heart can also cripple your progress if you don't establish one important fact before you start designing your impact. "Who are you going to serve?"

The natural response of the kind, compassionate creative is 'everyone!' You see needs everywhere and recognise hundreds of different ways your skills can align to make life better. This is incredibly honourable and beautiful. It's also a mistake. You cannot serve everyone well, and you will burn yourself out if you try.

Impact that is spread too thinly is really no impact at all.

Let me illustrate. Imagine a big nail laid flat on a piece of timber. You can bash that nail with your hammer as hard as you like, and sure, it'll dint the timber, but it's not going to penetrate into the wood and have the impact it was designed for.

However, if you turn that nail on its end, point down, one small tap will split the fibres of the wood and it will begin to penetrate toward its goal. A few more well-placed blows and it breaks through one level, then the next, finally achieving its purpose – connecting 2 members that eventually form the structure of a great building that will be enjoyed by many. That's impact. It needs to be focused to work.

WHERE TO FOCUS

Your 'sweet spot' is the overlapping zone between your gifts, talents, abilities, strengths and experience; AND another person or group whom you've been called to serve. If your Impact zone is family, then that's relatively straight forward. You know them well; and if you don't, well then that's your first mission! For a business, social enterprise, or community group, that's a little more vague. Our tendency is to go broad because we don't want to leave anybody out, but if you do, before you know it your focus is diluted, and your energy and resources spread thin.

To overcome this, I use a technique called Designing your Ideal Customer Avatar (or ICA). I first came across the ICA concept with Marie Forleo, who uses it as a part of her *B-school* (business) program.[1] It's a powerful marketing tool but it can be equally useful if you are designing a course, starting a business or social enterprise, or supporting a community group. It helps you to narrow your focus and answers that all-important question, 'who am I going to serve?'.

An Ideal Customer Avatar (ICA) is a semi-fictional character that you create who embodies the key characteristics and personal attributes of the people you are trying to serve. It is generally a compilation of people you know, including yourself a few years earlier, plus a few extra ideas from your imagination. When you first start authoring your ICA it feels ruthless. Age? Hair-colour? Social-media preference? Number of kids? Hobbies? Every decision feels like a cut to the core! You're pruning, cutting off more and more people, and it feels like you're cutting off limbs! It's painful because you don't want to leave people out!

Please understand, this process is not about saying who you *won't* serve; it's about refining exactly who you're aiming for so you can identify and find those whom you can serve best.

Imagine an archery target with your ICA's name on the bull's eye. That's what you're aiming at. Sure, there are others; similar people who are 1, 2 or even 3 rings out from the bullseye who are still excited by what you're doing. This is great. These people are still a part of your tribe. They're welcome to buy, or sponsor, or get on board with your enterprise. Of course you will help them, but don't be distracted by them. Stay focused on your ICA.

Seth Godin, in 'This is Marketing' says we need to identify a minimum cluster around our ICA and serve them. He calls this our 'Minimum Viable Audience'.[2,3]

When you are writing to define your ICA, it is important that you think creatively and use your intuition. Your ICA embodies *your people*. You know this person! You know more about them than your conscious mind realises. Despite being imagined, he or she is 'real'; at least as real as an un-bodied person can be!

I have a belief that has served me well. I can't prove it as true or not true, but my belief is that the *right people*, whom you are called to serve are out there and waiting for you – and it's like their collective voice is somehow reverberating in the atmosphere. (I know that sounds a bit woo woo, but it works!) As you tune in, and listen for what *that voice*, what that collective need is saying to you, you will find that the ideas for your ICA begin to flow, and before you know it you've written a page or two that rings true. When you read it back, you *know* that this is the person/people you're called to serve. Not only that, now you're getting excited! You can't wait to meet them in person!

Another great way to learn more about your ICA is to talk to them. Not the fictional paper-version of course, but when you have written a little, it usually doesn't take a lot of thought to come up with 1 or 2 people you know in real-life who resemble your ICA in some way. They don't have to be a perfect match. Your ICA might be a 34-year-old mum, called Sharron, with 2 kids aged 9 and 11 who is wanting to get back in shape. And you may know a 36-year-old mum, called Wendy, with 3 kids, 7, 10, and 13 who started trying to get in shape a year or two ago. Talk to her! See how it's going. Maybe she's had a breakthrough. Or maybe not. There is a lot you can learn on your quest for impact by asking good questions and then listening, really listening, to your ICA.

If you'd like a little help getting started with the types of questions to ask in this sort of conversation, you can download my 'Talk to your ICA Guide' at: www.thrivebydesignbook.com/resources

Once you know who you serve, cross reference this with the Identity work you did in Part 1: Maximised Identity. Where those 2 zones overlap, that's your sweet spot. That's where the magic starts to happen.

| 36 |

Impact Through Education

*Education is the most powerful weapon
we can use to change the world.*

NELSON MANDELA

    I know I'm biased, but I believe that one of the most powerful and profound ways that you can have an impact is through education. I'm not talking about going out and becoming a teacher, (although you could do that if you wanted to), I'm talking about 'education' in its broadest and most natural sense. A human-to-human exchange, one person imparting knowledge, wisdom, character and skills to another. Sharing life to make life better.

    In the same way that we can all be leaders because we all have a unique story to share, we also can all be educators too. We can all teach and learn from one another. One of the biggest challenges facing any leader is, how do you *scale* your impact? How do you expand influence and still maintain the essence and integrity of the message you are trying to share? How leaders have responded to this challenge have shaped our experience of 'knowing' in the world more than we realise.

THE EDUCATION SYSTEM - THEN AND NOW

Institutionalised education is the hierarchical solution to that question, 'how do you have impact at scale?' Developed initially in the 1800s to serve the needs of a rapidly growing industrial economy, it was implemented as a top-down, manager-centred affair. Sit down. Shut up. Listen, and (if you're lucky) do. This approach is still most people's prevailing experience of education. It's an attractive solution because (in theory) it's easy and uncomplicated to deliver, but at the same time, it robs the individual participants of agency and motivation.

In the traditional model, 90% of exchange is one way. Lecture style. A lot of 'teaching' gets done, but not a lot of learning follows. How do humans respond in any relationship that is disproportionately one sided? That's right, we resist. We seek to restore the balance of power. More than 100 years after the factory-style secondary education system was developed, this model is now *way* past its expiry date! And yet, it still continues to be the predominant methodology practiced in most schools and universities. It has become more and more redundant as more and more people come online and have access to free information. That's not to say there is no longer a role for educators. There is, but their role is different. It no longer makes sense for educators to stand at the front of a room claiming to be the purveyors of all knowledge. Not when almost everyone in the room has access to an internet-connected device (probably in their back pocket). Education has been irrevocably decentralised.

With all this new information comes unprecedented privilege and opportunity, and with that, comes unprecedented levels of risk and responsibility. Young people and adults need guidance as much as they ever have! The role of an educator must now shift from 'instructor' to 'guide'.

BECOMING A GUIDE

Becoming a 'guide' in your own unique way is a powerful path to impact. People need help, so this shouldn't be too hard, right? Wrong!

Unfortunately, education is carrying baggage from the past. People still envisage domination and control whenever they think about 'education'. To learn requires you to admit weakness and we consider that appropriate for younger children, but secretly are glad that we're past that! It's vulnerability. Jordan Peterson describes "every learning experience as a mini-death",[1] and so, the big problem leaders face is the conditioning of people by authoritarian social structures (including school) to resist help and to feign perfection. There are numerous stories of how this *learner-vulnerability* has been abused in the past by so called 'educators', and this provokes a visceral feeling of anger and injustice. Our collective social memory is stacked against us. In education, trust is the issue.

RECONNECTING

How do you overcome this? How do you lead/support/guide people who have hardened themselves to hearing?

Back when I was a part of this model, something inside me knew that it was fundamentally flawed. It didn't, and still doesn't, support authentic learning. Seeing my students (and myself) suffer, as we both tried to 'toe the line' and make that system work, I was compelled to go searching and to find something better. That's when I came across *life-coaching*.

Coaching sits at the facilitative end of the human-to-human continuum that includes counselling, mentoring, and teaching. There's a wide variety of definitions and interpretations on what coaching is, and much of this depends on the context. Skills & Performance coaching in the business setting are expected to be dogmatic and directive, providing instruction and advice necessary to improve performance. Developmental (or personal) coaching is more facilitative and holistic. Personal coaches use questioning, active listening, creative problem-solving, and client-directed goal setting to help people take self-directed actions and achieve better outcomes. They rarely instruct or give advice. Their primary goal is clarity of purpose and personal empowerment. From this, all other forms of success (including business and workplace success) flow. This is the essential nature of transformational leadership.

(I explore these ideas further in an essay, available at: www.thrivebydesignbook.com/resources)

Coaching (and Mentoring) is a facilitative form of education that takes people on a journey of personal growth. The person that emerges at the end of that process is not the same person that began the journey. I hope that is the case with this book. I hope that is the case with all of my programs. I position my youth programs as educational experiences because that is what parents want, or at least they think they do. We do cover traditional content, and the kids do learn, but my programs are not so much about 'education' as they are about 'transformation' – creating an immersive experience, stepping into a whole new way of thinking and being. My adult coaching programs are the same.

Remember back in Chapter 17: Design Thinking we looked at the role of the Designer as well as numerous other 'guiding' roles. There are so many different ways to take people on a journey. So many different paths you can take. Your experience makes you the expert on your path. What you have learned, from both your successes and your failures, enables you to be the right person to guide others. Moreover, that story, that includes heartbreak and defeat, is a story of vulnerability, and as such, it helps to overcome the resistance of the people you are trying to serve.

Last chapter we identified your 'Sweet Spot' – the special zone where your genius and experience overlap the wants, needs and desires of your ideal client. As you consider that Sweet Spot, also consider how you can use education to connect with, build rapport, and scale your impact to support those who need it most?

You might immediately think of what you can teach and what they could learn (i.e. traditional instruction). That has value for sure, but don't stop there. The information you have is likely available in several other places. What's unique is your story. Is there a process of transformation, a journey that your client needs to go on before they can have what they want? Telling stories, illuminating a path, that too is education. There is a convincing argument that anthropologically, that is how we are wired to learn – through stories and through relationships.

WHAT'S YOUR SPECIAL SAUCE?

How do you take people on a journey? What are the steps you will take?

People are much more likely to trust you (and follow you) if you can explicitly tell them what's going to happen and when. That's the Vision. I came across a great technique for designing a strategic vision from marketing expert, Frank Kern. I have used this technique numerous times, including the planning phase for this book! It's pretty simple.

Grab a blank A4 or A3 page. Turn it landscape. In the top left, draw a sad face, and then in the top right, draw a happy face. Just below the sad face, succinctly list or describe the pain points of your client/customer. Why are they hurting? What's wrong? What are they missing?

Then under the happy face, describe what thriving looks like. Describe the breakthrough that your ideal client/customer is longing for. Keep it to 1 or 2 sentences.

Then connect the 2 faces with a long horizontal line across the page. That's the journey between the two states. On this line, mark 5 circles or dots. These are like the Milestones we learned about in Chapter 19, The Anatomy of Strategy. They are the markers of progress. They help your client to understand the steps that they need to take. Understanding these steps makes the journey seem achievable. They begin to get excited about the destination that had previously seemed like a pipedream. Later, when you share about your own journey and your experience taking these steps before them, they recognise that you can be trusted to take them where they want to go. You have become 'the guide'.

In reality, any transformation rarely happens in 5 neat steps. Leadership is dynamic and requires you to be responsive and adaptable, but by having a framework to know where you are and what comes next, you can alleviate anxiety and focus on the work that needs to be done. By doing that, the battle is already half-won!

Use the rest of your page to label and flesh out the details of those five steps. It doesn't have to be five. It can be more; it can be less. So long as in the end there is a clear sequence that flows, from pain to breakthrough. A story that starts with heartache and concludes with a happy ending.

MX90

MX90 is my signature life coaching program for adults. It follows the 5-step outline I've shared above. The Pain-point, the Breakthrough, and the 5 steps that bridge the two, are outlined below. I share these as an example you can follow.

The Pain Points. Frustration, Self-doubt and growing Negativity. My client is typically a married, late 30s man or woman who has followed the traditional path all their life. They have studied hard, worked hard, and are good at what they do. In a lot of ways others would consider them 'successful', and yet they find themselves feeling lost and without purpose. Age 40 (or 50) is on the horizon and this growing sense of 'missing the mark' scares them. They want better and they are realising they need some help to get them there.

The Promise (or breakthrough). A clarity of purpose that brings confidence, motivation and a new sense of vitality and wellbeing. An inner transformation that leads to tangible, enjoyable success.

The Steps. (You will recognise some similarities here) We work from the inside out over the course of 90 days.

- Phase 1 is all about Identity. Who are you? Who are you called to be?
- Phase 2 is about Mindset. Developing positive mental habits and identifying limiting beliefs.
- Phase 3 is Strategy. Designing smart actions to reach your goals.
- Phase 4 is Habits and Accountability. Walking together, addressing issues as they arise and keeping you on track with your commitments.
- Phase 5 is Flying Solo. A gentle push out of the nest – you're ready to do this next 90 days on your own!

- And finally, I check in and review progress with you 6 months after beginning the journey. What went well? What needs to improve? Where to next?

You can see a full outline of MX90 at: www.blueprintlifecoaching.com.au/mx90

| 37 |

No Wrong Place

I am in the right place, at the right time, doing the right thing.

LOUISE HAY

Here we are. At the end of a journey, and like all endings, it is also a new beginning. You've come a long way! We've explored the core of your Identity. Listened carefully to the Call. We have confirmed that foundational, immutable truth; that you are precious beyond measure, no matter what you've done, or choose to do in the future. Your value is infinite. You are amazing – just as you are, and yet, you decided to pick up this book. You decided to embark on a quest for insight, and together we have travelled, from the inside-out...

From the Core to Mindset. From Mindset to Lifestyle. From Lifestyle to Leadership, and onto Impact.

On the way, you learned a little more about me. My highs, my lows; how I got this far, and my epic fails along the way.

You now know my mission. To co-create impact-driven success stories, with you, and others like you. To stretch the boundaries of what most people call 'education', and to help others to do the same. To challenge the dehumanising institutions of our society and foster warm, authentic human connections and communities in their place. I hope that this book has been an asset to that end.

I want to thank you for giving me some of your most precious resource – your time. I pray earnestly with all my heart that the moments you have invested here will yield an abundance of joy and freedom in whatever you choose to do next.

Now that we've laid out the map, you will know intuitively where you need to head off to next.

It may be back to the beginning, to dive deeper and discover more about yourself. It may be to get clear on the Call, the spark, the 'why' that moves you forward.

It may be back to the Dojo, the Mindset training gym to hone your mental acuity. It might be to back to 'The Anatomy of Strategy' and one of the 6 Lifestyle Domains. Perhaps one you haven't read yet, or perhaps you want to revisit the same one again, knowing there is still more to learn. Perhaps you'd like to review that section with a partner or friend? Someone you've committed to walking through life with together. It would make a lot of sense to design your lifestyle with their input!

Or perhaps, the next step for you is Leadership. Reviewing the 5 phases of Impact or exploring the bonus resources package.

Or perhaps you're ready to reach out and work with a coach to take your game to the next level?

Whatever you choose, I want to emphasise, that you are exactly where you're meant to be. There's no wrong place for you. You are in the right place, at the right time, doing the right thing, right now.

You belong. You are not alone. You are unique, but you share this adventure with millions of other kindred souls, who all have one thing in common…

You are, *designed* to THRIVE!

RESOURCES

Download at:
www.thrivebydesignbook.com/resources

PART 1: MAXIMISED IDENTITY
- Your Mission Notebook

PART 2: MAXIMISED MINDSET
- Brain Health Planner
- Neuro-chemical Profiles
- Happiness Boosters
- Review – Reframe – Breathe
- Divergent Thinking Challenges
- My Top 10 Inspirational Movies
- Mind Mapping Guide
- 16 Neuro Linguistic Programming Presuppositions

PART 3: MAXIMISED LIFESTYLE
- Mind Mapping Tools
- Maximised Strategy Framework
- Weekly Planner
- A2 90-day Planner
- Romantic Connection – The Feelings List

PART 4: MAXIMISED IMPACT
- Further Reading for Leaders Guide
- Talk to your ICA Guide
- Masters Essay

NOTES

PART 1: Maximised Identity

The Maximised Life

1. Lord, A. (Host). (2020, August 7). It's all about perspective: with Michael Crossland. The Blueprint [Episode 30]. Blueprint Life Coaching. https://www.blueprintlifecoaching.com.au/post/episode030
2. The Man Cave – https://themancave.life/
3. Lord, A. (Host). (2020, April 6). Success is sooo much more than money! (No. 12) [Audio podcast episode]. In *The Blueprint Podcast*. Blueprint Life Coaching. https://www.blueprintlifecoaching.com.au/post/episode012
4. Ray, S. (2017, July 15). The four key secrets to success – according to Oprah Winfrey. *Your Story*. https://yourstory.com/2017/07/secrets-to-success/amp
5. Alex Kendrick – this quote came from a DVD extras clip of Alex speaking to the cast of 'Facing the Giants' about adversity
6. *Holy Bible New International Version*. (2011). Biblehub. https://biblehub.com/niv/1_corinthians/4.htm

Let's Get One Thing Straight

1. Spector, D. (2012, June 11). The Odds Of You Being Alive Are Incredibly Small. *Insider*. https://www.businessinsider.com/infographic-the-odds-of-being-alive-2012-6
2. Brown, C.B. (2010). The power of vulnerability [Webinar]. TEDxHouston. https://www.youtube.com/watch?v=X4Qm9cGRub0

Where Do You Belong?

1. Peplau, L. A. (1985). *Loneliness research: Basic concepts and findings.* In I. G. Sarason & B. R. Sarason (Eds.), Social support: Theory, research and application (pp. 270-286). Boston: Martinus Nijhof.
2. Australian Psychological Society. (2017). *Australian Loneliness Report: A survey exploring the loneliness levels of Australians and the impact on their health and well-being* [PowerPoint Slides]. https://psychweek.org.au/wp/wp-content/uploads/2018/11/Psychology-Week-2018-Australian-Loneliness-Report.pdf
3. Cigna. (2020). *Loneliness and the workplace.* https://www.cigna.com/static/www-cigna-com/docs/about-us/newsroom/studies-and-reports/combatting-loneliness/cigna-2020-loneliness-factsheet.pdf
4. Peplau L., & Perlman D. (1982). *Perspectives on loneliness.* Loneliness: A sourcebook of current theory, research, and therapy. New York: Wiley.
5. Landsverk, G. & Michelson, A. (2020, November 25). When you're lonely, your brain craves social interaction like it desires food, according to new research. *Insider.* https://www.insider.com/loneliness-and-hunger-have-similar-effects-on-the-brain-study-2020-11#:~:text=Loneliness%20can%20trigger%20cravings%20for,to%2

Found

1. Brown, C.B. (2018, March 27). Defining Spirituality. *Brené Brown.* https://brenebrown.com/articles/2018/03/27/defining-spirituality/

A Tool for the Journey

1. Morristown Beard School. (2014). *Tapping Into Your Creative Potential.* https://www.mbs.net/morristown-beard-school-news/~board/news/post/tapping-into-our-creative-potential-september-19-2014
2. Robinson, K. (2007). *Do Schools Kill Creativity?* [Webinar]. TED Talks. https://www.youtube.com/watch?v=iG9CE55wbtY
3. De Bono, E. (1992). Serious creativity: Using the power of lateral thinking to create new ideas. London: Harper Collins Publishers doi: http://dx.doi.org/10.5204/jld.v8i1.230
4. Pressfield, S. (2002). *The War of Art.* Rugged Land.

A Quantum Leap

1. Bellisario, D. (March 1989 – May 1993). *Quantum Leap* [Television Series]. Belisarius Productions; Universal Television.

PART 2: Maximised Mindset

Your Amazing Brain

1. Kwik, J. (2020). *Limitless: Upgrade Your Brain, Learn Anything Faster, and Unlock Your Exceptional Life.* Hay House.
2. Scott, P. (2013). Redesign My Brain with Todd Sampson Season 1 [DVD]. Mindful Media.
3. Siberry, J. (2015). Redesign My Brain with Todd Sampson Season 2 [DVD]. Mindful Media.
4. Bolte, J.T. (2008, February). *My Stroke of Insight* [Video]. TED Conferences. https://www.ted.com/talks/jill_bolte_taylor_my_stroke_of_insight
5. Clark D. D. & Sokoloff, L. (1999) in Basic Neurochemistry: Molecular, Cellular and Medical Aspects, eds. Siegel, G. J., Agranoff, B. W., Albers, R. W., Fisher, S. K. & Uhler, M. D. (Lippincott, Philadelphia), pp. 637–670.
6. Vuleta, E. (2021, October 29). *41+ Absolutely Amazing Brain Facts.* Seed Scientific. https://seedscientific.com/brain-facts/
7. Queensland Brain Institute. (n.d.). 10 Amazing Brain Facts. The University of Queensland, Australia. https://qbi.uq.edu.au/10-amazing-facts-about-brain
8. Neurotracker. (2016, January 16). *10 Facts You Did Not Know About Your Brain.* https://www.neurotrackerx.com/post/10-things-brain
9. Buzan, T. (2006). *The Ultimate Book of Mind Maps* (p64). HarperCollins Publishers.
10. HealthDirect. (n.d.). *Drinking Water and your Health.* https://www.healthdirect.gov.au/drinking-water-and-your-health
11. Chang CY, Ke DS, Chen JY. Essential fatty acids and human brain. Acta Neurol Taiwan. 2009 Dec;18(4):231-41. PMID: 20329590.
12. National Institute of Neurological Disorders and Stroke (NINDS). (n.d.). Brain Basics: Understanding Sleep [Article]. Publication No. 17-3440c. https://www.ninds.nih.gov/health-information/patient-caregiver-education/brain-basics-understanding-sleep

13. Anderson E, Shivakumar G. Effects of exercise and physical activity on anxiety. Front Psychiatry. 2013 Apr 23;4:27. doi: 10.3389/fpsyt.2013.00027. PMID: 23630504; PMCID: PMC3632802.

Neurochemistry Insights

1. Owens, A. (n.d.). Tell Me All I Need to Know About Oxytocin. *Psycom.net.* https://www.psycom.net/oxytocin
2. *Adrenal Hormones.* (2022, January 23). Endocrine Society. https://www.endocrine.org/patient-engagement/endocrine-library/hormones-and-endocrine-function/adrenal-hormones
3. *Beware High Levels of Cortisol, the Stress Hormone.* (2017, February 5). Premier Health. https://www.premierhealth.com/your-health/articles/women-wisdom-wellness-/beware-high-levels-of-cortisol-the-stress-hormone
4. *The Effects of Testosterone on the Body.* (n.d.). Healthline. https://www.healthline.com/health/low-testosterone/effects-on-body
5. *5 Benefits of Testosterone for Men and Women.* (n.d.). LT Men's Clinic. https://ltmensclinic.com/5-benefits-of-testosterone-for-men-and-women/
6. Sherman, G. D., Lerner, J. S., Josephs, R. A., Renshon, J., & Gross, J. J. (2016). The interaction of testosterone and cortisol is associated with attained status in male executives. *Journal of Personality and Social Psychology,* 110(6), 921–929. https://doi.org/10.1037/pspp0000063
7. Adams, S. (2015, August 26). *Do Your Testosterone And Cortisol Levels Dictate Your Leadership Ability?.* Forbes. https://www.forbes.com/sites/susanadams/2015/08/26/do-your-testosterone-and-cortisol-levels-dictate-your-leadership-ability/?sh=2b6dc9437dbb
8. Norris, J. (2009, October 1). *Estrogen Plays Key Role in Male Brain Development.* University of California San Francisco. https://www.ucsf.edu/news/2009/10/103292/estrogen-plays-key-role-male-brain-development
9. Olds, J., & Milner, P. (1954). *Positive reinforcement produced by electrical stimulation of septal area and other regions of rat brain.* Journal of Comparative and Physiological Psychology, 47(6), 419–427. https://doi.org/10.1037/h0058775

10. Olds, J. (1956). Pleasure Centers in the Brain. *Scientific American*. Vol. 195 (No. 4), pp.105-117. https://www.jstor.org/stable/24941787
11. Healthdirect. (n.d.). *Dopamine*. Healthdirect. https://www.healthdirect.gov.au/dopamine#:~:text=You%20can%20boost%20a%20low,problem%20with%20the%20adrenal%20glands.
12. Cuddy, A. (2012, June). Your body language may shape who you are [Video]. TED Conferences. https://www.ted.com/talks/amy_cuddy_your_body_language_may_shape_who_you_are

The Happy Mind

1. Foster, A. (2018, April 18). Deadly Mistake That Changed Australian's Family's Life Forever. News.com.au https://www.news.com.au/travel/travel-updates/travel-stories/deadly-mistake-that-changed-australian-familys-life-forever/news-story/9a723a59ee4f9a37b720c3d6e8f5bb25
2. Wilczek, F. (2015, September 23). Einstein's Parable of Quantum Insanity. *Quanta Magazine*. https://www.scientificamerican.com/article/einstein-s-parable-of-quantum-insanity/
3. Frankl, V. (1946). *A Man's Search for Meaning*. Beacon Press.
4. Achor, S. (2010). *The Happiness Advantage: The Seven Principles of Positive Psychology That Fuel Success and Performance at Work*. Ebury Publishing.
5. Know Your Brain: Reticular Formation. (n.d.). https://neuroscientificallychallenged.com/posts/know-your-brain-reticular-formation
6. Kwong, E. (Host). (2020, July 15). Understanding Unconscious Bias [Audio podcast episode]. In *Short Wave*.NPR. https://www.npr.org/2020/07/14/891140598/understanding-unconscious-bias
7. McDougall, P. (2008, January 29). *Humans Can Only Think About Four Things At Once, Study Says*. InformationWeek. https://www.informationweek.com/it-life/humans-can-only-think-about-four-things-at-once-study-says
8. Cherry, K. (2020, April 29). *What Is the Negativity Bias?*. Verywell Mind. https://www.verywellmind.com/negative-bias-4589618

The Growth-Focused Mind

1. Briceño, E. (2012, November). *The Power of belief – mindset and success* [Video]. TED Conferences. https://www.youtube.com/watch?v=pN34FNbOKXc

2. Dweck, C. (2012). *Mindset – Updated Edition: Changing The Way You think To Fulfil Your Potential* (6th Ed.). Robinson.
3. This quote can be traced to multiple sources. It is most often attributed to Chuck R. Swindoll: https://www.goodreads.com/quotes/1169-life-is-10-what-happens-to-you-and-90-how
4. Hann, D. (2015). Life Coaching Lectures. Life Coaching Academy. https://www.lifecoachingacademy.edu.au/
5. Foster, M. & Krueger, G. (2008, June 11). *A Story about 1 Father and His 2 Sons with 3 Lessons for All of Us.* Bigg Success. https://biggsuccess.com/2008/06/11/1-father-2-sons-3-lessons-for-all-of-us/
6. Campbell, J. (2012). *The Hero with a Thousand Faces: The Collected Works of Joseph Campbell.* New World Library.
7. Pressfield, S. (n.d.). *The Villain Drives the Story.* Steven Pressfield. https://stevenpressfield.com/2017/12/the-villain-drives-the-story/
8. Duckworth, A. (2016). *Grit: The Power of Passion and Perseverance.* Scribner.
9. Tom, N. (2021, October 25). *Why Perfection is the Enemy of Progress for Entrepreneurs.* Real Business. https://realbusiness.co.uk/perfection-enemy-progress-entrepreneurs
10. Acuff, J. (2017). *Finish: Give Yourself the Gift of Done* (1st ed.). Portfolio.
11. Oppland, M. (2016, December 16). *8 Ways To Create Flow According to Mihaly Csikszentmihalyi.* PositivePsychology.com. https://positivepsychology.com/mihaly-csikszentmihalyi-father-of-flow/
12. Dietrich, A. (2002). Functional neuroanatomy of altered states of consciousness: The transient hypofrontality hypothesis. *Consciousness and Cognition, Volume* (12), 231-256. https://pages.ucsd.edu/~jpineda/COGS175/readings/Dietrich.pdf
13. University Bible Fellowship. (2015, October 15). *The Kingdom of God Belongs to Such as These (Lk 18:15-30).* University Bible Fellowship. https://ubf.org/resourcedetail/18253?source=HQ%20Education%20Study%20Team&genre=Gospels%20and%20Acts(NT)&bcode=142&chapter=18
14. University Bible Fellowship. (2009, August 1). *Become Like Little Children.* University Bible Fellowship. https://ubf.org/resourcedetail/17409?page=20&bcode=140
15. Kotler, S. (2014). *The Rise of Superman: Decoding the Science of Ultimate Human Performance* (Kindle 1st ed.). Amazon Publishing.

16. Waitzkin, J. (2008). *The Art of Learning: An Inner Journey to Optimal Performance* (37102nd ed.). Free Press.
17. Wheal, J. (2013, December 27). *Hacking the GENOME of Flow* [Video]. TED Conferences. https://www.youtube.com/watch?v=WqAtG77JjdM
18. Lord, A. (2021, September 13). Deciphering the Flowcode (Episode 71) [Audio podcast episode]. In *The Blueprint Podcast*. Blueprint Life Coaching. https://www.blueprintlifecoaching.com.au/post/episode071

The Positioned Mind

1. Fullan, M. (2016). The elusive nature of whole system improvement in education. *J Educ Change* 17, 539–544. https://doi.org/10.1007/s10833-016-9289-1
2. Griffin, D. & Stacey, R. (2015). *A Complexity Perspective on Researching Organisations: Taking Experience Seriously* (1st ed.). Routledge.
3. Knight, J. (2015). *Better Conversations: Coaching Ourselves and Each Other to Be More Credible, Caring, and Connected* (1st ed.). SAGE Publications.
4. Stronger Smarter Leadership Program. (2013-2022). Stranger Smarter Institute. https://strongersmarter.com.au/stronger-smarter-leadership-program/
5. Tolle, E. (2005). *A New Earth: Awakening to your Life's Purpose.* Penguin Books Ltd.
6. Safir, S. (2017). *The Listening Leader: Creating the Conditions for Equitable School Transformation* (1st edition). Jossey-Bass.
7. Ki-moon, B. (2011, October 12). *Remarks at the grave of Dag Hammarskjoldto commemorate the 50th anniversary of his death* [Written live speech]. United Nations. https://www.un.org/sg/en/content/sg/speeches/2011-10-12/remarks-grave-dag-hammarskj%C3%B6ld-commemorate-50th-anniversary-his-death
8. Ramsey, K. (2019, March 17). *The Presuppositions of Neuro-Linguistic Programming.* Medium. https://medium.com/achology/the-presuppositions-of-neuro-linguistic-programming-b2b0649cabe7
9. De Bono, E. (2017). *Six Thinking Hats.* Penguin Books Ltd.

The Abundant Mind

1. Howes. L. (Host). *Transform Your Mind to Manifest & Attract Financial Abundance*. School of Greatness: Episode 1288. https://lewishowes.com/podcast/transform-your-mind-to-manifest-attract-financial-abundance-with-dr-joe-dispenza/

Mind Mapping

1. Cognitive Psychology Students. (2020, January 28). *Can Colour Coding My Notes Really Get Me Better Grades?*. Thinking About Thinking. https://thinking.umwblogs.org/2020/01/28/can-color-coding-my-notes-really-get-me-better-grades/
2. Blaus, B. (2013). *Multipolar Neuron.* [A detailed image of a neuron]. Wikipedia. https://commons.wikimedia.org/wiki/File:Blausen_0657_MultipolarNeuron.png
3. Genovese, J. (2013). *Don't understand something? Break it down with mindmaps.* [A mindmap about mindmapping]. Learning Fundamentals. https://learningfundamentals.com.au/dont-understand-something-break-it-down-with-mindmaps/

Design Thinking

1. Schwarz, J.O., Gordon, A.V., Rohrbeck, R. (2019). *Technology Innovation Management Review*, 9(8), 30-42. DOI:10.22215/timreview/1259
2. Whitmore, J. (2017). *Coaching for Performance: The Principles and Practices of Coaching and Leadership, 5th Edition.* John Murray.

PART 3: Maximised Lifestyle

The Anatomy of Strategy

1. Gerber, M. E. (1995). *The E-Myth Revisited: Why Most Small Businesses Don't Work and What to Do About It.* HaperCollins.
2. Herman, T. (n.d.). *90 Day Year Small Business Playbook Program.* 90 Day Year. https://www.90dayyear.com/sbe-program
3. Acuff, J. (2017). *Finish: Give Yourself the Gift of Done* (1st ed.). Portfolio.

Fun & Adventure

1. Roy's story is found here: Lord, A. (2019, November 25). *A Medical Miracle – Meet Roy*. The Blueprint: Episode 003. https://www.blueprintlifecoaching.com.au/post/episode003
2. Lord, A. (2021, September 6). *If You Can Dream It, You Can Do It!*. The Blueprint: Episode 070. https://www.blueprintlifecoaching.com.au/post/episode070

Health & Fitness

1. Lord, A. (2020, January 13). *3 mindset principles for a Happy, Healthy lifestyle (with Sarah Moss)*. The Blueprint: Episode 006. https://www.blueprintlifecoaching.com.au/post/episode006
2. Lord, A. (2020, February 10). *5 keys for living with health and vitality*. The Blueprint: Episode 008. https://www.blueprintlifecoaching.com.au/post/episode008

Romantic Connection

1. Ribar, D.C. (2004, January). *What Do Social Scientists Know About the Benefits of Marriage? A Review of Quantitative Methodologies*. (Discussion Paper 998). https://dx.doi.org/10.2139/ssrn.500887
2. Tourtellotte, B. (2011, November 18). *Demi Moore, Ashton Kutcher call it quits*. Reuters. https://www.reuters.com/article/idINIndia-60593220111117
3. Holy Bible New International Version. (2011). *Matthew 6:33*. Biblehub. https://biblehub.com/niv/matthew/6.htm
4. Silk, D. (2016, June 22). *PART ONE – 4 WAYS TO SPOT POWERLESSNESS*. Loving on Purpose. https://lovingonpurpose.com/blog/becomingapowerfulperson1/
5. Chapman, G. (2016). *The 5 Love Languages: The Secret to Love That Lasts*. Moody Press, US.
6. Celebrate Love Seminar. (2005). *L.I.F.E Framework*. In Rekindle the Fire: Couples Pack. (Ed.).
7. Chausis, C. (2010, August 19). *Teachers Are Like Gardeners* [Video]. YouTube. https://youtu.be/aT_121H3kLY

Family Life

1. Oxlad, V. (Series Producer). (2021-). *Parental Guidance* [TV Series]. Channel 9 Television.
2. Tsabary, S. (2015). *The Conscious Parent: Transforming Ourselves, Empowering Our Children.* Hodder & Stoughton
3. I learned the terms Triangle & Circle to describe a phenomenon I'd been seeing for years in the Stronger Smarter Leadership Program https://strongersmarter.com.au/stronger-smarter-leadership-program/
4. Harris, B. & Harris, G. (2020). *Raising Kids to Do Hard Things: Seven Biblical Principles to Encourage and Motivate Your Kids.* Multnomah.
5. Singhal, M. (2020, July 22). *3 Keys to A Happier Family: Love, Limits and Laughter.* Parent Circle. https://www.parentcircle.com/interview-with-dr-justin-coulson-about-how-to-be-a-happier-family/article

Work, Business & Finance

1. Pape, S. (2017). *The Barefoot Investor: The Only Money Guide You'll Ever Need.* Wiley.
2. Pressfield, S. (2018). *The Artist's Journey: The Wake of the Hero's Journey and the Lifelong Pursuit of Meaning.* Black Irish Entertainment LLC
3. Delosa, J. (2021, November 27). A common misconception about alignment. [Status update]. Facebook. https://www.facebook.com/photo.php?fbid=447874810036745&set=pb.100044426889749.-2207520000..&

Mastering Your Calendar

1. Gilbert, D. (2004). The surprising science of happiness [Video]. TED Conferences. https://www.ted.com/talks/dan_gilbert_the_surprising_science_of_happiness?language=en
2. Lord, A. (Host). (2020, June 29). Unlocking your success using neural programs. The Blueprint [Episode 24]. Blueprint Life Coaching. https://www.blueprintlifecoaching.com.au/post/episode024
3. Le Cunff, A. (n.d.). *The planning fallacy: why we underestimate how long a task will take.* Ness Labs. https://nesslabs.com/planning-fallacy

Habits & Systems

1. Lord, A. (2020, January 13). *Scaling Your Impact with Systems (with Dave Jenyns)*. The Blueprint: Episode 075. https://www.blueprintlifecoaching.com.au/post/episode075
2. Sather, A. (2021, May 27). https://einvestingforbeginners.com/compounding-interest/. Sather Research.
3. Duhigg, C. (2012). *The Power of Habit: Why We Do What We Do in Life and Business*. Random House.
4. Clear, J. (2018). *Atomic Habits: An Easy & Proven Way to Build Good Habits & Break Bad Ones*. Avery.

PART 4: Maximised Impact

Stepping Up

1. Safir, S. (2017). *The Listening Leader*. John Wiley & Sons Inc.
2. Harari, O. (n.d.). *Quotations from Chairman Powell*. GovLeaders.org. https://govleaders.org/powell.htm
3. Full Sail University. (2012, June 19). *Sir Ken Robinson Speaks at Full Sail University* [Video]. Youtube. https://www.youtube.com/watch?v=PHi-AikHVFI

Impact is a Process

1. The Nobel Prize. (n.d.). *Albert Einstein Biographical*. The Nobel Prize. https://www.nobelprize.org/prizes/physics/1921/einstein/biographical/
2. Reuters. (2013, March 16). *Oprah named most influential celebrity for second year*. Reuters. https://www.reuters.com/article/us-mostinfluential-idUSBRE92E0YM20130315
3. South African History Online. (2019, August 27). *Nelson Mandela: Father of the Nation*. South African History Online. https://www.sahistory.org.za/article/nelson-mandela-father-nation
4. Mandela, N. (1995). *Long Walk to Freedom: The Autobiography of Nelson Mandela*. Back Bay Books.
5. Lexico. (n.d.). Diligence. In *Lexico.com dictionary*. Retrieved May 31, 2022, from https://www.lexico.com/definition/diligence

You Will Face Resistance [But You've Got This!]

1. Peterson, J. (2018). *12 Rules for Life: An Antidote to Chaos* (1st ed.). Random House Canada.
2. Jordan B Peterson. (2014, March 2). *2014 Personality Lecture 13: Aleksandr Solzhenitsyn (Existentialism)* [Video]. YouTube. https://www.youtube.com/watch?v=8u3aTURVEC8&t=1s
3. *Holy Bible New International Version.* (2011). Biblehub. https://biblehub.com/niv/proverbs/13.htm
4. Collins, J. (n.d.). *The Stockdale Paradox.* Jim Collins. https://www.jimcollins.com/concepts/Stockdale-Concept.html

Who Are You Going to Serve?

1. Forleo, M. (n.d.). *B-School.* Marie Forleo. Retrieved June 2, 2022 from https://www.marieforleo.com/bschool#how-does-bschool-work
2. Godin, S. (2018). *This is Marketing: You can't be seen until you learn to see* (1st ed.). Penguin UK.
3. Godin, S. (2019, March 20). *The minimum viable audience.* Seth's Blog. https://seths.blog/2019/03/the-minimum-viable-audience-2/

Impact Through Education

1. Peterson, J. (2018). *12 Rules for Life: An Antidote to Chaos* (1st ed.). Penguin Books Limited.

Andrew Lord is a renegade school teacher turned life-coach and lifestyle entrepreneur who is committeed to helping men and women dream bigger and shine brighter as they seek to make the world a better place.

He is happily married to Sofia and the proud dad of 5 beautiful children - his greatest treasures.

Andrew is always thinking outside the box and is on a mission to co-create 'impact-driven success stories'. He is consistently stretching the boundaries of what most people call 'education' and challenges common dehumanising practices and structures, supporting schools and organisations to create warm, authentic communities instead.

You can connect with Andrew online inside the THRIVE BY DESIGN book community or his Blueprint Life Coaching pages.

www.ingramcontent.com/pod-product-compliance
Lightning Source LLC
Chambersburg PA
CBHW070248010526
44107CB00056B/2381